BRADFORD V

Bradford in flood. The bottom of Silver Street on 16 June 1903. The fine building on the right is the Lamb Inn, which closed in 1914. Note the pestle and mortar above the doorway of the adjacent shop. This was Willson, the Chemist. On the near left, the cast iron structure by the bridge parapet is a men's urinal.

BRADFORD
VOICES

*A Study of Bradford on Avon
through the twentieth century*

Margaret Dobson

EX LIBRIS PRESS

Published in 1997 by
EX LIBRIS PRESS
1 The Shambles
Bradford on Avon
Wiltshire

Design and typesetting by
Ex Libris Press

Cover printed by
Shires Press, Trowbridge, Wiltshire

Printed by Cromwell Press
Broughton Gifford
Wiltshire

ISBN 0 948578 89 0

© Margaret Dobson 1997

*Erratum: page 165, second paragraph
from the foot of the page, re "Orpins".*

"This house...is owned by the church
and administered by a charitable
Trust."
Please add, "This house is now
privately owned."

Contents

Foreword

by John Chandler, BA, PhD

BRADFORD ON AVON, if you are exposed to it for any length of time, can easily become an addiction. I have known many Bradfordians, new and old, who show signs of this condition (several are in this book); and I am certain that I too, had I the privilege of living in this unique town, would rapidly become a hopeless case. Addicts perhaps, but certainly not sufferers – there are no unpleasant side-effects. Enthusiasm for Bradford engenders contentment.

If you doubt me, then read this book. Here is the story of a small Wiltshire town over a hundred years, told largely through the memories of some fifty of its inhabitants. Times of peace and conflict, work and play, poverty and affluence – the stuff of any history – are here spiced with graphic freshness tempered with fond reflection such as only mature reminiscence can convey. There are images of compassion, robustness, and quiet humanity; there are carefully crafted phrases which might grace a poem; and there are moments of wonderfully unexpected trivia which, looking back, were perhaps significant after all – the midnight milkman, footprints in the mud settled on the swimming pool floor, hymn-singing in the mushroom quarries during an air raid, mice in the sweet-shop after dark.

Margaret Dobson has written a remarkable social history. It is scholarly and reliable, detailed but never dull, and it flows seamlessly and fairly through all the events and issues of Bradford's recent past, bringing them (and us) firmly into the present. It is the distillation of some eight years' affectionate, painstaking and enthusiastic work on the author's part, and of a collective total of several thousands of years, I suppose, in the memories of her interviewees. The result (if I may borrow her description of a coronation celebration) may best be described as, 'satisfyingly splendid'. If you were not already addicted to Bradford on Avon, you soon will be. And if you were, this book will prove irresistible.

John Chandler
East Knoyle, Wiltshire
October 1997

INTRODUCTION

Much of the heart of Bradford has changed very little in the last hundred years. Ancient houses still line its streets and jumble together along its lanes and in its secret alleyways. The sense of the past is very strong in the town, not only in its buildings but also through the many families here which can proudly claim to have been part of Bradford for centuries. Bradfordians' recollections, together with their memories of their parents and grandparents go back to the earliest days of the twentieth century. These rich and varied stories are too valuable to be lost. It is the intention of this book to try and record something of the social fabric of Bradford as it has altered over the last hundred years. Fortunately it is still possible today to wander around Bradford in the same streets and to see many of the same houses and cottages which constantly bring the past back to life.

At the beginning of the twentieth century Bradford was a self-sufficient entity. People lived, worked and shopped in the town for all their needs. Apart from special outings, usually organised on a yearly basis by businesses and churches, nearly all entertainment also took place within the town itself. Even significant national events, such as Royal funerals and coronations were marked by solemn processions through the town and thus became local events as well. It was only some years after the Second World War that Bradford's inward-looking economic and social patterns began to disintegrate. Transport systems changed dramatically and the town also had to accept an influx of 'incomers', many from the south-east, who seeking a quieter life were delighted by the architectural charms of the town and attracted by its reasonable house prices. It is, in part, their money and enthusiasm for old Bradford which has helped to preserve it. The town is now part of a much wider world; many of its inhabitants work and shop outside of its boundaries: but it remains a special place, created by the many, many generations of those who have lived and worked here over the centuries.

My first tape recordings of Bradford people talking about their lives date back to 1989 when I was working with so many others towards the production of the Community Play, *Under the Fish and Over the Water*. As a raw 'incomer' I did not contemplate doing anything more than that, knowing I was quite unqualified to say anything interesting or useful about my new home. But I retained a strong feeling that Bradford's life through the twentieth century should be recorded in such a way that others could share in its past before some of it disappeared. I am very aware that I know far less about the town than anyone who has been here for a long time. But sometimes it happens that those who have always lived in their familiar world take it for granted and it is the incomer who appreciates new surroundings with a fresh and delighted eye. This book is my tribute to the town.

People have been very generous, welcoming me, a complete stranger, into their homes and into their lives. I have now spent eight years listening to Bradford voices, recording some of them and fashioning them, with as much accuracy and attention to detail as I can manage into a permanent record. Where there are mistakes, they are all mine.

It is impossible to thank everyone for the help they have given me, but some people who have sustained me throughout this enterprise must be mentioned. Frederick Fielding has become an especial friend who has encouraged me throughout. Without his quiet and steady persistence it is unlikely that this book would ever have been completed. Jack Stafford has been a most constant and reliable source of information. Jo Uncles has also contributed most helpfully throughout this long period of preparation. Mary Ashton has spent many hours at the Local Studies Centre on census returns and other related matters and her detailed help is much appreciated. She has also been a careful commentator on each chapter as it was written. I have been particularly glad that a Bradfordian, Jack Mock, was prepared to write most of chapter four about Bradford during the Second World War, thus adding his sound local knowledge to my endeavours. Frances Richardson's help over the specialist and time-consuming task of creating the index has been absolutely invaluable. There are many others and I am grateful to them all, each and everyone.

Then there has been the challenge of finding photographs to bring to life various aspects of Bradford's which might be unknown to readers fresh to the town while, at the same time, providing unfamiliar material to interest those who have lived in it all their lives. I wanted to show people going about their normal affairs in the town as the century has progressed as well as recording local buildings and the changes to them. Many Bradfordians, and sometimes their relations now living elsewhere, have hunted through their albums, their cupboards and even their attics to help in this task. Such kind and patient response has been much appreciated and has greatly enhanced the book.

Fred Fieldings's collection of Bradford scenes and people has been a major contribution to this photographic record. Chris Penny and Philip Davis have also loaned interesting and unusual views of the town from their collections. As film was difficult to obtain during the Second World War, it has not been easy to provide suitable material of that period, but the Wiltshire and Swindon County Record Office generously provided some useful material from their Wiltshire Times file and the interest and response from the Local Studies Centre, Trowbridge has been similarly helpful. Peter Maundrell's professional contribution to the later chapters is a great help and my son, Robert, is another valued contributor to the final chapter.. Avon Rubber most readily and generously provided several photographs of the rubber works and the town centre. Beamish, the North of England Open Air Museum has also allowed reproduction of some of their material and the Bradford on Avon Preservaton Trust has provided several interesting views of the town. The book ends on the positive note of looking to the future which must surely come through Bradford's three schools. The immediate and involved way all three responded to my urgent demands for practical assistance in providing suitable photographs *at once* convinces me that our town's young people are in very good hands.

I would also like to acknowledge the professional assistance received from Colin Johns and the Bradford Town Scheme, Major John Peters, Royal GBW Museum, Salisbury and the Imperial War Museum, Lambeth, London

Margaret Dobson
Sladesbrook, Bradford on Avon
October 1997

About the author

Margaret Dobson studied for her degree in English literature at Birkbeck College, London University, and took her research degree through Southampton University. After a long period as Head of English in an Inner London Comprehensive she became a Senior Lecturer in English and Education for 16 years at Middlesex Polytechnic, later Middlesex University.

She is now an English Tourist Board Guide for the West Country. She is also Archivist to the Bradford on Avon Preservation Trust and its Chairman.

She has two sons, Paul and Robert.

LIST OF CONTRIBUTORS

Many people have given time and trouble in creating this book and it is impossible to name everyone. But I am grateful to them all. Here is a list of those whose contributions appear most directly in the text.

Miss Mary Ashton
Mrs.Winifred Bancroft (née Millard) (WB)
Mrs. Joyce Baumann (JB)
Mrs. Sally Beale
Mrs. Ursula Boulding (UB)
Mrs. Edith Budds (née Ratcliffe) (EB)
Mrs. Noreen Cambourne (née Bryant) (NC)
Mrs. Isabelle Carter (née Heavyside) (IC)
Mrs. Peggy Cussins (PC)
Mr. Michael Darlow (MD1)
Mr. Martin Davies (MD2)
Mr. Philip Davis
Mrs. Margaret Dobson (MD3)
Mrs. Molly Dotesio (née Dunn) (MD4)
Mrs. Mavis Earnshaw (ME)
Mr. Frederick Fielding (FF)
Mr. John Fielding (JF)
Mr. Harry Fox
Reverend Gordon Green (GG)
Mrs. Sue Griffiths
Mrs. Joyce Gridley
Mrs. Joan Hanney
Mrs. Dione Hartnoll (née Moulton) (DH1)
Mr. Reg Hayter (RH)
Mrs. Doreen Hemming
Mrs. Lily Holbrook (née Banks) (LH)
Mr. Clifford Holsgrove

Mr. Dick Huntley (DH2)
Mrs. Phyl Huntley (née Powney) (PH)
Mr. Colin Johns (CJ)
Mrs. Vicky Landell Mills
Mrs. Hilary Lywood (née Chard) (HL)
Mr. John Ludlow (JL)
Mr. Roger Mawby
Mr. Jack Mock (JM)
Mrs. Gwen Mortimer (née Lailey) (GM)
Dr. Alex Moulton (AM)
Mrs. Diana Newman (DN)
Mrs. Rose Niblett (née Bennett) (RN)
Miss Mabel Pearce
Mr. Christopher Penny
Mrs. Anne Riley
Mr. Geoffrey Saxty (GS)
Mr. Jack Stafford (JS)
Mr. Henry Stevens (HS)
Mr. David Stokes
Mr. Sidney Stone (SS)
Mr. Jack Symes
Mrs. Isla Tuck
Mrs. May Turtle
Miss Joyce "Jo" Uncles (JU)
Mr. Donald Vass (DV)
Mrs. Elsie Wilkins (née Bainton) (EW)
Mr. Tim Williams (TW)

One feature I am only too conscious of is that voices on the tape recordings have a warmth and vitality it is impossible to reproduce on the printed page. I have not tidied up the original transcripts of the tape recordings too much since it seems right to keep the flavour of spoken language as much as possible. All individual voices are in italics which I hope will help make different contributions clear to the reader.

The initials in brackets at the end of each piece will help you to identify who is speaking and the year in which the tape recording was made, e.g (WB89) = Mrs. Winifred Bancroft speaking in 1989: (MD2/97) = Mr. Martin Davies speaking in 1997.

CHAPTER ONE

1900 - 1913
A New Century Opens:
The Character of a Provincial Town

Bradford in 1902 at the Coronation of Edward VII ~ The Town's Sense of Self-Identity and its Modern Amenities, the new Technical Institute and the Swimming Baths ~ Shops, Churches and Schools ~ Poverty in the Town ~ Spencer Moulton as major employer in Bradford ~ Avoncliff Workhouse & Town Charities ~ Church Lads Brigade and Territorial Army Recruits ~ Organization of Town Affairs ~ The Purchase of Westbury House and Gardens by the Urban District Council ~ Town Celebrations for the Coronation of George V in 1911

IN THE PICTURE OPPOSITE SOME of the townspeople of Bradford on Avon are standing at the entrance to the Shambles. It is the 9th of August 1902 and, arrayed in their best clothes, they are gathered in the centre of the town to watch some of the triumphant processions slowly moving along Market Street to mark the coronation of King Edward VII. Coronation Day had been declared a Bank Holiday and every business in the town was closed. The detailed newspaper reports suggest that every single one of Bradford's 4,500 inhabitants must somehow have been involved. Mr. John Moulton was, of course, Chairman of the Managing Committee for the Coronation celebrations. Then there were special sub-committees for such important activities as Illuminations, Bonfire, Fireworks, School Children's Tea and – that essential component of all celebrations of the time – Medals. The *Wiltshire Times* tells us that: 'All the inmates of Bradford on Avon workhouse (excluding vagrants) were given a Medal to mark the Day.'

There were two sets of prizes for the most effective displays of private illuminations and it seems generally agreed that these were as good as the many displays by shops and commercial establishments. Indeed the Coronation edition of the *Wiltshire Times* hardly knew how to describe the efforts at decoration by Bradford's loyal and patriotic householders: 'The private residents in Trowbridge Road came out quite strong with their decorations, there being several veritable exhibitions: the same might be said of the various thoroughfares through which the procession passed.'

It must have been quite a scramble to get everything organised in time because every street in the town was in chaos until the very last moment. The new main drainage system was being installed throughout the town and the main sewer was not put under the town bridge until Coronation week itself. But fortunately all was well and the necessary thoroughfares were clear for the great day. The local paper claims that some twelve hundred school children[1] took part in the procession which must have taken much of the morning to wind itself around streets on both sides of the river. No doubt the entire town also joined in the celebrations in Priory Park, the large area of open ground on the hillside above Newtown which belonged to the Priory and which the owner, Mrs. Collett, usually made available for grand open air public events. No one was left out and the *Wiltshire Times* could report that the youngest and the oldest members of the community had been especially rewarded: 'The juveniles had their promised tea and the aged poor were entertained at the Town Hall to a repast which cheered and benefited them.'

Traffic outside the Town Hall when the century opens. The Town Hall was designed by Thomas Fuller of Bath and built in 1854. After Bradford Urban District Council moved out in 1911 it eventually became a public hall used for dances and other social events. It also served as the first cinema in the town.

The "aged poor", some flashing their medals, would be filing up the steps and into the somewhat flamboyant public building opposite the Shambles for their festive repast. Built by a private company, the Town Hall Company, and let to the town on a long lease, this large structure, so unlike the sober architecture of most of Bradford, had been the centre of local affairs for nearly fifty years. It incorporated the Town Hall, the Fire Station and the Police Station; it also included a magistrates' room and dwellings for the police. Bradford was divided into two administrative districts. One was the densely packed urban parish defined as the area enclosed within a circle of one mile radius of The Swan in Church Street; the other rural area called Bradford Without was made up from outlying settlements such as Cumberwell, Bradford Leigh and Trowle.[2] Both the Urban District Council (U.D.C.), and the Rural District Council held their monthly meetings in the Town Hall.

The new General Post Office, seen in the picture on the right of the Shambles, had just been completed in 1901 and this ensured that Bradford could boast an up to date national postal service which we, nearly a century later, can only envy. In 1903 the Post Office, presided over by Miss Lydia White, was open from 7 in the morning until 9 at night right through from Monday to Saturday and also for two hours on Sunday mornings. Letters were dispatched from Bradford eight times a day and delivered around the town three times daily, the first delivery being at 7 a.m. Parcel dispatches and delivery services, on a separate timetable, were equally frequent.[3] Miss Lydia White also supervised a telegraph service and so, with the opening of a telephone exchange by the National Telephone Company in 1898, Bradford could surely feel it was keeping up to date with modern improvements.

At the beginning of the twentieth century Bradfordians had a clear sense of their own identity and reason to feel some satisfaction with their town. There were some other public buildings which contributed to the modernity of the town, for Bradford was fortunate in having two wealthy local benefactors who gave generously to public causes.

Mr. John Moulton, already mentioned as Chairman of the Managing Committee for the Coronation festivities, Justice of the Peace and joint owner of the Spencer Moulton Rubber Works, was a very significant figure in the town's affairs. With his wife and two young sons, he lived in The Hall, the late sixteenth century building which still adds its imposing presence to the town's landscape.

Lord Edmond Fitzmaurice of Leigh (1846-1935), had particular concern for the many poor in Bradford. He was the second son of the fourth Marquis of Lansdowne, the family which had owned Bowood near Calne since 1754 and which still owns it today. The family had always been active in political affairs and Lord Fitzmaurice was a distinguished Liberal, who after earlier service as

Above: Mr. and Mrs. John Moulton's sons, John (b.1886) and Charles Eric (b. 1889) in the grounds of The Hall. Both boys served in the First World War. John became an eminent botanist. He married and had three children, the youngest of whom is Dr. Alex Moulton. He died in 1926. Charles Eric was killed fighting in France in 1915.

Below: The Technical Institute in Junction Road as it appeared in 1905. Some Trowbridge Road houses can be seen in the background on the left.

Under-secretary of State in Gladstone's government in the 1880s was re-elected as member for the North Division of Wiltshire in 1898. Chairman of the Wiltshire County Council, he lived at Leigh House, on the northern side of the town, now an hotel, Leigh Park House. In spite of his busy political life, he still devoted much of his time and money to local concerns. Lord Fitzmaurice had been the principal contributor to the Technical Institute in Junction Road, formally inaugurated and handed over to the town in 1897 and described by the *Wiltshire Times* as "the focus of the Technical Education movement in the district". The new County Day School for both boys and girls was designed as part of the same complex, which also included further facilities for Bradfordians to enjoy such as a fully equipped gymnasium. The buildings later became the Grammar School and still stand, a century later, as the central area of what is now Fitzmaurice Place retirement apartments.

With no children of his own, Lord Fitzmaurice went out of his way to give financial help where needed. School uniforms, extra books, years of study up to University level – Lord Fitzmaurice would listen and contribute. He also funded two scholarships to the County Day School. There are many stories of his quietly funding those in need. But not everyone could accept this generosity:

He used to pay for a lot of people to go to the Grammar School. My sister passed – I didn't – and he offered to pay for her. But my mum wouldn't accept charity and she wouldn't let her go. He paid for a lot of poor people in Bradford, though. He was a really lovely man. He was good to everyone. (LH97)

Throughout his long life, Lord Fitzmaurice continued to allow the children in the locality the run of his gardens on Friday afternoons. Mostly they were quiet, grateful for a chance to play on smooth grass instead of in their usual rough fields; it was an unfamiliar pleasure to roll down the slope from one lawn to another and to explore round the summerhouse. But Mr. Rawlings, the head gardener, was not so enthusiastic. A bucket of drinking water and a white mug were always placed near the big mulberry tree for the children's use and there are several accounts of his battles to stop the children picking the fruit. Mulberry leaves, which a boy might need for his silkworms at home in a box, were another source of dispute. Jack Stafford still has vivid memories of warfare with Mr. Rawlings:

He was very strict. He always carried a dutch hoe and he'd give you a poke with the handle if he thought you were out of line. In those days Lord Fitzmaurice's grounds came as far as the roundabout in Sladesbrook and we used to wait there to go in a door in the high wall and up the long path to the garden. While we were waiting for the door to be unlocked some of the older boys would be climbing on the wall and old Rawlings would creep down and give you the edge of his tongue and another good prod if he caught you.

We weren't big enough to get up to real mischief but we'd run around the shrubbery and leave a track through the ivy under the shrubs. So he put wires across to trip us up. He was full of things like that. (JS97)

One hopes the butler was more tolerant.

We went there carol singing one night, us girls, we used to have candles then and the candle fell and set fire to the mat. So the others ran away and left me to put it out. But I left it and joined the others round the front and went on singing. And the butler came out and asked what is it. Lord Fitzmaurice said they've been singing lovely, and the butler said yes, sir, I heard them. So he gave us half a crown after burning his mat. What he said in the morning when he saw that mat burned I don't know. (LH97)

Bradford townsfolk could also boast of another newly acquired amenity which Trowbridge, the much bigger rival town three miles down the road, could not possibly match. To commemorate Queen Victoria's Diamond Jubilee in 1897, Mr. John Moulton and Lord Fitzmaurice had contributed generously to the building of the Public Baths in Bridge Street which opened a year later at the total cost of £1,200. Since bathrooms did not exist for the vast majority and since it was commonplace for one outside privy to be shared by the inhabitants of as many as five cottages, the provision of this new amenity was taken up with enthusiasm by all: 'a very pleasing feature being the general support extended by the working classes who gave according to their means, the result being that the baths have been handed over to the town entirely free from financial liability beyond the actual working expenses,' proclaimed the *Wiltshire Times*. (WT11.6.98)

Mr. Moulton had already created a small public pleasure ground on the land between the site of the Baths and the town bridge, replacing the old dye house and timber yard which previously stood there. Nowadays we would find these old buildings interesting and picturesque but attitudes have changed. The *Wiltshire Times* commented: 'The Baths stand at the east end of the Pleasure Gardens, where Mr. Moulton has created a bright spot in place of the dilapidated buildings which formerly spoiled the appearance of the locality.' The Public Library and a car park are now on the site, but the fine iron railings alongside the river which carry the initials JM on each post are part of the original fittings which Mr. John Moulton put in place.

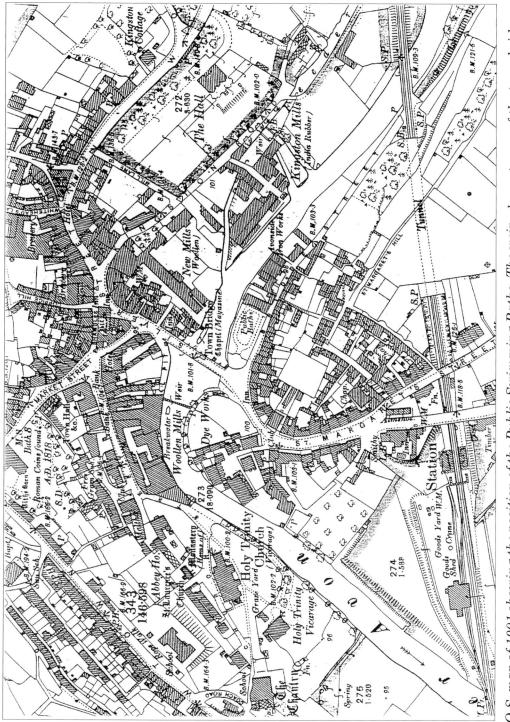

O.S. map of 1901 showing the position of the Public Swimming Baths. The weir, downstream of the town bridge, was a temporary structure erected and removed when necessary.

Some major landmarks in Bradford on Avon as they appeared at the beginning
of the twentieth century.
Above: The town bridge with its blind house (lock-up), sometimes called "the chapel".
Below: The Norman parish church, Holy Trinity. On the right is the Saxon church,
which was probably rebuilt in stone as we see it in the tenth century. After several
other uses it was rediscovered in the 1850s. Behind the two churches lies the
upper part of Church Street.

The Baths, equipped with seventeen curtained dressing-boxes and a hot and cold shower, contained a heated swimming pool where 'those who relish a plunge may dive into six feet of water'. The shallow end was three feet six inches. Everyone could now enjoy the novelty of a private bath (either first class costing 4d (2p) or second class costing 2d (1p) with hot water on tap. The balance sheet giving 'the actual working expenses' for the six months ending September 1900 provides interesting details on the uses made of the Baths, and shows that the men of the town took to these new facilities more quickly than the women. The Urban District Council, clearly a prudent body, laid down 27 bye-laws[4] regarding use of the Baths with penalty of £5.00 for any offence against them. Mr. Joseph Heavyside with his wife Julia became Superintendent of the Baths and Pleasure Grounds at the wage of £1.00 per week in May 1909[5] and it was in his time that a new water supply was piped to the Baths from Ladywell and Barton Orchard in 1915. It took sixteen and three quarter hours to fill the Swimming Baths each time from the new supply. It is not surprising that the water was only changed twice a week.

The self-sufficient nature of the town can also be easily appreciated from a simple tally of the range of shops in the Shambles in 1900.[6] Around ten different establishments managed to crowd themselves into this small space: William Summers, baker & confectioner; C. Hart, jeweller & watchmaker; Thomas Coupland, grocer & patent medicines; Elizabeth Rudman, china & glass dealer; Emma Fishlock, pork butcher; Ellen Caball, another confectioner from 1903; William Bailey, hairdresser & toy dealer; A.W. Wheeler, outfitter; Mrs. K. Adams, grocer; William Earle, ironmonger and William Bowden's fish shop on the corner with Market Street which would be replaced by the new General Post Office the following year.

This immense variety of domestic goods and services literally on the doorstep becomes even more astonishing to our modern eyes when one considers the many more shops and services available all over the town – along Newtown, Market Street, Church Street, up Silver Street, up Whitehill and over the town bridge into Bridge Street, St. Margaret's Street, Frome Road and the Trowbridge Road. For example, Silver Street alone could provide the following: Messrs. Knees (Complete House Furnishers and General Ironmongers), together with two chemists, four butchers, two meat companies, three bootmakers, three drapers as well as a tailor, an ironmonger, a stationer, a plasterer, a grocer & fruiterer, a provision store, a baker & confectioner, three public houses, one wines & spirits and the early telephone exchange.

Lists of tradesmen and services in the town which appear in the Trades Directories of the early 1900s seem endless. When one adds to this the nine churches, the Technical Institute, the five schools (a figure which does not take into account private educational establishments) and 21 public houses, it would seem Bradfordians had no reason to go out of their town unless they chose to do so.

There were nine places of worship in the town, two of them Church of England and seven Non-Conformist. Six schools served the town in general, but a number of private schools also flourished. But while no doubt many enjoyed their modern lifestyle of 1902, and some families had enough income for private education and piano lessons, the vast majority of the townsfolk could not have found life easy. The Coronation edition of the *Wiltshire Times* tells us that there are 3,688 diamonds in Queen Alexandra's crown. The very next item of news is that food is dearer than it has ever been over the previous 25 years. Was some covert criticism on the distribution of wealth intended here? The eulogistic and patriotic tone of the newspaper would suggest not. The sharp contrast in wealth and comfort was simply a statement of fact and something that most people seemed to take for granted. Here is a description of life for one Bradford family from someone whose husband, Ernest Bancroft, was born in the first decade of the twentieth century:

> *My husband was one of the youngest in a family of 14 children and his father had been one of nine. There was about 18 months or two years between babies – that was the usual thing in those days They lived in Newtown at the bottom of Wine Street; the house is still there now. Of course by the time my husband was born the older ones were getting married. But Ernest's father was in the building trade, a stone mason, and before he went to work in the morning he used to go out chimney sweeping for extra money. (WB89)*

Nowadays, as we look at the interesting little houses full of 'character' in Newtown, Middle Rank and Tory it is almost impossible to imagine the state of these dwellings at the beginning of the twentieth century. Multiple occupation was the norm. The steep hillsides upon which Bradford houses are built encouraged such use. Much of the inner part of the town, including houses in Barton Orchard, Coppice Hill and Whitehill, had been built on 'a cottage upon a cottage' kind of system. For example, many of the houses in Tory have their front door on one level and their back door two storeys above. In 1900 this back door would probably be the entrance to the meagre dwelling of a totally separate family. Nor would occupants be the owners of the properties. Landlords tended to be living elsewhere, simply extracting rents from their tenants and maintaining the houses in the most minimal fashion. Built into the hillsides, and with little in the way of modern foundations, these old houses inevitably oozed damp through their floors and walls. Lack of piped water indoors, little heating and even less sanitation were a natural part of daily life for large families crowded together in tiny rooms. We can only speculate on what it was like to live in such conditions. But first hand descriptions of living in Bradford in the 1920s and 1930s can be found in chapter three and give us some notion of domestic life before the amenities we take for granted were readily available.

Bradford had been a flourishing town since the middle ages with its success founded on the clothmaking industry. The height of its prosperity came during the late seventeenth and eighteenth centuries – as the Georgian houses in the town, built by the clothiers who organised and profited from this trade bear ample witness. Daniel Defoe had visited Bradford around 1725 and recorded his amazement at their wealth, stating that in Bradford: 'it was no extraordinary thing to have clothiers worth from ten thousand to forty thousand pounds a man,[7] still a substantial sum today and a lordly fortune at the time. But the cloth industry was always vulnerable, dependent upon factors outside the control of those who worked within it. There is a long history of boom times and slumps in the demand for Bradford cloth, depending on alterations in trade agreements, changes in fashion and the development of new processes within the industry.

The nineteenth century records a steady decline in the local cloth trade[8] as customers moved to the Yorkshire mills which offered modern production methods and lower prices. National demand was also growing for material which was lighter in weight yet Bradford persisted in the manufacture of traditional and heavier broadcloth. Abbey Mill in Church Street was built as a new cloth mill in 1875: but it was forced to close by 1902.[9] The last dye-house, which is now St. Margaret's Hall, closed in 1903 and two years later Greenland Upper Mill, the last cloth mill in the town, also stopped production. Although other traditional trades – notably stone quarrying – provided employment, there was much poverty as the staple industry of the town declined and finally died. For some Bradfordians the only solution to intolerable conditions was to seek a new life elsewhere. The newspapers of the time continually carry advertisements for workers abroad. To emigrate to an unknown and uncertain future in America or one of the colonies of the British Empire was preferable to staying in Bradford.

There was one longstanding source of employment in the town. By far the greatest contributor to Bradford's economy in 1900 was the Spencer Moulton Rubber Works on the five and a half acre site along by the river just upstream from the town bridge. It was established in 1848 when Stephen Moulton returned to England from America, intent on setting up a manufactory for the then new invention of vulcanised rubber. It may have been a personal contact with the owner of Woolley Grange which caused him to choose Bradford. He bought The Hall and began manufacture in what had been the cloth-making Kingston Mill in his grounds. With true entrepreneurial speed he was exhibiting at the Great Exhibition of 1851 and was awarded a Prize Medal for his manufacture. Isambard Kingdom Brunel thought highly of the new Bradford enterprise, writing personally to Stephen Moulton for technical assistance on the development of rubber plates and flanges which were then supplied for his third and last great shipbuilding project, the *Great Eastern*.[10]

Producing army goods, such as capes and rubber backed groundsheets in their thousands, for the Crimean War[11] provided further work, but Moulton's main business was in supplying equipment to railways all over the world. After varying fortunes, the firm amalgamated with George Spencer & Co. of London in 1891 when it became George Spencer, Moulton & Co. At this point, the workforce numbered 78. By the beginning of the twentieth century it was a flourishing commercial operation producing a wide range of items, although still mostly for the demands of the railway industry. By the end of 1900 its employees numbered 164, rising 5 years later to a total of 184 as shown below.

Number & range of Spencer Moulton employees in 1905[12]

	Young persons		Above 18 years Years	Total Male &
	Male	*Female*		*Female*
1. Mixers, Washers and Cutting Shop	2		49	51
2. Hose Room	1	14	21	36
3. Heater	2		37	39
4. Fitters, Smiths, Joiners, Pattern Makers & Enginemen	1		28	29
5. Trimming Shops	1		20	21
6. Messenger & Watchman			2	2
7. Stores			6	6
Total	**7**	**14**	**163**	**184**

In 1906 another rubber manufacturer came to Bradford, taking over the empty Greenland Upper Mill. The Sirdar Rubber Company (which would be bought out by the Avon Rubber Company of Melksham nine years later) installed the most modern machinery of the day and went into full production, thus considerably boosting the town's economy. But Spencer Moulton, now run by Mr. John Moulton, Stephen Moulton's youngest son, remained the dominant employer in the town, paying good wages and with a close, paternalistic relationship with its workforce. In June 1902, for example, Spencer Moulton employees went up to London in the special train hired as a yearly event for the firm's annual outing. They were accompanied on their trip, as usual, by the Bradford on Avon Amateur Brass Band, which had just become the Spencer Moulton Brass Band. The morning's parade from Kingston Mill across the town bridge to the railway station was good practice for the coming Coronation.

Another aspect of the town in Coronation year is provided by a booklet published by Bradford on Avon (Poor Law) Union for 1902.[13] Six adjacent parishes were linked into Bradford to provide relief for those in dire need. The Union Workhouse which had been at Avoncliff since 1841 still housed 92 persons as "indoor paupers" who were visited once a month by a changing rota of Poor Law

Bradford on Avon Brass Band in 1902, pictured in Temple Field. This was a field along the Holt Road just beyond The Hall. Originally an amateur band, it was enlarged in 1902 and affiliated to the Spencer Moulton Rubber Works.

HALF=YEAR ENDED LADY=DAY, 1902.

Number of Paupers Relieved.

BRADFORD-ON-AVON UNION.	In-Door				Out-Door				Total Relieved by In-door and Out-door Relief	Relieved In and Out-door	Total Relieved during Half-year
	ADULTS		Children	Total	ADULTS		Children	Total			
	Males	Females			Males	Females					
Bradford-on-Avon Union	59	37	15	111	64	118	80	262	378	12	361
Vagrants	...	...	...	227	...	...	...	...	227	...	227
Total											588

Details from the published information and accounts of the Bradford on Avon Union Workhouse, 1902

ATTENDANCES of GUARDIANS & RURAL DISTRICT COUNCILLORS

DURING YEAR 1901-1902.

	Board Meetings	Rural District Council	Assessment Committee	School Attendance Committee	Finance Committee	House Committee	Contract Committee	Total Number of Meetings attended	Total Number of Meetings held
No. of Meetings held	28	21	8	12	8	18	3		88
Mr. F. Applegate	21		3	4	2	9	1	31	67
,, F. Austin	26							26	28
,, J. H. Beaven	22			9				33	41
Mrs. M. I. Beaven	26		7	11				40	43
,, A. M. Beddoe	20							21	31
Dr. J. Beddoe	28		7			12		53	81
Mr. T. Moore	27		7	6		10		44	55
,, F. Rich	21				1			28	49
,, A. T. Scrine	27							27	43
,, T. W. Copland	18							18	27
Canon Hon. S. Meade	14	11	4					29	27
Mr. J. Gillman	23	17	5	6			1	40	57
,, G. Gingell	20	16	5	3			3	47	49
,, G. Hayward	14	11		9				32	69
,, B. C. Mattick	25	19						61	72
,, J. H. Bishop	19	15	4					34	72
,, G. Gerrish	16	11				8		27	49
,, W. Webb	7	7			1	1	1	14	49
,, E. P. Alexander	25	19	7	10	8	8		73	88
,, A. J. Beaven	18	15		6	1			84	52
,, J. Sawtell	18	10	3		3	7		34	61
,, J. Mole	21	18						44	65
,, A. Wallington	9	7	1	1	1			17	61
,, S. G. Kendall	6	13						10	49
,, L. Mizen	4	6						37	63
,, E. Burbidge	18	18	2		2		3	17	61
,, T. Rudman	8	6		3				23	49
,, J. Marsh	13	18	1			1		29	49
,, D. Windo	16	18		4				8	57
,, J. T. Pike	4	7				3		15	57
,, F. W. Woods, Jun.	7	4	3					48	61
,, R. Edmonds	22	16				7		43	70
,, W. J. Wilkins	18	15	5		0	4	1		76

* Appointed 13th September, 1901.

Dr. *Particulars of the Common Charges for*

	£	s.	d.	£	s.	d.
To In-maintenance	479	4	3¼			
— Salaries of Workhouse Officers ..	83	8	1			
— Rations ,, ,, ..	83	15	4¼			
— Salary of Chaplain of Workhouse	30	0	0			
— ,, Medical Officer of Workhouse	20	0	0			
— Carpenter's, Engineer's, Mason's and Plasterer's Work and Materials for Repairs	177	18	7			
— Blankets, Sheeting, Bedding, Furniture, &c., for the Workhouse	62	12	5½			
— Rates, Tithes and Insurance ..	21	1	2			
— Lamps on Aqueduct	15	4	4			
— Right of Way over Aqueduct ..	2	10	0			
— ,, ,, into Workhouse	0	10	0			
— Master's Petty Disbursements ..	3	0	1			
				979	4	3¾
— Out Relief	513	5	5¾			
— Boarding out	79	3	3			
— Non-resident Relief	69	9	10			
— Paupers in Institutions ..	35	2	2			
— Lunatics	543	10	11			
— Extra Medical Fees	3	0	0			
— Salaries of Clerk and Relieving Officers	113	9	0			
— ,, ,, Medical Officers ..	100	0	0			
— Collector's Commission	7	7	3			
— Superannuation	42	18	5			
— Rent, &c., of Board Room, Office, &c., at Town Hall	15	17	6			
— Loss on Oakum Account	3	15	2			
— Expenses under Union Assessment Acts	26	6	6			
— Contribution to the Bath Mineral Water Hospital	7	0	0			
— Contribution to Bath Eye Infirmary	3	0	0			
— Settlement and Removal Expenses	0	14	6			
— Clerk's Petty Disbursements, &c. ..	4	6	11½			
— Advertisements, Printing & Stationery	105	18	0			
— Audit Stamp	5	0	0			
— Legal Expenses	2	6	6			
— Vaccination Fees and Expenses ..	38	2	0			
— Registration Fees and Rent of Office	26	5	0			
				1745	18	5¼
				£2725	2	9

the Half-year ended Michaelmas, 1901. Cr.

	£	s.	d.
By Treasurer Grants from County Council ..	807	13	4
— Wood Account Profit	0	13	0
— Pig Account ditto	29	17	2
— Garden Account ditto	5	15	8
— Fractions Unpaid	0	0	10¼
— Collector of the Guardians' Account	73	12	6
— Sale of Rags, &c.	0	2	0
— Payments to Master of Workhouse for Maintenance, &c.	14	16	6
— Contributions under Poor Law Officers' Superannuation Act, 1896	11	1	7
— Grant under Agricultural Rates Act, 1896 ..	216	16	11½
	1160	9	6¾

— Parishes, their proportions, according to their Assessable values:—

	Assessable Value.						
Atworth	£2240	£71	5	10			
Bradford-on-Avon ..	19268	613	4	11			
Bradford Without ..	3112	99	0	11			
Broughton Gifford ..	3927	124	19	9¼			
Holt	5084	161	16	2			
Limpley Stoke ..	4301	136	17	9			
Monkton Farleigh ..	2505	79	14	7			
South Wraxall ..	1298	41	6	3			
Westwood	1473	46	17	8			
Winkfield	1641	52	4	7			
Winsley	4312	137	4	9			
					1564	13	2¼
	£49161						
					£2725	2	9

Guardians. But attitudes had changed in the sixty years since it was set up and the Bradford Union was now favouring "outdoor relief", providing money and occasionally food and clothing for the needy living in the area. Co-operation between local towns meant that arrangements were often made to send the poor or disadvantaged to appropriate Institutions, even when outside the Bradford Union. Thus their 1902 booklet lists the names of the fifty "Lunatics" being kept at the Wiltshire County Asylum in Devizes at a weekly rate of maintenance of just under 10s 0d (50p). Five of them had their maintenance paid by their families, seven were partly maintained and the Bradford Union paid all other dues – a hefty annual sum of money to which the town's ratepayers were obliged to contribute.

This is, of course, the reason why the business affairs of the Union were made so very public. The names of the Guardians and Officers, their expenses and remuneration, the number of meetings held and the individual attendance record of each Guardian and Officer are fully recorded. We know that Fred Watts, the Master of the Workhouse, received £60 per annum, his wife Ellen who was Matron received £30. There were four other staff receiving in total £95 per annum as well as Edith Latham whose heavy duties as General Servant brought her a return of £13 a year. There were other items which the Board of Guardians thought worth paying for. A little headline in the *Wiltshire Times* for 4 August 1906 reads MUSIC AT THE WORKHOUSE and, reading on, we learn that Miss Tonkins of Avoncliff who has played the harmonium in the workhouse chapel 104 times in the past year will now be paid £4 per year to continue to do so. This was not sufficient diversion for Miss Mabel Monger, who resigned earlier in the same year after two and a half years as an assistant nurse. She declined a higher salary, saying she 'could not stand the deadly monotony of the place'. (WT26.4.06)

Full lists of those receiving relief were also published together with details of what they received. Thus the troubled circumstances of individual families were known to all. One large family[14] certainly had difficulties: Cora, aged 11, and Rose, aged nine, were being fostered in Monkton Farleigh; Joseph , aged 12 and William, aged seven were being fostered by a different family in Bradford Leigh; Florence was being trained and maintained at an Institution known as the Wiltshire School of Cookery and the Wiltshire County Asylum was caring for another Cora who, one assumes, might well have been the children's mother.

The published accounts provide a further picture of life at Avoncliff. Paupers in the Workhouse contributed to their upkeep by picking oakum,[15] keeping pigs, selling wood and garden produce, raising £36.5s.10d by their efforts in six months in 1901. Their co-operation was part of the system, but some resisted; two reports from the Magistrates' Court make the point:

*'Fourteen days hard labour to two inmates for refusing to pick oakum.
(DWG30.3.11)'*

*William Bartlett, a vagrant, sentenced to 21 days hard labour for refusing
to do his allotted task at the workhouse. Defendant admitted offence and said
he strongly objected to working in a cubicle – he had no objection to working in
the open air.(DWG23.3.11)*

Jim King, a Bradford man born in 1900, could remember seeing some of the
inmates when he was about eight years-old. They used to deliver kindling wood
from the Workhouse to the council offices in Market Street, having pushed it on
a handcart all the way from Avoncliff. Also loaded on the handcart, he remembers,
was a large bound ledger book from the workhouse master for inspection by
council officials. The half-year ending Michaelmas 1901 required an expenditure
of just over £2,725, an enormous sum of money at a time when a group of four
cottages in the Winsley Road could be sold at auction in the same September for
a total of only £139. (WT 27.9.02)

Bradford on Avon.
Old Men's Almshouses.

*Hall's Almshouses in Frome Road. The gabled houses in the background in St.
Margaret's Street were demolished in the 1960s.*

There were several long established charities to help the aged poor of the
town, notably Hall's Almshouses in Frome Road for four old men (who were
allowed to have their wives with them) founded in 1700 and restored by Horatio

Moulton in 1890, and also St. Catherine's Almshouses, rebuilt in the nineteenth century and housing four old women.[16] All those over 70 had good news in 1908 when the Liberal Government brought in the Old Age Pension Act through which they were to receive 5s.0d (25p) a week, provided they had less than £21 per year coming to them from any other sources. The first payment was on 6 January 1909. The almswomen in the St. Catherine's Almshouses who already received a weekly stipend of 4s.0d (20p) found this was reduced to 2s.0d as a result. There seems to be no public record of whether the old men in Hall's Almshouses had the same treatment. Their weekly allowance in 1908 was 7s.6d (37p) but records show that 27 years later they were receiving only 5s.0d (25p) a week. 'The poor old women', as they were invariably called, continued to receive the 2s.0d that had been their lot since 1908.[17]

There were, of course, plenty of other interests and preoccupations in the town. For example, the Church Lads Brigade had recently been formed under Mr. O.P. Skrine who later became the owner of Kingsfield Grange. The boys, numbering eventually as many as 50, could engage in boxing, football, rifle practice and general army training. With their own bugle and drum band plus their handcart they appeared in all the parades and processions which took place yearly in the town. Together with other local companies, they enjoyed training camps at Dawlish and other coastal resorts every summer from 1909 to 1914. Their hut was replaced by a splendid HQ in New Road in 1914 built at Captain Skrine's own expense. Its drill hall, recreation room and rifle range some 23 yards in length remained in use for many years. Its remnants are still to be seen, now forming part of a commercial garage on the same site. Captain Skrine was to become a very significant figure in town affairs in 1916.

Their elder brothers, aged seventeen and a half and over, might be found exercising at the big Drill Hall in St. Margaret's Street which had previously been the dye house, learning about Territorial Army life in G Company, the 4th Battalion of the Wiltshire Regiment, commanded by the Earl of Radnor. Following the Boer War and probably aware of future European troubles, Parliament had passed Lord Haldane's Territorial and Reserve Act in 1907. There was a long history of local military units in Wiltshire, the Wiltshire Volunteers having been formed as far back as 1860. But the Wiltshire Territorial Association was inaugurated after a meeting in Trowbridge in 1908 and created as two major army units. One was the new 4th Battalion, an infantry unit, and the other was the Royal Wilts Imperial Yeomanry, a highly prestigious cavalry unit[18]. This also stemmed from an long established Yeomanry force and was now based at Chippenham where it was initially commanded by the Marquess of Bath. Bradford became central to its activities when he was succeeded in 1911 by Lieutenant Colonel G. Llewellen Palmer.

Above: The Church Lads Brigade returning from camp in about 1910. They are drawn up in the station car park with railway wagons in the shunting yard behind them. The Chantry and Well Path cottages are in the centre of the background, Wilkins Brewery on the left and Tory on the skyline to the right. The haystack on the right suggests the rural nature of the town.

Below: Territorials G Company of the 4th Battallion of the Wiltshire Regiment in camp about 1911. Frederick Fielding is standing fourth from the left. The small boy is one of the Stevens family, his father, without army headgear, sits behind him.

G Company was a strong branch of the 4th Battalion. Here was provision for friendship groups to meet and enjoy sporting events, practise in a flourishing shooting club and take part in training sessions and camps across Wiltshire and down to the sea. At a time when little organised entertainment was available for the young, this must have been a rare chance to have fun and activity at no personal expense. Consequently it flourished.

In many respects the town continued to conduct its own affairs as it always had done without too much outside interference. The Lay Lord of the Manor in 1902 was Sir Charles Parry Hobhouse of Monkton Farleigh, a title and office which had been purchased by the Hobhouse family from the Methuen family in the middle of the previous century. The formal public bodies which governed the town and its surroundings were Bradford Urban District Council, Bradford Rural District Council, the County Magistrates for the Division of Bradford and the Board of Guardians of the Workhouse. All held their meetings in the Town Hall and proceedings were reported in the local papers, sometimes with an unexpected informality. For example, the Master of Avoncliff Workhouse at a monthly meeting of the Board of Guardians:

> The Master said most of the tramps were strangers to him. Chairman: Any genuine fellows? Master: Yes sir, the last (sic) part of them. Our tramp wards are not inviting. The tramps are searched when they come in and they have their bath and do not get much sympathy from me. But when I see a genuine workman, I act up to the order and let him go. (DWG 9.3.11)

In the seventeenth and eighteenth centuries, town affairs had been in the hands of the wealthy clothiers. The situation was not so different in 1900 when prominent Bradford inhabitants, mostly men with businesses of their own to manage, gave their free time to serve on a range of committees to improve town amenities, administer law and order – and possibly protect some of their own interests. The same names appear across a wide range of local affairs. Clearly well known to each other, they have time and space for banter or personal comment in meetings. This is frequently reported in newspapers, adding a touch of entertainment in the solid columns of newsprint. The development of newspaper photography and all the diversity of newspaper layout which naturally followed was still a long way in the future.

Serving in public office was no sinecure. The Minutes of the U.D.C. are full of heated discussions over the sewage works being installed with so much complication near to the Kennet and Avon canal beyond the town. The narrow streets of the town gave cause for much anxiety, especially since petrol-powered vehicles were beginning to appear, sometimes driven at the reckless speed of 20 miles per hour. There were discussions of possibilities of widening such thoroughfares as Newtown, Silver Street and St. Margaret's Street. In bad weather road surfaces suffered extra damage as teams of horses struggled to drag their heavy loads up the slippery hills. Drainage and lighting were further concerns. In 1911 the Town Council admitted that Bradford was one of the worst lit towns in West Wiltshire and double gas burners were put into the gas lamps at the end of the Shambles and by the weigh house at the top of Masons Lane. But the town was full of darkness. More lights were placed in such areas as Huntingdon Street and up Woolley Street – although one councillor grumbled that this was lighting the suburbs and not the town itself! Then there was the constant problem of keeping the river clear.

The Highways Committee, for example, would 'call attention to the unsightly collection of mud in the bed of the river near the Town Bridge and to the bad smell arising therefrom.' This seemed to be a yearly problem, exacerbated by the mills and other trades in the town which used the Avon as a convenient way to dispose of waste or effluent. Both Mr. Crisp, the ironfounder in Bridge Street, together with the Great Western Railway, were accused of throwing cinders, ashes or rubbish into the river. The GWR indignantly denied the charge, but Mr. Crisp hit back. 'Mr. Crisp said he had better use for the cinders, and also asked the Council to remedy a complaint at Tayler's Court in Bridge Street, heaps of filth being deposited under his office window. It was a disgrace to the good old town of Bradford.' (DWG 26.1.11)

Dirt, smoke and smells were unavoidable in such a densely packed industrial little town. But residents were ready to stand up for themselves. Messrs. Wilkins & Hudson's brewery in Newtown is now long gone but in 1906 it was in full swing:

Mrs. L. Colhoun complained of smoke issuing from Messrs. Wilkins Brewery chimney. More than eight months had elapsed since several of the residents in the neighbourhood appealed against the nuisance but far from being remedied it was, if anything, worse than before. During the week previous to her letter her house was filled with smoke with scarcely any cessation. (DWG 26.4.06)

Mr. Wilkins' response was diplomatic but firm:

We are most anxious to cause as little annoyance as possible to residents near the Brewery and we have endeavoured to lessen smoke with some success. When a limit has been fixed by the Council as to the time of day allowed for the emission of black smoke from <u>all</u> the chimneys in the town, our firm will be pleased to fall in line...The Brewery has been in existence for something over

Above: The long range of buildings which made up Wilkins Brewery in Newtown, together with their public house, The Seven Stars. The terrace of three houses in the centre of the photograph was demolished soon after this was taken. Railwaymen cultivated their individual allotments on the land between the wire fencing and the railway tracks.

Below: Part of the procession for the memorial service in Holy Trinity Church to mourn the death of Edward VII in May 1910. The Scouts and the Church Lads Brigade are followed by town dignitaries. The two buildings on the immediate right have greatly changed since then. The next building with a blank wall at ground level and lattice work above was also later replaced.

100 years and surely in selecting a residence within a short distance from so large a chimney the possibility of a nuisance from the same should be taken into consideration. A great quantity of steam is required in a brewery and unfortunately it is impossible to produce the same without smoke. (DWG 26.4.06)

As Bradford had a sturdy number of tall chimneys belching black smoke from its mills along the river, as well as two other breweries – Ruddles on Coppice Hill and Spencers on Whiteheads Lane – Mr. Wilkins' generous offer to fall in line with the town's non-existent smokeless zone was not taken any further.

In 1910 and 1911 two matters were central to all public deliberations in Bradford. One involving much controversy was the proposal by the Urban District Council to move itself out of the Town Hall which it had always rented from the private company, the Town Hall Company, and to buy Westbury House for £1,000. The Town Hall was proving to be too small for the number of functions it had to serve. The U.D.C. argued Bradford would gain an imposing municipal building which would house Council officials on the upper floors and provide a basement for the storage of municipal documents, together with a depot for Council stores at the rear. The acquisition of Westbury House gardens was seen as an opportunity to demolish its high boundary wall beside St. Margaret's Street and to widen the main street on the south side of the town bridge, thus opening up a new town vista across the river. A further proposal was to turn the gardens themselves into a public park. At the end of the twentieth century we may take the little public park by the river as our natural right, unaware of the dramas surrounding its purchase. The full sum required for this imaginative development in the centre of the town was £1,400 – a substantial sum at the time. This would necessitate a loan of over £900, upon which ratepayers would pay the interest. Not surprisingly this provoked a very public debate.

The Local Government Board Enquiry held on 22 March 1911 was fully reported in the *Wiltshire Gazette*. The strong body of opposing ratepayers had hired a barrister, Mr. Vachell, to represent their interests against those of the U.D.C., led by the Clerk, Mr. Compton, and the Chairman, Mr. John Moulton, J.P. Mr. Compton argued that Westbury House was in reasonable order, having been bought by Mr. Adye the County Surveyor in 1893, the inference being that such a man would naturally choose to purchase a sound property and would maintain it. But Mr. Vachell treated the UDC case with some derision. He argued:

...that there was no fair reason why a little town... should wake up to some unnatural sense of importance and say it must have municipal buildings. Only one argument had been advanced, and that was that there was no safe place for the safe custody of the valuable documents (laughter). It was all very well if

municipal buildings were presented to a town, though, even then, presents were often white elephants (applause). It was not fair to those who had to struggle to make both ends meet. Westbury House was very old, nearly 300 years old, and its day had gone; its life had been lived. There were signs of decay and desolation in the house and to ask the Local Government Board to grant the loan to buy the house was preposterous. The basement where the documents were to be kept was the place where the floods entered. (DWG 23.3.11)

Mr. Vachell, with most of the large audience on his side, then turned to the proposals for Westbury House gardens:

...a laudable idea, but to call it a pleasure ground was mere nonsense. He dared say elderly people could sit in the damp there and contemplate the river and the passing traffic (laughter). He then presented a petition signed by 200 people against the proposal, which was displeasing to the majority of the ratepayers.

The Congregational Church in St. Margaret's Street had an enthusiastic drama group, led by Mrs. Richard the minister's wife. This is the cast for their production in about 1912.

Various prominent townsmen spoke up, Mr. John Moulton and Lord Fitzmaurice being fully in favour of the move. But others were not convinced.

Opinions over the virtue of buying and maintaining such an old building differed. Then there was the question of possible flooding and the great floods of 1823 and 1882 were referred to several times. The enquiry lasted four and a half hours, with tempers rising. Innuendoes were made about the reasons for moving, which included suggestions of friction between the Magistrates and the Town Hall Company. It was true that now the long lease had expired the Town Hall Company would only give the U.D.C. continuing occupation on the basis of a yearly tenancy agreement. This must have produced an uncomfortable feeling of insecurity which no District Council would find agreeable. However, Mr. Compton was clear where the real opposition to the proposal actually came from:

> *Mr. Compton said if they took a vote of the electors he had no hesitation in saying there would be a majority in favour of the scheme ('No'). A great deal of the opposition had been got up by the shareholders of the Town Hall Company ('No'). You see the heat...if there had been a question of buying the Town Hall for £1,400 and it would be a cost on the rates there would not have been anything like the opposition there is to Westbury House. (OWG 23.3.11)*

The Inspector went away to consider the proposal and, fortunately for us, came down in favour of the purchase and the loan. After more opposition over the rate of interest ratepayers would be asked to bear, Lord Fitzmaurice and Mrs. Gerald Fitzgerald, another local resident and sister to Mr. O.P. Skrine, advanced the required sum still outstanding at the interest rate of three and one quarter per cent, half a per cent less than could be obtained elsewhere. At their first meeting in Westbury House in October the U.D.C. considered the case of Caroline Robinson, found drunk and twice convicted of keeping a brothel on St. Margaret's Hill. They also debated the problems of motor lorries on the narrow, twisty, steep gradients of the roads and began on the process of arranging improvements in St. Margaret's Street. Thus this street was widened and Westbury Gardens was created as a public space. It was to see much use over the next few years.

The second, far less contentious issue in 1911 was how best to celebrate the forthcoming Coronation of George V and Queen Mary. At the beginning of the twentieth century a Coronation was not a distant London matter to be watched in the home on television. Every town and village provided its own personal show of patriotic enthusiasm and the royal event was a local celebration as well, with everyone out on the streets, participating in the solemnity and the entertainment of the occasion. Plenty of ideas were offered and, since the suggestion of buying Westbury House and its grounds had already been mooted at the UDC meetings, this was proposed as a permanent memorial for the occasion. Interestingly Mr. Ambrose Elton wrote to the UDC proposing :

> ...that the best memorial would be to start a fund for the preservation of the ancient buildings of that almost unique town, which were every day condemned as being unsafe and were therefore being destroyed. (DWG 23.3.11)

This enlightened suggestion was ignored.

They set up a Committee to look into the possibility of a Cottage Hospital, they debated the need for a recreation ground for the children of the town or a pedestrian bridge across the river. And they considered the detail of the celebrations themselves: 'that some scheme should be instituted by which the lives of the poorer inhabitants could be brightened on the day, so that they could look back upon it with pleasure as a red letter day.' Although more permanent schemes came to nothing and it would take several more royal and national events to bring some of them to fruition, the eventual celebrations, spread over the two days of 22 and 23 June were satisfyingly splendid.

As was then the custom for any significant events in the town, the main streets both sides of the bridge were embellished with triumphal arches of greenery. These provided the dignity of setting considered suitable for the parades which seemed to pass constantly through them. The eight subcommittees in charge of events had a great many different sections of townsfolk to organise. The day started with peals of the parish church bells in the early morning and special 10 a.m. church services at Holy Trinity, Christ Church and the Wesleyan Chapel in Coppice Hill – all the Non-conformists coming together for this special occasion. At 11.15 all the Sunday Schools and Societies assembled in the Poulton Field, off the Trowbridge Road, and formed into a procession. At the risk of being tedious, it seems worth detailing the organisations which took part because this shows the variety of groups within the town: The Urban District Council, Parish Church School, Spencer Moulton's Brass Band, Christchurch School, Ancient Order of Foresters, Independent Order of Oddfellows, Bradford Fire Brigade, the Brotherhood, Bradford Cricket Club, Church Lads' Brigade and band, Wesleyan School, Congregational School, Countess of Huntingdon's School, Boys' Brigade and band, Zion Baptist School, Old Baptist Chapel School, Providence Chapel School, Church of England Men's Society, United Patriots, Wiltshire Friendly Society, Wiltshire Working Men's Benefit Society, the cyclists and finally, the Scouts. (DWG 23.6.11)

As in 1902, the *Wiltshire Times* tells us that some 1,200 children took part in this morning parade, 'the infants being accommodated in gaily coloured wagons'. They would certainly have needed this transport for everyone in the procession must have walked miles – from Poulton Field, Trowbridge Road, St. Margaret's

Above: Bradford on Avon Cycling Club in 1907. With dropped handlebars and without mudguards, these bicycles seem remarkably modern. The same young men appear in photographs of local football and rowing teams throughout this period.

Below: Bradford and District Motorcycle Club outside The Swan on 12 April 1912. Details in a West Wilts Directory explain that the club "embraced a radius of 8 miles around Bradford". Chairman of the Committee was Mr. Alex Wilkins and the Captain was Mr. John Selfe.

Street, Silver Street and Woolley Street to the Temple Field in the Holt Road, which belonged to Mr. John Moulton. There the children sang the National Anthem and walked all the way back to their respective schoolrooms, where each child was presented with a Coronation mug. Meanwhile the adults had stayed in Temple Field for a grand public luncheon, music from the brass band and further entertainment provided by the 'All Black' Minstrels – who figure in many local shows of the period. Later in the afternoon the children walked back again to Temple Field, sang several hymns and got ready for the sports competitions, which were the next feature on the programme.

Some of the children who took part in the Coronation procession in 1911 when George V was crowned. They are pupils at Miss Cockrom's private school in St. Margaret's Street. This was a well established school, especially popular with the traders of the town and the better-off families living south of the river.

Reading the newspaper reports of the time, it becomes clear why they needed eight subcommittees to arrange the festivities. There was a Grand Bonfire in Priory Park and various Bradford householders illuminated their homes for the occasion. Given that electricity was only for the very, very affluent and would not reach the majority of Bradford houses for another fifteen years, this must have required some considerable ingenuity. Evidently learning from the enthusiasm of those who illuminated their houses in 1902, there was another organised competition this time with prizes for those judged to be the best in two categories of entry: (those above the rateable value of £10 and those below).

All prizewinners were, of course, duly reported in the *Devizes and Wiltshire Gazette* and *Wiltshire Times*, both papers carrying detailed reports of all the festivities:

> *At dusk there was a grand illumination of the town, including the bridge, the baths and river, over 3,000 lanterns and fairy lights being used. (DWG 23.6.11)*
>
> *Another charming feature of the rejoicings was a lantern procession in which 50 specially prepared and beautifully silhouette (sic) lanterns were carried, these being designed by Mr. E. Hopkins, who threw great energy into the festivities and headed the parade in the character of a Chinaman. This started from and terminated at the new Territorial Drill Hall. (WT 24.6.11)*

On 23 June there were even more celebrations – no doubt all eight subcommittees had thought up too many entertainments for just the one day. Again the Spencer Moulton brass band performed morning and evening:

> *In the afternoon there was a freak cricket match, ladies v. gentlemen. The latter had to bat with broomsticks and field left-handed...in the evening there was a dinner with musical entertainment for the aged people of the town...250 attended and 1s.6d (7.5p) was given to the 60 who were unable to come. (WT 24.6.11)*

And as a final highlight the manager of Lloyds Bank in Church Street, Mr. E. Hopkins, still dressed as a Chinaman, led his lantern procession around the town yet again. Bradford now stood ready to enter its new Georgian era.

A rare view of what was once Horse Street, i.e. the narrow part of Market Street. The photo can only be dated from a study of the shops on either side. Knees (China & Glass) on the right did not come to that site until 1908. The Colonial Meat Company on the left, run by A.T. Scrine, was still there in 1916. By 1920 Fitz Henry Benjamin had moved his refreshment rooms next door (just visible on the left) into Mr. Scrine's shop. The traffic in town is so slight that it seems an extra stall can be set up in the road in Market Street itself.

CHAPTER TWO

1914 -1918
Bradford and the Great War

Normal life ~ Emigration ~ Responses of Bradford to the War ~ Patriotism ~ The Fortunes of Bradford men, especially those in the Wiltshire Regiment ~ Escalation of Casualties ~ The Impact of the War on Bradford Life ~ Local Tribunals ~ Avoncliff Hospital ~ The End of the War ~ 'Flu Epidemic and the Toll of the War Years

IN EARLY 1914 DAILY LIFE seemed to be continuing in its usual way. There were the inevitable winter floods over the town bridge. Dr. Adye, the Medical Officer for the town, reported in April that he had inspected 186 houses in poor condition and twenty were so bad that closing orders had been issued and many of them demolished; Mr. Fitzgerald, another local benefactor, gave several of his cottages to the poor; the residents of the Shambles complained to the U.D.C. that rubbish and ordure piled up in their street and was not removed; Mr. Heavyside got his licence for music and dancing at the Baths renewed. And the local newspapers continued to provide advertisements and information for workers wanting to emigrate to Canada, New Zealand and Australia:

> *S. Australia grants cheap passages to rural workers and their families, to domestic helpers and other approved emigrants, especially plasterers, bricklayers plumbers, iron workers, and boiler makers and there is sometimes a scarcity of such men...W. Australia offers assisted and nominated passages at £3 a head to female servants between 18 and 35 years of age. (DWG 15.1.14)*
>
> *BRADFORD Intending emigrants to Canada should apply to Raymond Harris, Wiltshire Shipping Agency, Timbrell Street, Trowbridge. sole agent to the Royal Line, sailing direct from Bristol to Canadian ports. (DWG 26.2.14)*

To this day many Bradford families have relations all over the world whose greatgrandparents and grandparents answered such advertisements and started new lives away from the close-packed streets and terraces in which they were born.

Above: Trowbridge Road in 1914. The railings on front garden walls survived the First World War but were mostly removed in the Second World War.
Below right: Emigration. This and other similar advertisements constantly appeared in local newspapers throughout the period.

My husband had two brothers, Osborne and Reg, who used to work for Spencer Moulton. Os asked for a rise, he thought he deserved it, but the manager said that the factory couldn't do that, there wasn't the money. So Os thought about it and went down one day and said I'm leaving sir, and I'm taking five of your men with me. They offered him a rise then but it was too late. He went out to Australia with his brother and the others and built his own factory. They wanted my husband to go but he wouldn't leave his widowed father so he stayed at Spencer Moulton. It must have been hard going for them. Os and his wife, Dolly, had three children. Dolly used to come back occasionally when they got on their feet and she said she used to cry every night to come home. (LH97)

CANADA
WANTS MEN
TO TILL THE SOIL

Farming in Canada
means
100% Annual Profit.

Get a piece of the earth—in the Empire—under the Flag. Canada's land is freehold land. Two years' rent of a British Farm will purchase improved land of equal area in Canada—Britain's nearest overseas dominion. 160 acres Government land free for farming. Work for all farm labourers and domestic servants guaranteed.

For free maps, pamphlets, and full particulars, apply to Mr. A. McOWAN, Canadian Government Agent, 81, Queen St., Exeter ; or to Mr. J. OBED SMITH, Assistant Superintendent of Canadian Emigration, 11 and 12, Charing Cross, London, S.W.

As the European situation grew ever more grim and Germany steadily built up its armaments, preparations for war were continuing all over England. In Wiltshire arrangements were put in place for a supply of arms, clothing and equipment for members of the National Reserve in preparation for mobilisation. Many young men could not wait to go. Mrs. Gwen Mortimer, born Gwen Lailey in 1911, was the daughter of the local blacksmith, Albert Lailey, who had his important forge and business in Bridge Street. Here she talks of her brother, Albert William:

My oldest brother, he wanted to be a soldier, he joined the cubs under Mr. Harvey. Mr. Harvey took them to London and they wiped the board up there with their drum and pipe band. When my brother was 15 he joined the Territorials and went to camp. Nothing would do but what he'd join the regular army. At 16 he joined the Gloucesters and said he was 18. He went to India, Egypt, China and Singapore. He was only 16 but he was a man when he came back. (GM93)

While the Territorials continued their regular manoeuvres and the Royal Wiltshire Yeomanry were in camp for 15 days near Tisbury in May, some young Bradford men looked for even more prestigious regiments. In 1914, Frederick Albert John Fielding, born in 1896, was working with his father, a carpenter and wheelwright at nearby Chalfield Manor. Frederick Albert's son, also Frederick, who has kindly allowed the use of his father's army records, describes something of his father's early life:

He'd been in the Church Lads Brigade and joined the Territorial Army in 1911 – there was quite a strong branch in Bradford – and he went on 3 TA camps in 1911, 1912 and 1913. Then before the war even started he decided to join the Coldstream Guards, which was unusual because most young men joined the 4th Battalion of the County Regiment. Possibly they persuaded him to join the Coldstream Guards because the guardsmen were all over 6 feet and my father was 6 feet one and a half inches. Apparently he was always one for uniforms and that may have been another draw. (FF96)

Frederick Albert Fielding was examined at Devizes on the 9 July 1914, pronounced fit and sent directly to Caterham. Some three weeks later Private Fielding was in the 4th Battalion of the Coldstream Guards

July brought the usual town entertainments – a school treat with a parade to Priory Park, then the Regatta later the same month with the Spencer Moulton band playing by the riverside. Many interested and curious townsfolk turned

An intriguing photograph, date uncertain, taken outside the Swan Hotel of "the first bus to Bath". Joseph Heavyside, who became Superintendent of the Baths in 1909 and who died in 1919, is one of the inside passengers. As electric cars do not have radiators "Bath Electric Tramways" may only be the name of the Company. However there seems to be extra mechanical gear on the underside of the vehicle. Note the gable of another building reflected in the right hand window of the bus.

up at the unsuccessful attempt to auction the premises and contents of Spencers' Brewery in Whiteheads Lane, a long established local business now absorbed by Ushers of Trowbridge. The Bradford Horticultural Society held its Annual Flower Show in the grounds of The Hall on the first Tuesday in August. Here, once again the Spencer Moulton band was playing and there were competitions in the usual categories including one for the Best Cottage Front Garden. But the talk must have been on far more alarming events. Germany had declared war on France two days previously and now declared war on Great Britain on the evening of Tuesday 4 August 1914. The local news was that the 4th Territoral Battalion of the Wiltshire Regiment, including G Company which contained many Bradford men, had been ordered out of its training camp on Salisbury Plain and sent to Devonport. Meanwhile Private Fielding was already in training to cross to France with the British Expeditionary Force. His son continues the story:

That was the force that was termed "the Old Contemptibles". The Kaiser called it "a contemptible little army". There were a lot of soldiers over there apparently but quite a lot were in the background. My father went straight into the fighting. Men who actually came under fire in those early days had a little tiny rosette to add on to their medal strip so my father gained that as well. He was there until Boxing Day of 1914 and then he came home for 4 months. (FF96)

On Sunday 18 August the Bradford National Reservists were at Holy Trinity church:

There was a large muster and the parade was witnessed by a big crowd. Westbury House (the Urban District Council Office) is being used as a military and public service office, in order to give information to the public. There seems no likelihood of distress at present in Bradford. Messrs. Spencer Moulton works, which are in full swing, employ most of the men in Bradford. Their firm have a number of men away on Army service and have promised to look after their wives and families in their absence. Miss Gilder of Woolley Street is the local secretary of the Soldiers' and Sailors' Families Association. (DWG 18.8.14)

Two days later a thousand people gathered outside the old Town Hall for a recruiting meeting. Mr. John Moulton presided and the meeting was most enthusiastic. By 27 August Spencer Moulton had repeated their promise to provide for families of their workers who had volunteered, and a War Relief Committee, under the Chairmanship of Mr. John Moulton, was in place to look after other families in the town. This speedy response was necessary for on 3 September many members of both the 4th Battalion and the Yeomanry found they had volunteered for service at the Front. The usual Army practice was followed in that if a man was <u>not</u> prepared to volunteer, then he had to take one pace forward from the ranks. Many men found they had not moved. Extra leave was granted to men who had volunteered: but those staying on Home duty were given no leave. Some who had stepped forward changed their minds and decided to go.

Over the next few weeks the *Devizes & Wiltshire Gazette* published a Roll of Honour containing the names of all the Wiltshire men who had answered the nation's call so quickly. More than 200 Bradford men came forward in the first three weeks and their names, which appeared on this Roll of Honour, can be found as Appendix II. 120 men volunteered from Spencer Moulton's works. The size of the workforce had greatly increased since 1905, but this was still a substantial proportion of its employees. The men had been promised £10 each – £5 from the firm and a further £5 personally from Mr. John Moulton. The

A Soldier
of the
KING.

AFTER the War every man who has served will command his Country's gratitude. He will be looked up to and *respected* because he answered his country's call.

The Regiments at the Front are covering themselves with Glory.

Field-Marshal Sir John French wrote in an Order of the day,

"It is an Honour to belong to such an Army."

Every fit man from 19 to 38 is eligible for this great honour. Friends can join in a body, and serve together in the same regiment.

Rapid Promotion.

There is rapid promotion for intelligence and zeal. Hundreds who enlisted as private soldiers have already become officers because of their merits and courage, and thousands have reached non-commissioned rank.

Enlist To-day.

At any Post Office you can obtain the address of the nearest Recruiting Office. **Enter your name to-day on the Nation's Roll of Honour and do your part.**

GOD SAVE THE KING.

euphoria and energetic excitement of the time comes over dramatically in photographs of these early days and in newspaper reports where each new group is given full praise for their patriotism. When 30 Bradford men who had joined the 4th Wiltshire Regiment left on 7 September the Spencer Moulton band, playing martial tunes, accompanied them to the railway station.

Although many Bradford men naturally joined the 4th Battalion of the Wiltshire Regiment at the start of the war, the Army dispersed them over the six, later the seven, Battalions of that Regiment. But one unit did remain grouped in its geographical basis. This was G Company of the Territorial Battalion, made up of Bradford and Melksham men who found themselves part of the Wessex Division on the *Kenilworth Castle* troopship which sailed eastwards early in November via Gibraltar, Malta and the Suez Canal to defend British interests in India. Compared with other volunteers they were lucky. By the time they arrived at Delhi Fort in December 1914, the 1st Battalion of the Wiltshire Regiment had been badly mauled at Mons in one of the early offensives and the 2nd Battalion had fared even worse, being almost annihilated at Ypres in October.[1] We have a record from the *Devizes & Wiltshire Gazette* of one local man who survived that October onslaught:

24 December: Private Gilbert Burton of the 2nd Wilts Regiment arrived home in Bradford. He was wounded at Ypres with lyddite in the right side of his chest and later when seeking shelter in a turnip field he was so severely injured in the left leg by shrapnel that the leg had to be amputated. Burton, who was a reservist, was called up in the early stages of the war and was employed at Messrs. Spencer Moulton. After lying in the Princess Christian Hospital at Weymouth for some time he was brought to Bradford, Mr. Sydney Spencer very kindly motoring to Weymouth and bringing the injured soldier home. Burton went through the South African war possessing 2 medals and five clasps. Under Dr. Flemming he is now going on as well as can be expected.

The 2nd Battalion was reinforced, only to be in the forefront of the heavy fighting at Neuve Chapelle, 'while the actual taking of Neuve Chapelle on 10 March 1915 cost us less than 3,000 casualties, subsequent fighting ran up the bill to close on 13,000.' The *Devizes & Wiltshire Gazette* goes on to report that some time later, after a concert behind the lines, 'the spirits of the men however do not require any stimulant as a more cheerful crowd does not exist in France either in or out of the trenches.' No doubt they were just glad to be still alive but one wonders if their anxious relatives at home were reassured by such statements.

Life in Bradford must have been a strange mixture of sitting around just waiting for news and yet being busy with wartime civilian life. As patriotic symbols, the five national flags of the Allies were purchased and placed on the central Drill Hall (now St. Margaret's Hall).[1] Meanwhile the current Roll of Honour of Bradford's serving men was completed in March, at a cost of £7.14s.9d, collected by

Left: Sitting around on Barton Steps. An undated photograph in which the steps look freshly cleaned. For many years, the little building above the steps and to the left was a sweet shop.

public subscription by Mrs. Goodall, and placed on public display in Westbury Gardens. Fundraising concerts became a feature of Bradford life. Not every family in the town could benefit from Spencer Moulton's promise to care for its volunteer workers' families so, for example, the Soldiers' and Sailors' Families Association organized a concert at the Baths in February 1915 to assist townsfolk in need.

Then there were new people, brought to the area through the war. Other towns such as Corsham, Chippenham and particularly Bath, were filling up with Belgian refugees. Bradford had none but it still had plenty of new faces There was an influx of Yeomanry soldiers, and at the end of February some 230 soldiers of the 27th Cyclist Division also arrived in Bradford and were billeted in one of the factories vacant at the time. Not entirely exhausted by exercises up and down Bradford's steep hills, some of their excess energy was diverted into football matches on the Spencer Moulton sports ground in the Trowbridge Road.

Such a drastic change in population prompted the magistrates to decide to close all the local pubs and licensed houses at 9 p.m. This cautious step, which had already been taken by Melksham and Trowbridge, did not go down at all well. This was the exact time when the Spencer Moulton shift ended and workers were suddenly deprived not only of their normal refreshments but also of their usual places to gather and talk – a routine which must have been even more valuable in such crisis times. The newspapers continually report rowdy behaviour in the streets.

As the heavy fighting continued, names of the killed and wounded began to mount up. Private Daniel Brown, younger brother of the captain of the town football team, left a widow and three children and Sapper Herbert Lane of Trowbridge Road, 1st Wessex Royal Engineers, who had received severe injuries at the Front, died in Kings College London and had a full military funeral. Private Fielding of the Coldstream Guards, who had spent the first four months

Left: Three soldiers in the Horse Artillery. Bert Crisp born in 1896 into the family of iron founders which had commercial premises in Bridge Street is the one in the centre.

of 1915 back in England and was not keen to return to the carnage across the channel, was sent out again at the beginning of May, destined to stay in front line fighting for nearly another full year. Recruiting meetings became familiar sights, many of them led by the militant Bishop of Salisbury who could put forward five reasons for pressing men to volunteer. Sometimes the results were dramatic. The *Devizes & Wiltshire Gazette* reports one such meeting with the band playing:

> *A dustman had been listening to the speeches and the music. Suddenly he left his cart and grimy as he was raced up to the sergeant. A farewell word to his mate and he quitted his dustcart and turned his face for, it may be hoped, the final dustup in Berlin. (DWG 3.6.15)*

Meetings were held in the town to organize all possible resources towards the war effort. At the instigation of the Reverend A.T. Richardson, vicar of Holy Trinity, a War Loan Syndicate was formed under Mr. J. Moulton's leadership and the initial sum of £500 swiftly donated. The same meeting also began to enrol people into the National Guard for home defence and decided to get a list of signatures of those who were willing to carry home their parcels from shops. This proposal, enthusiastically passed by all, which seems so curious to our eyes, illustrates how different life was in 1915. In the days when all goods were delivered, it was, of course, a practical move to dispense as far as possible with male labour, thus making more men available for the war.

The 5th Battalion of the Wiltshires was sent to the Gallipoli Peninsula to face the Turks, and Private Peter Hill of Newtown was killed at the Dardanelles on 9 August. Aged 19, he had worked at the Sirdar Rubber Works, Greenland Upper Mill, and his brother, Tom, had been killed a few months before. It was almost impossible to keep track of all the men who had gone and were still going. The local printer William Dotesio began production of another Roll of Honour, 'a handsome parchment covered book which will sell at 6d in aid of Red Cross funds.' Anxious that no names should be omitted, since the Town Council's Roll of Honour was quickly out of date, he asked relatives and friends to send him details. But accurate information on recruitments, casualties or prisoners of war was not available, especially since the 1st, 2nd 6th and 7th Battalions of the Wiltshires constantly remained in the centre of fighting. Reports on officers were relatively more speedy and accurate than reports on men in the ranks: thus the news came through that Captain Richardson, son of the Vicar of Holy Trinity, Bradford, had died in June in more heavy fighting. The principal family in Bradford also had much to grieve over. Here are some details from the obituary for Lieutenant Charles Eric Moulton which appeared in the *Wiltshire Times* on 25 September 1915.

Above and below: The Press Bureau granted the Daily Mail *the exclusive right to market "Official War Postcards, sold in packets of eight cards for 6d. Half the net profits were donated to military charities.*

THE LATE LIEUT.C. E. MOULTON

When the sad news became known in Bradford that Lieut. Charles Eric Moulton of the 6th Wilts Regiment, youngest son of Mr. and Mrs. Moulton of The Hall had been killed in action, it created a deep feeling of regret, coupled with sympathy, among the whole of the inhabitants, and especially those whose daily duties are connected with the rubber mills of Messrs. G. Spencer, Moulton & Co....

Whilst on work in connection with the improvement of a communication trench, and in charge of a detachment he was hit by a rifle bullet and died almost immediately...He was popular with officers and men, especially those soldiers who lived in Bradford...

Lieut. Moulton, who was aged 26, was educated at Eton College and afterwards served for three years as an apprentice at the engineering works of Messrs. Stothert & Pitt, Bath. Subsequently proceeding to London University, he for twelve months studied chemistry and later succeeded to the post of Assistant Works Manager at the Bradford Mills. Here he soon made himself extremely popular with the employees and was held by them in the highest esteem. With Mr. Sydney Spencer he was instrumental in forming the firm's Recreation Club and took a great interest in the laying out of the grounds at Poulton. One of his ideals was the betterment of the conditions of employment, his opinion being that much better results are obtained from a contented and united band of employees whose interests the people they labour for make their own.

When war broke out he, with many others from the firm, patriotically offered his services to the War Office and obtained his commission as second lieutenant September 22, 1914. He was gazetted to the 6th Wilts. Regiment and promoted to lieutenant July 17th, 1915.

Although his inclinations lay in other directions, he nevertheless threw his whole energies into his military training and in a short time proved himself a capable and painstaking officer. He took a keen interest in the welfare of the men of his own platoon. Their troubles were his, and he entered wholeheartedly into their joys and recreations, large packets of cigarettes and tobacco, which constantly arrived from his parents at The Hall, being distributed with a lavish hand.

Over 80 years after Lieutenant Moulton's death, Dr Alex Moulton has explained further what a serious blow this was to the family and to the future of the town:

He was my uncle and he was being deliberately trained up to run Spencer Moultons. He'd spent three years in the engineering world in a different firm so he'd learned a lot from that. Then he'd studied chemistry which is what rubber production is all about and when he came into our firm he really got to know the men and understand the work force. We were devastated as a family – and it was a tragedy for Spencer Moulton and the town as well as for us. (AM93)

Mr. and Mrs. John Moulton's elder son, Lieut. John Moulton, was serving in India where the the 1st and the 2nd Regiments in the 4th (Territorial) Battalion continued to be stationed. Their work in India included route marches, inter-company competitions, musketry practice, bayonet fighting and – hardly something to look forward to in temperatures of 105 degrees F in the shade – a 10 mile marching contest in full marching order. Staff Sergeant D.H.Powney sent a steady stream of letters to the *Devizes & Wiltshire Gazette* describing their life in camp and their rare furloughs in the Himalayas. There is also a very interesting account of the impact of such a different way of life on ordinary Wiltshire men, many of whom had probably never been further than Salisbury, Bath or Weston super Mare in their lives. It might seem comparatively stress-free far from the European battle lines; but doubtless not to Sergeant H.Stafford of Bradford, who was serving in India when he heard his son Edward had been killed in France.

The *Salisbury & Winchester Journal* 18 September 1915 reported news at the national level:

LORD KITCHENER IN THE HOUSE OF LORDS

Lord Kitchener told the House frankly that the provision to maintain the strength of the forces in the field...had caused him anxious thought and he made it clear that this anxiety was largely due to the recent falling off in the numbers coming forward to enlist...a large addition to the numbers of recruits would be needed and the problem of how to secure an adequate supply was receiving close attention and would, he hoped, soon be solved...He did not for one instant doubt that whatever sacrifices may prove necessary to bring this gigantic war to a successful conclusion would be cheerfully undertaken by the people of the country.

Mr. Asquith let it be known that we had now not far short of 3,000,000 fighting men.

Lord Derby, who had taken over the post of Recruitment Director for the country, couched his demand for further keen volunteers in language which, with our hindsight, is difficult to tolerate. He called for 'every effort to stimulate recruiting in order to provide Lord Kitchener with the 30,000 men he requires to enlist every week to make good the wastage of war.' Some local repercussions were predictable The rally at Chippenham in October showed that the excited mood of the first year of the war had vanished:

> *As the hour approached for the meeting to be held, it was remarkable to see the numbers who were walking across the bridge in the opposite direction. The sound of martial music played by the band of the 2nd Wilts. Regiment had no effect on their patriotism. (DWG 21.10.15)*

The tone of the speakers had changed too. For those who had not yet volunteered there were such phrases as 'a load of shame and disgrace for the rest of their lives,' or 'those who hid behind the flounces of women,' 'shirkers', 'Are you a fighter or a blighter? asked one speaker. 'Do you want to be branded C for coward?' (DWG 21.10.15). There seems no evidence of white feathers being handed out in order to embarrass and shame men into joining the services, but the language at the meeting certainly had that intention.

Mr. A.W. Long, who organised the Bradford recruiting meeeting two weeks later, took a different and more sucessful line. Bradford loved parades. So the Trowbridge Company of the National Guard marched over and was met at the entrance to the town by the band from the Devizes Military Depot and, headed by the band, there was a torchlight procession around the town. Stirring addresses encouraged 30 men, many of them married, to volunteer, mostly for the Wiltshire Territorials in India. Their wives must have thought this the most prudent step they could take. Thus by the beginning of 1916 the Secondary School had 42 names on its Roll of Honour and William Dotesio's Roll was published (no copy of this seems to exist) and now recording the deaths of 21 Bradford men.

January 1916 brought in the Military Services Bill (called by energetic campaigners such as the Bishop of Salisbury "The Slackers' Bill") compelling unmarried men between the ages of 18 and 40 to come forward when they would be deemed to have enrolled. The word "conscription" seems to have been avoided. Those in essential occupations, an only son, a man unmarried but with dependent parents and also conscientious objectors would not be called up. Tribunals were set up to consider the cases of men who were not prepared to go. Bradford selected nine members for its panel, including a representative from the Workers' Union. Given that the losses in France at Loos in January were over 60,000 killed, wounded or missing, and that the 5th Battalion of the Wiltshires continued to sustain very heavy casualties against the Turks,[2] the consequent turmoil in every family which had men still at home is almost unimaginable. Pressures upon those serving on the tribunals and sometimes making life and death decisions on neighbours and acquaintances must also have been intense. Mr. Skrine, Captain and inspiration of the Bradford Church Lads Brigade, was one of the men put into this unenviable position.

The cases which came before tribunals were reported in the local papers so the details of each man's circumstances were there for all to see and comment upon. Here is a representative selection from March 1916:

> BRADFORD Three months exemption to Donald R.Keates – motor cycle agent – though he said it was no good to him as his business would have to go.
>
> Jesse Dicks, 40, was represented as necessary to the public: he delivers coal to the poorer people and no one else can be found to do so dirty a job – one month's exemption. The Manager said he would appeal to a higher tribunal.
>
> One month exemption to Dr. Flemming's chauffeur, the Dr. pointing out the current strain on the medical professsion and saying a lady driver would not be suitable.
>
> Edward A. Ruddle, 36, given 6 months exemption because he would have to close his brewery, with which there were several licensed houses.
>
> Mr. Moulton's gardener, William H. Matthews, pleaded domestic grounds and was refused.

Inevitably there was sometimes outside interference such as that endured by the Pickard family in Wingfield. Mrs. Pickard's statement reported in the local paper that she had 14 children and pleaded that the son now before the tribunal should be granted total exemption because she had six other sons already in the Army brought a swift response from her neighbours. Under the heading FOOLED BY A WOMAN the next week's paper gave a full account of further proceedings:

> Mr. Skrine said the 6 sons had dwindled down to three. The feeling in the village was very great and the person who wrote to him said the man ought to go...As a matter of fact the woman had 10 children herself, and of those 5 were girls, so she could not have 6 sons serving. The Chairman: Considering the feeling in the village and the facts before us, I ask you to reconsider the case. If there have been lies told it is right these lies should be exposed. Mr. Skrine...We have had so many of them lately. (DWG 16.3.16)

The Church Lads Brigade grouped outside their HQ in New Road. Captain O.P. Skrine is on the left of the drum. This side of the building with its corrugated iron roof can still be seen today.

But for the third week running, there was yet another report on Mrs. Pickard's family affairs. Further investigation revealed that she had married a widower with four children and that 10 of the subsequent 11 children they had together were still living. So the six sons included the stepsons and was an accurate family picture. Mr. Skrine pointed out angrily that Mrs. Pickard had been held up to odium because of the previous week's publicity. Her son was given one month's exemption as a result – but one wonders if the Pickard family eventually recovered from these events and whether neighbours in the little village of Wingfield could ever be reconciled.

The news throughout 1916 was disastrous. Britain now had 36 Divisions across the Channel. Much of the French army had been pinned down by the Germans and so British forces took over the front line around Arras and the surrounding area in a steady war of attrition.[3] In February 1916 the British front extended from Ypres to the Somme. While the Territorials remained in India, and the remains of the 5th Battalion of the Wiltshires fought on in the Dardanelles, other Battalions of the Wiltshires continued fighting in France.

On 28 March 1916, Private Fielding of the Coldstream Guards was hit in the right shoulder while fighting in the field and was sent back to England to

Above: The Wiltshires cheering during the Great Advance – another official War Postcard.

Below: 8th Wilts working staff with some of the tools of their trade. These include, among others, a tailor, a boot repairer, a barber and a carpenter.

recuperate. The battle of the Somme was launched on 1 July 1916 and raged on until October without achieving any appreciable breach in the German defences. All home newspapers were full of lists of dead and wounded from this, the worst of battles. So it is not surprising that Private Fielding went missing on 24 August. As his son says, 'It appears that Father was wounded and he didn't relish going back.' The astonishing thing is that he was brave enough to return to duty one week later. As punishment he was sentenced to 348 days in detention. But Britain could not spare its cannon fodder. Experienced men were needed at the front: so he was posted back to France a mere three weeks later, all credit for the 638 days he had already served his country now forfeited. This time he was placed in the 5th Battalion of the Coldstream Guards and would fight on in France without remission for another eleven months. He was hit again in July 1917 while wearing a bandolier full of bullets: one pouch exploded against his body and some of the shrapnel imploded into him. So he was brought home in July 1917 and remained in England until his final release well after the end of the war in April 1919.

Censorship prevented details but long lists of casualties were eventually printed, sometimes long after the actual battle. It is hard to feel reassured by the cheerful reports from the Front which sometimes found print. For example, the *Devizes & Wiltshire Gazette* 13 April brings news of the 2nd Battalion:

> *The last account of this comparatively new Battalion which has arisen with renewed vigour from the remnants of the almost annihilated original one, is most satisfactory. They had had two months trench duty and were now resting...the weather and the trenches were both deplorable, and there was a good deal of sickness but now they are very fit and quite happy and looking as brown as gypsies after the recent glorious spell of sunshine. (DWG 13.4.16)*

In England 1916 brought Zeppelin raids in the Midlands, a new wartime threat. The first night this happened, in February. 'The information reached Bradford just before midnight. All public lamps were extinguished and the employees of the rubber works on the night shift were sent home, the town being in darkness by 12.05.' Such a swift reponse suggests much attention had already been paid to lighting restrictions and blackouts. For the rest of the war various Bradford inhabitants were to come before the magistrates for lax responses to these new regulations. The UDC also organised Air Raid Precautions.

> *When the alarm is sounded, the hooter at Sirdar Rubber Works should be sounded as a warning to the Gas Company and private individuals to*

extinguish lights…The Clerk said the hooter is now not sounded after 6
p.m. so if it did so, people would know something was up. The steam would
be kept up all night and a man would be at the Works ready to sound the
hooter which would go for 3 minutes.' (DWG 10.2.16)

In the same year Spencer Moulton, busy producing both solid and pneumatic
rubber tyres together with tubes and other army equipment, put forward its
plans for a new two-storey building directly by the Town bridge. Perhaps the
innovative choice of reinforced concrete as its building material was influenced
by the new ways in which enemy Zeppelins could threaten strategic factories in
England. This building, called the Lamb Factory to commemorate the Lamb
Inn which had previously occupied the site, was one of the first to use such
modern building methods. It still stands by the town bridge today, the
circumstances surrounding its erection now forgotten.

The Wiltshires were right at the forefront of the advance just south of Thiepval
in July which resulted in terrible casualties. When this was followed by the
news a week later that all field officers and half the men of the Wiltshire Battalion
in the Dardanelles were killed on their first landing, it is not surprising that
there had to be plenty of efforts to keep up the morale of those waiting for news
in Bradford. There was a large Patriotic Demonstration in early August in
Westbury Gardens with an orchestra and services at both the parish church
and the Wesleyan chapel. Then there was the usual August Garden Fete at The
Hall with a baby show where: 'The skipping competition for girls attracted a
good deal of attention, and Olive Holbrook, the first prize winner, skipped 676
times before breaking down…Mr. E. Holdom's orchestra provided music for the
afternoon and the Spencer Moulton band played for dancing in the evening.'

Normal features of daily life occasionally provided some relief and
entertainment for those who read the paper:

NEIGHBOURS QUARREL

Arising out of a neighbours' quarrel at Whitehill, Mrs. Anne Caines was
summoned for using threats towards Lucy Mayo and for assaulting George
Smith; Emily Smith and Annie Caines were charged by George Smith with
assaulting him. Mr. E.J White (Trowbridge) appeared for Mrs. Caines and
Mrs. Smith. The cases were all taken together.

The evidence showed that George Smith's daughter threw a bucket of dirty
water over Mrs. Smith, his sister-in-law, and the latter mopped it up and threw
it back. Smith then went to Mrs. Smith's house, where Mrs. Caines hit him on
the head with a teapot. The pot was broken and Smith had been under the

doctor ever since, and appeared in court with a bandaged head. Mr. White
said his clients submitted that Smith was the only aggressor.

The magistrate decided that all the parties had gone outside the bounds for
keeping the peace and all four would be bound over in £5 each to keep the
peace for 12 months. (DWG 27.7.16)

The papers were full of other items more closely connected with the war. The
U.D.C. was concerned that "soldier lunatics" were to be charged upon the local
poor rates rather than supported by national funds. Grim entertainment was
available in November when the Palace Cinema at Chippenham showed the
official pictures of the British Army at the Battle of the Somme in which both
the bravery and the losses of the Wiltshire Battalions had been so pronounced.
Making this film was a disaster for the authorities. It had a terrible effect on
recruitment and was consequently taken out of circulation.

It was time to push for even further efforts at home. Bradford had by now
amassed nearly £2,000 in the War Loan Syndicate. Men who had not been
"deemed to have enrolled" were asked to join a newly formed Volunteer Corps
for their towns. Trowbridge, almost three times the size of Bradford, already
had a force of 80: Some 50 Bradford men came forward. Production of munitions
and other war essentials manufactured in Bradford factories therefore grew
even more intense.

Reports of the activities of the tribunals continued. Difficult cases went on
to a higher panel and exemptions were sometimes given, when a good argument
was put forward:

BRADFORD An interesting case was heard at the County Tribunal when
Nelson Howard Uncles, 37, married and passed for general service was appealed
for by his father, Mr. B. Uncles, a local ironfounder, in which business it was
claimed that the son was indispensable as a fitter and turner. ...It was shown
that a brother had recently joined the Colours and that this man's services
were in request as he had considerable expert knowledge of agricultural
machinery. Mr. Stratton supported the appeal from an agricultural point of
view. Speaking as a steam plough owner, he expressed the belief that motor-
ploughs were likely to make considerable headway in the future. It was essential
to have a firm in the locality which could provide small parts, as this firm did,
and there was not another firm of the kind for many miles. The Chairman
announced that it was prepared to grant conditional exemption if the man
would enrol as a war munition volunteer. That meant that if he were considered
indispensable he would remain; if not, of course he would be taken. The father
gave the necessary undertaking and the exemption was granted. (DWG 21.12.16)

As a member of the tribunal, Mr. Stratton supported other agricultural workers against the army authorities:

FARMER THOUGHT HIS PLACE WAS ON THE LAND

The military appealed to the County Tribunal against Albert Knight, Frankleigh Farm. He has passed for general service, is 39, married: his farm is 170 acres of which 60 are arable, 37 cows, 28 in milk. He took over the farm from his father (aged 77) in March 1916. There are 4 men on the farm, including Albert Knight.

Mr. Stratton said the farm was understaffed.

Mr. Warren asked the man if he had never considered the question that he ought to go out and fight? Albert Knight said he had not, he thought he was doing his work on the land.

Mr. Warren: "I don't think you are much of an Englishman if you haven't thought of joining the Army."

Mr. Stratton protested against this: the man thought as a farmer, he was not called upon to join. If every farmer went to France it would be a bad job for the country.

Adjourned to give the military an opportunity to call up the man when the new regulations were issued by the authorities. (DWG 15.1.17)

In March 1917, Albert Knight was given exemption for four months.

The constant drain on manpower in the town and surrounding countryside brought inevitable problems. The three bakers of Bradford – William Henry Burgess, Hubert James Penny and Charles Dainton – were constantly being called before the tribunal. Strong words were said on their behalf in March 1917: "If the tribunal took away these three bakers, or half the bread supply of the town, half the people would be practically starving". This same battle with the military was fought and won at three monthly intervals throughout the rest of the war.

But the military had to persist in requiring men to join the Services. Two further cases in 1917 not only highlight the circumstances of the individuals concerned: they also illustrate the needs of the town as it struggled to survive from day to day. Stephen Reginald Keates, cycle and motor engineer of Bradford, was 19 and single. His sister appeared before the County Tribunal when the army yet again required him to enrol. She argued his case well:

It was pointed out that the respondent was carrying on a business in Bradford which was the only shop in the town where motor cars could be repaired, and the bicycles of a large number of munition workers could be attended to during their working hours. The military authorities on the other hand contended that Keates was a young man, unmarried, and had had nearly a year's exemption. It was absolutely in the national interest that he should now be called up for service. Keates' sister stated that the business now belonged to a brother who was called up and joined the service last August. She was looking after the financial side of the business and the respondent, a younger brother, was looking after the work in the shop. They only had a boy 16 who had recently come for cycle work, and she assisted as far as she could when they were very busy. She had two brothers besides her sister who were serving. Her sister had been in Kitchener's Hospital in France for a year and was now in Salonika as a trained nurse. The tribunal dismissed the military appeal. (DWG 7.6.17)

Albert Charles Dodge, boot and shoe repairer, of Silver Street, aged 38 and passed for general service, did not get quite such sympathetic treatment. The Bradford tribunal had given him an exemption, because he was in a certified occupation. As his work was continuous they had thought it useless to give him only a short exemption. But the Army was not satisfied. At the County Tribunal in Trowbridge presided over by the Marquess of Bath, Captain Morley, appearing for the Military, was more pressing:

Capt. Morley – How many boot repairers are there in Bradford?
Dodge – Three, I think.
Capt. Morley – Are there not the Co-operative, Uncles, yourself, Batchelor, and Andrews?
Dodge – Yes. But we have more work than we can all do. Now that boots are so dear, people are having more repairs done.
Capt. Morley – Who does the most?
Dodge – I should say the Co-operative. They have two men.
Capt. Morley – Will you take it from me that Uncles does the most?
Dodge – I should not have thought so. I find it impossible to cope with the work and though I work until 10, 11 and even 12 every night, I always leave 20 or 30 pairs over. (WT 6.6.17)

Charles Dodge argued that as new boots had almost doubled in price since the war started poor and middle-class people were now obliged to have their boots repaired as long as they could. Therefore his work was of great national importance. But the Tribunal was not convinced, the Chairman commenting that any man passed for general service would have to be called up before long. He was given one month to make necessary arrangements after which he would have to go into the army.

MY WASH WORK DONE WHILE YOU DO GUARD WORK.

AT night, silently, swiftly, Rinso does the washing while the housewife sleeps and the Volunteer is on guard. The good wife who uses Rinso greets her husband coming off duty with a smiling face on wash-day morning and is free to attend to his comfort, for she has only to rinse the clothes and hang them out to dry.

Rinso is the cold water washer. It is just as effective in cold water as other and more costly preparations are in hot. It saves the cost of coal, the bother of the copper fire, the dangers and unpleasantness of steam.

Soak the clothes in cold water and Rinso overnight. Rinse and hang to dry in the morning. That's all.

In 2d. and 1d. PACKETS EVERYWHERE.

THE DIRT DISPELLER

R. S. HUDSON LIMITED. LIVERPOOL, WEST BROMWICH & LONDON

Left: Rinso advertisement aimed at the housewife. It exploits the problems of the times but now provides some interesting social comment on domestice life during the Great War.

Of course women had taken over men's work in all manner of ways. But not without a struggle, particularly in rural occupations. The previous year Lady Hobhouse of Monkton Farleigh had put forward the names of 16 women in her village ready to help with milking in order to release men for active service. This initiative had been treated with some public derision at the Bradford Rural Council Meeting. But gradually there had been a grudging acceptance of the value of women's labours. However Wiltshire farmers, although hardpressed, remained most unwilling to apply for help in heavy work from soldiers made available from the Army barracks at Devizes. Perhaps farmers such as Albert Knight preferred to struggle on undermanned, feeling that thus they were safer from tribunal directives.

Food supplies were becoming increasingly difficult. In June 1917 it was announced that in the previous week German mines and submarines had sunk 27 of our merchant ships over 1,600 tons. It might be expected that such devastating news would be censored but immediate measures were needed to ensure that food supplies at home were sufficient. 'There is no cause for dismay,' said the *Devizes & Wiltshire Gazette* cheerfully,' but economy in food and all requirements of daily life is as urgent as ever.' A food control scheme came into operation and preparations were made to break up 85,000 acres of Wiltshire grassland in order to grow corn, much to farmers' alarm. A subsidy was introduced to encourage the growing of sugar beet. Private land in Bradford such as at French Grass and Avon Field was to be commandeered for allotments. This raised strong protests, especially from one man in the Trowbridge Road who feared his one acre of land, once taken, might move out of his control. He fought the U.D.C. on this issue for the remainder of the war and, through procrastination, kept his plot of land intact. Elsewhere in Bradford, new allotments sprang up so that more people could feed themselves. Serious rationing of staple items, such as sugar, was introduced on 30 December 1917 and prosecutions for food hoarding were swift to follow. "Gross profiteering" was already an offence. Edwin Slade & Son, grocers of Trowbridge and Bradford were fined £25 for selling 2lbs of green gooseberry jam for two shillings (10p) when the Jam Prices Order decreed one shilling and sixpence halfpenny (just over 7p) to be the maximum price allowable. A heavy fine indeed at the time. Charles Dunning in the Winsley Road was also prosecuted for selling potatoes at a halfpenny above the fixed price of 2d (1p) a pound At the other end of the social scale the *Devizes & Wiltshire Gazette* announced a little later that: 'Lady Mabel Gore Langton, daughter of the late Earl Temple, has been fined £80 for food hoarding. It was stated she had in store enough tea to last the household a year.'

Everyone had to suffer.

In April 1917 Mr. John Moulton was selected as High Sheriff for the County, a position of more than usual responsibility in wartime. However he was still working on Bradford's needs three months later when the U.D.C. arranged for a supply of coal to the Bradford poor for the following winter but at the current low summer prices:

> *This was Mr. John Moulton's doing. He accompanied a deputation to interview the coal merchants with the result that they agreed to deliver coal next winter at the rate of one hundredweight a week at today's price to a list of poor people, those on parochial relief and old age pensioners...As the merchants have agreed to deliver coal which in some cases will be difficult and requires strong men the Council passed a resolution in favour of the merchants being allowed to retain the men now employed by them, instead of having them taken for military service. (DWG 5.7.17)*

There were several coal merchants based in the goods yard by Bradford railway station. They fought many a local tribunal to try to keep their young employees from being sent to the war in their employ. No doubt they found this deal, which had the High Sheriff's support, was well worth any commercial expense.

Another event of major significance to the town was the decision to close the workhouse at Avoncliff, mostly by moving inmates to other local institutions. This left the buildings available for use as a Red Cross Hospital for convalescent soldiers. In May "the scheme was approved – committees were appointed for the management of the hospital. It was announced the children of Christchurch school had offered to fit up one of the wards and a hope was expressed that others in the town and villages would emulate their example." (DWG 24.5.17)

Bradford town dignitaries connected with the war effort, together with Red Cross nurses at Avoncliff Hospital outside Fitzmaurice Grammar School.

Red Cross hospitals had been created and in use in nearby towns such as Corsham and Devizes almost since the beginning of the war, but Bradford had not provided such a service before. The call was taken up with great enthusiasm and exemplary speed. Three months later the first patients arrived by train at Bath station and were immediately transported by canal to the newly appointed hospital which had Sister Ponsford as its trained Matron. As a place for convalescent soldiers, little active nursing was required and so the rest of the nursing staff were volunteer V.A.D.s, organised by Mrs. Helen Douglas of Belcombe Lodge, assisted by Mrs. O.P. Skrine. Miss Foxcroft of Hinton Charterhouse was another of the many local people who devoted the next two years of their lives to the organization and daily duties in Avoncliff Red Cross Hospital. Here is her previously unpublished eyewitness account of the way they received first convalescent soldiers.[4]

ACCOUNT OF ARRIVAL OF FIRST PATIENTS IN 1917 TO AVONCLIFF HOSPITAL

On Monday July 22nd, a picturesque sight was witnessed on the Kennet and Avon Canal when the Red Cross Barge The Bittern belonging to the Bradford on Avon Red Cross Volunteer Aid detachment made its maiden voyage from Bath to bring the first convoy of wounded to Avoncliff Hospital. The Barge was under the Command of Mrs. Fletcher of Bradford, to whose, and Colonel Fletcher's energy the Hospital owes this novel and enjoyable means of transit. Mr. Weston of Bradford, an adept at this art, kindly volunteered to steer the Barge to and from Bath – there were also Miss Young, Miss. P. Skrine, Mr. Starr (who form the crew) Colonel Fletcher, Mr. O.P. Skrine, two members of the Bradford men's VAD, Sister Ponsford, Matron of the Hospital, and a VAD nurse.

The day was perfect and all agreed that the trip was most enjoyable. The wounded soldiers, 28 in number, embarked at the Sydney Wharf, Bath, leaving about 2.30 and arriving at Avoncliff at 5.30. Mrs. Vilven came down to Sydney Wharf and presented fruit and cigarettes to the men before starting. A substantial tea was provided for the men on board and a few minutes halt being made at Dundas Aqueduct, from thence onwards, a number of interested pedestrians on the tow path followed the course of the Barge – one kind friend presenting a basket of strawberries to the men as they passed. Those who witnessed the arrival at Avoncliff describe it as a most picturesque scene, when with the sound of singing from the Crew, the Barge with its Red Cross on the white awning hove in sight. A crowd including all the hospital staff had gathered to witness the arrival. The patients were quickly disembarked and comfortably settled in their new quarters.

Further comforts for these soldiers, in their bright blue convalescent uniforms were provided in the town, a large room at the Baths being altered into a canteen with a recreation room for wounded soldiers. Special seats being set up either side of the Town bridge and also in Avoncliff Lane. On Sundays some of the less wounded men would be brought into Bradford on The *Bittern* and entertained by local people in their houses. At least two of them returned to Bradford after the war and spent the rest of their lives in the town.

By January 1918, the hospital had between 80 and 100 patients and staff and there were plenty of wounded servicemen needing its gentle care. By February battalions of the Wiltshire Regiment were at war in France, Greece, Palestine, Mesopotamia, India and with the Egyptian Expeditionary Force in Egypt. The 2nd Battalion was once more in the thick of savage fighting at the

AN
EXHIBITION

OF

Soldier's Needlework,

FROM THE

AVONCLIFF

RED CROSS HOSPITAL,

WILL BE HELD AT

THE BATHS,

On Wednesday, March 20th, 1918,

from 2 to 5 p.m.

There will be a few Articles for Sale made by the Patients, the proceeds going to the Needlework Fund.

Wm. DOTESIO, Printer, Bradford-on-Avon

Soldiers were encouraged in needlework as an early form of occupational therapy. Not surprisingly, one of their main interests was in recreating their regimental crests in embroidered form.

The Church Lads Brigade boys stand to attention at the front entrance to their HQ. It is 6 May 1917 and their war memorial, adorned with flowers, is already in use. This memorial remained there until after the Second World War. In more recent years this front entrance to the building has been replaced by large garage doors.

battle of San Quentin in March and again had to be reformed after heavy losses. The 6th Wiltshires suffered a similar fate.[5] Each week the closely printed War Office Casualty List, the notification of killed and wounded sent to families, steadily grew longer – each page was fifteen inches long and ten inches wide and consisted of three columns of names densely printed in very small type. There were 30 full pages for the week ended 20 April, rising to 54 pages for the six days 29 April to 4 May. Many Bradford and Trowbridge names were among them. William Dotesio had to record that his second son, Corporal John Holmes Dotesio, in the Somerset Light Infantry, was killed in September. Fighting was bitter until the very last minute on 11 November 1918 and each week's lists show this in deadly detail. The *Devizes & Wiltshire Gazette* for 31 October 1918 announced: 'The casualty lists for the week ending 22nd October are again tragically long. In fact the total War Office publication of killed and wounded for that week totalled 60 pages – a formidable publication.'

Nor could people at home relax at the cessation of fighting. Lists of killed and wounded continued to appear – 50 pages on 14 November and another 52 pages a week later. The Wiltshire Regiment had been well represented in the last great offensive and Trowbridge and Chippenham families suffered particularly in the casualty list for the final week of that terrible month. It is a relief to turn from these relentless lists to the simple, moving letter written by Major W.S. Shepherd, 2nd Wiltshire Regiment to General Sir J. Hart Dunne, Colonel of the Wiltshire Regiment, back in England. The 2nd Wiltshires had endured heavy shelling on 4 November and were part of the final advance from Cambrai to Mons. They were at Mons on the day of the Armistice:

The day was very quiet for us. Everyone I think was rather stunned by the news and only too glad to spend the day in complete restfulness. The villagers had buried their church bell four years ago to preserve it from the Huns. This we unearthed and re-hung, and the only noisy time of the day was at 11 o'clock when this bell was rung as hard as it would go and the Drums beat up and down the main street of the village. (DWG 28.11.18)

In June Bradford U.D.C. had arranged to have the town's Roll of Honour Board renovated and the trees surrounding it in Westbury Gardens cut back. Some had achieved especial honour, for example Lance Corporal H.N. Mock of the Wiltshire Regiment who had been awarded the Distinguished Conduct Medal for gallantry. At some much later time in the century, this Roll of Honour was removed and eventually found a resting place in the skittle alley of the Liberal Club in St. Margaret's Street. When these premises were sold late in 1997 it was, by good fortune, removed and restored for full public viewing. It contains the names of 488 Bradfordians who served in the war. See Appendix V.

Then, as the servicemen slowly began to return, they found their home town suffering, along with much of the country, in the great epidemic of Spanish influenza which spared neither the armed forces nor civilians. Mrs. Mortimer, the blacksmith's daughter in Bridge Street, was 6 at the time:

I remember all the flags flying for the Armistice – and the great 'flu epidemic afterwards. One of our neighbours, a mother and father died, they had four children. And six of us were in one room with the flu, and the doors were left open for the doctor to walk in and walk out. Me, my mother and father and three brothers, we all got the flu together. There wasn't much they could give us. I remember I had croup badly and my mum got up and went for the doctor,

dear old Dr. Adye, he was lovely. He said,"My dear woman, you'll kill yourself."
She said "What was I to do? There's no one would come near you." It was a
really bad time – they reckon more died from that than was killed in the Great
War. (GM93)

People began to count the terrible cost of the past four years and to plan their
war memorials. One family's account might stand for that of many Bradford
families:

My mother's family name is Hill. There were four sons and four daughters
in the family. All four of her brothers served in the war and the youngest one
put his age on to get into the army. One died in the Dardanelles – he was only
just 19. He is commemorated on a memorial stone out there and I have a plan
of the area where the stone is. But he was just lost – no remains. Another
brother has a grave near Boulogne. So one brother died in the Dardanelles,
one died in France, one was a prisoner of war and the fourth brother came
home. (FF96)

The Spencer Moulton Rubber factory had lost 46 of its work force, including
the young man the Moulton family was training to be its future Managing
Director.

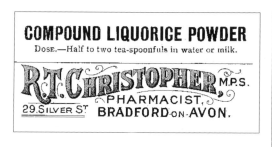

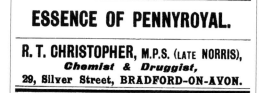

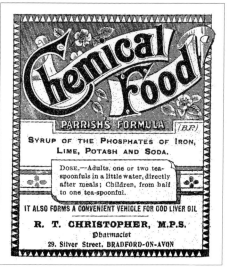

Labels from medication which was available from Mr. Christopher's pharmacy
in Silver Street.

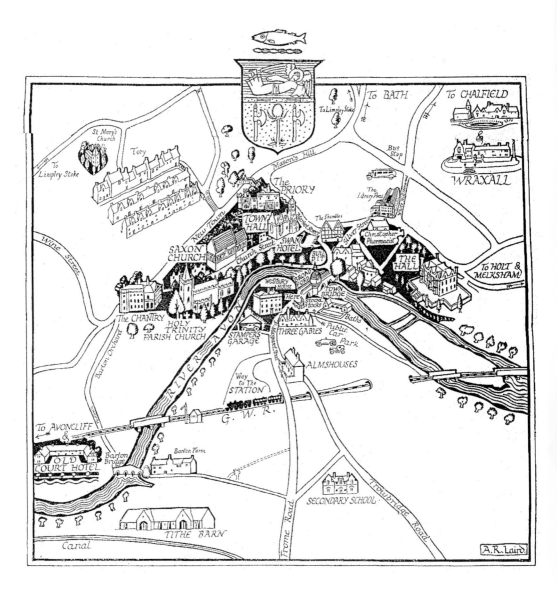

Part of one of the brochures printed by Dotesio, the local printing firm, in the 1920s and 1930s promoting the town and its facilities. Note the official public car park outside the gates to the swimming baths.

CHAPTER THREE

1919 - 1938
Social Life between the Wars

War Memorials ~ Animals in the Town, especially Horses ~ The Baths ~ Social Distinctions between Schools ~ Trowbridge Road and its Residents ~ Churches and Sunday Schools ~ Separate Communities and Sounds that drew them together ~ Domestic Toil and the Arrival of Electricity ~ Goods Delivered to the Door ~ Bryants Travelling Shop ~ Railways ~ Local Entertainments ~ Working at Spencer Moulton ~ Other Trades ~ Ring of Gentlemen's Residences around the north side of the Town

---

THE FIRST FOUR YEARS AFTER the Great War were marked with the new memorials to those who had served and those who had died. Spencer Moulton mounted a memorial to its own employees on one of its major buildings and this was ceremonially unveiled in 1919. The same year saw the installation of a drinking fountain and tall street lamp in the wide road space in Church Street opposite the Swan, donated by the Dainton family in memory of the boys of the town and especially of Lieutenant Howard H. Dainton of the 4th Gloucesters who died of wounds in 1918.[1] This remained in place until after the Second World War. Then came the dedication of the war memorial shrine in Holy Trinity Church in June 1920. There were other individual monuments, including the memorial window, also in Holy Trinity, dedicated, 'In loving memory of Reginald John Yerbury, Lance Corporal who died of wounds in France – Somme 1916.' Memorial windows in the Wesleyan chapel were unveiled on 6 October 1921.

Christ Church also commemorated the town's loss of life. The Moulton family built a Lady Chapel as a memorial to Lieutenant Charles Eric Moulton, and Brigadier General Sir Llewellen Palmer, a near neighbour to the church in his house at Bearfield, added a peal of eight bells in 1923. As an especial and individual token of remembrance, a bronze war medal, designed by Mrs. Miriam Christopher, wife of the local chemist, was struck in 1921 for every Bradfordian who had served. Each medal was individually named and given to the person or to the family involved. The *Wiltshire Times* for 7 May 1921 says that about 700

Above: Even in the 1930s there is plenty of space in Market Street to use the drinking fountain erected as a memorial to Lieutenant Howard Dainton and his friends.

Right: Unveiling the town's war memorial in Westbury Gardens on 2 August 1922. There are several accounts of people fainting with emotion during the ceremony.

medals were presented in this way. This may well be journalistic exaggeration. But the official Roll of Honour with its 488 names still contains over 10% of the town's population of 4,501 in August 1914.

The town war memorial took a little longer to create. The design finally accepted in August 1921 was by the architect, Alexander Dunn of Birmingham, brother of Mr. Arthur Dunn of Avonfield Terrace, Trowbridge Road, which thus gave it an especial local connection. Costing £600 in all, the base is in blue Bristol pennant stone and the monument itself in the best white Portland stone. It was unveiled and dedicated at an impressive and moving ceremony in Westbury Gardens on 2 August 1922.

A different kind of memento, namely a large German gun which had been presented to the town, proved quite a problem as the U.D.C. could not decide what to do with the gift. Melksham had received a similar trophy which its local inhabitants had unceremoniously dumped in the river. So the Bradford gun remained hidden in a store-yard at the back of Westbury House for some considerable time. Eventually it was positioned in the public grounds beside the Baths. It remained there for many years, until the Second World War when it sold for scrap iron, raising the sum of £4.

The Church Lads Brigade in 1920. They are grouped in Sandy Leaze, the backs of Wine Street buildings behind them. This area was built over in the 1970s.

Meanwhile ordinary life had to go on. Animals of all kinds were a natural part of town life. On Tuesdays sheep and cattle from farms north of the town might come wandering down Market Street and across the bridge on their way to the large weekly market in Trowbridge. Hopefully there was always the prospect of drama:

> Mrs. Dainton, wife of Mr. Dainton, baker of Bridge Street, had a remarkable escape from serious injury on Monday. Whilst a number of cows were being driven through the town by Mr. Day, farmer of Winsley, one of them, apparently infuriated at the sight of a dog which Mrs. Dainton had with her, made a rush at her. With commendable presence of mind she seized the animal's horns and held on until the drover beat it off. (WT 14.6.19)

There is an eyewitness account of bullocks being taken to a slaughter house just on the north side of the town bridge: one of the animals broke loose and went right through a shop window. A tiny entrance to a different abattoir behind a butchers in Silver Street still exists. It is no longer in use of course, but Mrs. Wilkins describes it for us:

> I can remember a couple of cows being pushed up the alleyway beside that shop in Silver Street. They killed cattle up there behind the butcher's shop and then hung the fresh meat straightaway. It's a tiny little passage way, and you can't imagine it, but I've seen it. (EW89)

Mrs. Holbrook, born Lily Banks in 1909, has even more gruesome memories of the same place:

> My parents allowed me to play with Mary Seymour whose family had the meat shop in Silver Street. We had to be in by half past eight, if not my dad used to come down and get us, but we were only playing down the shop. The slaughterhouse was round the back on a slope and we used to watch the cows being killed. They used to chop them down through the head. There was a big place where the blood used to collect down this slope and a great big sink with a tap. We weren't allowed down there, we used to watch from the bedroom window, I don't expect they ever knew we watched.
> Weren't we bloodthirsty girls though! Weren't we horrible! I couldn't watch it now. (LH97)

In January 1921 Mrs. Watson was summoned for leaving a donkey and cart unattended in Market Street:

Inspector Reed said the donkey and cart were straying about the street...Mrs. Watson had been previously warned as the donkey was often wandering off by itself and was once found on Mr. Moulton's lawn [laughter]. (WT1.1.21)

The next month George Wheeler was summoned for leaving a horse and cart uncontrolled on 3 February at noon in Newtown:

P.C. Stanley had the vehicle under observation from 12.04 to 12.24 when the defendant came out of the Bell Inn[2] and said he'd only been in for the ash bin. Mr. Doel the defendant's employer said some consideration might be shown as the defendant was engaged on a dirty job and started at 7.30 a.m. He only stopped 20 minutes and the thoroughfare was not a busy one. (WT 12.2.21)

The magistrates were not impressed and fined George ten shillings (50p)
Bradford's transport system had not changed much from before the Great War, although petrol driven vehicles were growing in number:

I can remember when the buses started running to Trowbridge in the early 1920s. We all used to go down to the gate and see one when it went by, it was such a novelty. It was a single decker, everybody said no, you couldn't have double deckers in Bradford, too dangerous, over that bridge. (MD4/97)

Many people had bicycles, but the horse was still the major means of transport. Mr. Albert Lailey, the town's blacksmith, was kept fully employed in his forge in Bridge Street. His daughter, Gwen, born in 1911, remembers it well:

I was nearly seven when we came to the forge in Bridge Street. I've seen as many as four horses at a time in the workshop and there was another shop above that where they used to do the wheelwrighting and all the general iron work. Wheelbonding was a big thing – all the wheels on the carts were wood with an iron bond. And in the forge the wall was covered with ready made horseshoes. I've seen Bridge Street lined with gypsies and their caravans waiting to bring their horses in to be shod. It was really a busy town. The gypsies came to our forge when they were passing through, especially when they came for Bradford Leigh Fair, which was always held on the last Monday in August. They used to have all their babies christened up there on the Sunday by the vicar of Christ Church. People did go up there to see all the babies being christened and to walk round and see what was going on. (GM93)

While Bradford Leigh Fair was taking place in a field alongside the Corsham

Left: Taking a horse to Lailey's forge in Bridge Street.

Below: Advertisements for local businesses from a guide book of 1923.

NICHOLS & BUSHELL

LIMITED

Family Grocers

and

Provision Merchants

Established 1886

WINES and SPIRITS,
BRUSHES and BROOMS
PATENT MEDICINES

Fresh Roasted Coffee a Speciality

Competitive Prices

Regular deliveries by Motor to :
*Holt, Corsham, Warleigh
Chalfield, Wraxall, Bathford
Atworth, Monkton Farleigh
Freshford, Iford, Winsley,
Westwood, Wingfield and
Hinton Charterhouse.*

'Phone : 26

THE MARKET PLACE
BRADFORD-ON-AVON

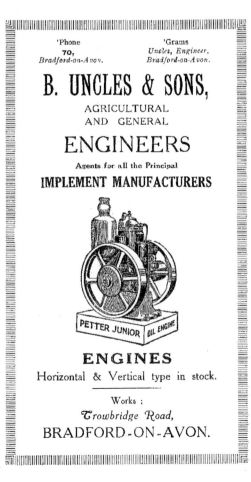

'Phone   'Grams
70,   *Uncles, Engineer,*
Bradford-on-Avon.   *Bradford-on-Avon.*

B. UNCLES & SONS,

AGRICULTURAL
AND GENERAL

ENGINEERS

Agents for all the Principal

IMPLEMENT MANUFACTURERS

PETTER JUNIOR OIL ENGINE

ENGINES

Horizontal & Vertical type in stock.

Works :
Trowbridge Road,
BRADFORD-ON-AVON.

Road at Bradford Leigh, one of the bus companies ran a single decker bus to and from the town during the evening. The fare was less than 1p. Today the only remembrance of this fair which was an annual event for over 150 years is in the name of the farm and its surrounding grounds – Fair Field.

Young Gwen Lailey knew every horse in the town:

> *Behind The Three Horseshoes was the stables for all the horses for the Great Western Railway and the LMS. They were used for deliveries from the station yard. That big yard, the station car park, was the coal yard for the town. The horses took all the coal from the railway up to Spencer Moulton and to the other rubber factory, Sirdar, at the far end of Bridge Street ... Every business, every butcher, grocery, everything was delivered by horse-drawn van...the Co-op had a stables in Whitehill. There were all the brewery horses – and the barges up and down the canal they were all horse-drawn as well. Then of course all the farmers used horses, the shire horses pulled the ploughs. (GM93)*

As far back as 1911, the U.D.C. had urged the need for a 10 m.p.h. speed limit in Bradford because of exceptionally steep hills on the north side of the town. Nothing came of this of course, and the narrow junction of Market Street with Newtown and Masons Lane with high walls on either side remained a particularly hazardous spot. It was only the sale and demolition of much of The Priory at the end of the 1930s which provided a long sought opportunity for the road and pavement there to be widened. Deep ruts and potholes were another constant problem, as the frequent deliberations of the UDC over road maintenance make only too clear. At one meeting it was stated that it was impossible for two horses with an ordinary load to get up Wine Street, which was of course a road for two-way traffic.

Chippings of carboniferous limestone from the Mendip hills – still the best material for motorways a century later – provided the basic material for repairing the roads. The introduction of tarmac did not solve the difficulties because in its early days this smooth surface could only be used on fairly level roads. It was an additional hazard for horses since their shoes could not find any grip on such a slippery surface, especially in wet weather. Nowadays Masons Lane is the main northern road out of the town. In the early part of the twentieth century the main route, especially for heavily laden horse-drawn carts and waggons, was up Silver Street and Woolley Street with a very narrow entrance into New Road; then it was left along to Mount Pleasant and right, onto the Bath Road or the Winsley Road. The sharp and narrow bend on Woolley Street where it leaves the Holt Road was known as Frying Pan Hill. It took all the traffic in both directions (the modern broad alternative road at Springfield did not exist) and was the scene of many accidents, as cumbersome waggons made this difficult turn. When motor vehicles began to appear on the roads, the problems became even worse.

Sometimes other animals, such as mules, were used, for example by Ruddles Brewery, now mostly an empty space on the right hand side going up Coppice Hill; Here Jack Stafford, born in 1912, recalls memories from his boyhood:

Where the flower shop now is in Silver Street there was a great pair of wooden doors to the brewery and an arch and that's where the mules brought the carts in. There were staves[3] all round the carts and the men rolled the empties off and the full ones on. And as you walked by on the pavement in Silver Street you could smooth the noses of the mules. That part was later turned into Scrine's first chemist shop, but they later moved next door to the shop they have today. (JS96)

Stables and sheds were packed in all over the town and there was a plentiful supply of animal droppings along the streets. Since so many people grew their own fruit and vegetables there was sometimes fierce competition for this free fertiliser. For example behind the long row of houses on the Poulton side of the Trowbridge Road was a corresponding long row of allotments. There are several accounts of householders lurking in their front gardens, bucket at the ready, poised to race into the road and shovel up manure before their neighbours could get to it.

The Baths continued to be as much a focal part of town life as they had been for the past 20 years. Mr. Heavyside the Superintendent died in 1919 but his wife and two young daughters, Phyllis and Isabelle, were allowed to stay on. Mrs. Isabelle Carter tells us more:

I felt sorry that mother had to work so hard. She ran it on her own with the help of a retired naval man who came in to see to the boiler and to change the water twice a week. The Baths opened at seven in the morning until nine at night and she would be on duty all those hours, 14 hours a day and six days a week. People could hire towels when they came and my mother had to wash all these towels afterwards in a big old fashioned copper boiler. She also sold the tickets and she had to make sure the five private baths were clean as well. She never had a holiday or went anywhere but I expect as a widow she was grateful for the job and thought the Council were good to keep her on. In 1921 she got thirty-five shillings (£1.75p) a week but she got the house and didn't have running expenses. So I expect that's what she was working for – to keep Phyllis and me. (IC96)

Above: Competitors and officials grouped at the shallow end of the swimming baths for Trinity Boys Senior School swimming sports in July 1938. Mr. Musselwhite, a longstanding teacher at the school, is the barechested man in the third row from the front.

Right: Boys beside some of the "17 curtained dressing boxes" which surrounded the bath.

Below: View of the Baths with members of the Heavyside family in the alcoves. The public entrance was in Bridge Street on the right of the photograph.

Children were given free swimming lessons as part of their school programme – surely a most enlightened attitude for the times. Jack Stafford and his friends made great use of it:

There was a good springboard and either side of it four or five steps for high and low dives. The water was changed twice a week, fresh water put in on Sunday for Monday...then Thursday they renewed it. Us boys we used to go in on Saturday mornings because it was cheapest then... we had a school class, then we had to pay ourselves on Saturday. We always got there first on Saturday, the ones I went with. All the muddy water where people did get in with dirty feet from Thursday and Friday was settled on the bottom, you couldn't see no white tiles. So the first person to get in and go walking across with the water up to say 4 feet, you'd see their footprints across the bottom.. And within half an hour to an hour the water would go completely misty and it was all churned up. (JS96)

By 1923 the school leaving age had risen to 14. Apart from private establishments, the infants and juniors went to one of the two National Church of England schools, either Trinity in Newtown (where The Rope Walk flats are now) or Christchurch at Mount Pleasant (now the Mount Pleasant Community Centre). There was also the non-denominational British School on Masons Hill. At the age of 11 some pupils went on to the County Day School (also known as the Fitzmaurice Grammar school) which had previously been the Fitzmaurice Technical Institute. Everyone else went on to the Senior Trinity National School in Newtown. To a little girl who lived in Woolley Street, Newtown was a long way off:

We usually mixed mostly with our own. I always thought we were a little village apart from the town. Christchurch School served this half of Bradford and Trinity served the other half. At Trinity (where the Rope Walk now is) they had infant and junior girls in one building and the boys in another. But we were mixed in Christchurch and we were mixed when we went on down to Trinity for those two senior years... there was a free scholarship to go to the Grammar School but not many only about six of the very top people were entered from our school. Of course we could go if our parents paid. Most business people in the town's children went. But nearly all paid you see. My mother was quite willing, but it was quite strange because my friend I used to walk up and down to school with she didn't want to go there – and neither did I. Her sister and my cousin went there, but it always seemed a bit snobbish to me in those days. And I as a child was a little bit shy and quiet. Of course we had a bit more of a sheltered life then. (EW89)

Above: Miss Jackson, of Trinity School in Newtown with one of her classes in the 1930s. This was taken in the school yard. Miss Jackson was 93 years old when she died in January 1996.

Below: Huntingdon Street as it remained until after the Second World War. Mrs May Turtle was born in No. 1, the three-storey house on the left, in 1907, and still lives there in 1997. The field in front of her house was a paddock and allotments until the bungalows were built on the site in the early 1960s. Before that, Mrs. Turtle could stand at her door and wave across the field to her friend, Mrs. Webb, living in one of the weavers' cottages in the Winsley Road. In her youth, the shop on the right belonged to Mr. Viner, "He used to put sugar in blue bags, do bran for the rabbits and corn for the chickens."

It has to be said that there were strong social distinctions between schools and Trinity School was, in general, not held in very high regard. Jack Stafford is quite direct about it:

Bradford boys went to the one in Newtown. That was, well, all the slums of Bradford went there....Wine Street, Tory, Middle Rank, Bridge Street. People down the town they didn't want their children to go there, too low for them, so they sent them up to Christchurch.

However Trinity School, with only limited land in Newtown, did have a playing field:

The Trinity School playing fields were up at the top of Wine Street – as you go along the Winsley Road past Wine Street the gate was just on the corner on the right. The entrance is still there but there's a house in there now. That's where we used to go and play football. No facilities whatsoever there – just a field. All sorts of kids went there but Trinity was a rough school. If you were a little more on the upwards you went on to the Grammar School. It was a complete division of what class you were really...my sister passed to go to the Grammar School but she couldn't go because we couldn't afford to buy the uniform. My mother had two sets of twins fourteen months apart and things like clothes, well, I was brought up wearing other people's cast-offs. I can always remember my boots never had any bottoms in them, always holes in the bottom of my boots – and I did walk in from Winsley!! That's how we were brought up...I wouldn't have had it any other way really. Looking back, I've gone from the depths to as high as I've got and I'm quite happy. When you can look back and see what you've got now and what you had when you were younger, which was absolutely nothing...But, oh dear, poverty is terrible. (DH97)

Poverty could be very humiliating as well:

Mother and I lived with my mother's parents in Ashley Road. My mother had a very rough life. We used to go to the Town Hall where she'd get parish money; they used to allow you so much for to live. She used to do a bit of charring for a Mrs. Price along the Winsley Road just past Wine Street. This particular day she'd been there and washed four blankets by hand, put them through the mangle and dried them and the lady gave her 6d. And mother said to me, is there anything you would like John and I said I'd love some chewing gum. It only cost about a farthing or a halfpenny. So she went into Fanny Pinchin's, the sweet shop in Market Street. It's now an antique shop but in those days if you looked through the window at night you could see the mice running all over the sweets. Anyway, she bought me this chewing gum. When she went to claim her parish money I went in with her and the chappie said to me what are you chewing and I said chewing gum. So he said to my mother – and he made her cry – if you can afford to buy him chewing gum I don't want you coming in here again trying to claim money to live. I always remember that, it's always stuck in my mind because she cried. That was probably about 1933 or 34. (JL97)

The County Secondary School ("the Grammar") served a wide catchment area and pupils travelled in by train from as far away as Westbury and also from Melksham. Mrs. Dotesio, who was a pupil there from 1917 to 1923, remembers the more leisurely school procedures of the day:

People came on bicycles and by train. And if the train was late, the Head always said, 'We won't start yet – we'll wait for the train people.' (MD4/92)

John Ludlow, second left, enjoying a sweet cigarette, one Boxing Day morning in the early 1930s. His mother stands behind him. They are surrounded by some of the Hinton family, their great friends, who were living in this cottage, 13 Bearfield Buildings.

Since the Grammar School pupils were the wealthiest as well as some of the cleverest children of a district which reached well beyond Bradford, inevitably social distinctions were widened: The pupils themselves emphasised this:

The Grammar School was snooty, anybody who went to the Grammar School looked down on Christchurch and Trinity and I went to Christchurch. But I also went to a woodwork class at the Grammar School. It was in a hut up behind the main building, and we used to be abused by the snobbish Grammar School boys, shouting abuse and throwing stones at us; I'd go over there on my bike and they'd throw our bikes about and ride on them. (JS96)

The rivalry was mutual. Pupils at Trinity School had for generations taunted the Grammar School pupils with the nickname "Tech snobs". This term of abuse goes back to the beginning of the century when Fitzmaurice was a Technical Institute.

As Bradford extended on the south side of the river, especially along the Trowbridge Road, there was an obvious need for another primary school. In the educational reorganisation which took place in the late 1920s, a new school – Trowbridge Road Junior School, now called Fitzmaurice Primary School – was built to answer this problem. During the 1930s the north side of the town expanded slightly along the Bath and Winsley roads, but the Trowbridge Road, a straight, open and relatively flat thoroughfare, was the favoured area for the homes of the traders and business people of the town. Its social status was well understood:

Trowbridge Road was different – it was called Piano Row because people living there were well off enough to have pianos: it was considered, just, well different. (EW89)

Some of the fine houses, many in pairs, on the eastern side of the road had belonged to Sir Charles Hobhouse and had been sold off to private residents on his death in 1917. Behind them lay large gardens, some extending as far as French Grass. By 1935 owners of houses in Trowbridge Road included, among others, a County Council doctor, three bank managers, three agricultural engineers, the headmistress of the local primary school, a water diviner and land agent, two of the foremost builders in the town, the station master of Bradford on Avon, a foreman and other managerial staff from Spencer Moulton. Smaller terraced houses had been built along the western side of the road, using local stone quarried from Jones Hill, on the southern side of the canal. The earliest block of these houses was built just before 1895, other blocks being gradually added in 1898, 1900 and later until they extended in a continuous row along the road. With their good, regular back gardens and substantial allotments, they too were owned by the more flourishing members of the community, such as a solicitor, the minister of the Congregational church and a wide range of owners of the larger shops in the town – Summers (cakes and tea shop), Uncles (shoe shop), Burgess (another cake shop), Taverner (barber), Coupland (grocer), Scrine (chemist) and the manager of one of the Co-op shops, Mr. Varnam.[4]

Unlike many townsfolk across the town bridge, most residents here owned the properties they lived in, thus emphasising in many people's minds the clear distinction between north and south of the river.

A sale of work on the lawn in front of the Bearfield Congregational Chapel in Huntingdon Street. This event was always held in the week nearest to Midsummer Day and helped to provide much needed funds. A flourishing church, it had a thriving Sunday School and took part in all the Sunday School Anniversary celebrations which were constant features in the town's calendar.

The two buildings on the right were a bakery and the baker's home. These were demolished after the Second World War, being replaced by new houses. Their gardens became the access road to Church Acre when that estate was built in the late 1960s.

In 1935 there were still eight different churches and chapels in the town, most with a Sunday school offering instruction and activity for the children and no doubt domestic respite for some hard pressed parents. The annual processions which marked many town events always included such bands of children, dressed in their best clothes and looking forward to the teas, picnics and other Sunday school treats:

At the Congregational Church we always had a Sunday School outing every year sometimes to Westbury White Horse or by train or coach to the seaside. When my sister was at Sunday School, they used to have outings on a canal barge. They used to scrub out the coal barges and go for an outing down to Dundas - pulled by horses. A Sunday School outing was a treat because that was the only time many children went for the day. Then we always had a Sunday School party at Christmas.

Then there was our Sunday School Anniversary every year with 60 or 70 children, girls in white dresses, boys in white shirts sitting on a tiered platform at the front of the church. They sang special Anniversary hymns which had all been learnt by heart in the weeks before. The children had three services on Sunday and one on Monday evening for prize-giving of books, and a bag of sweets for attendance at practices. On Sunday afternoon the children came from all the other Sunday Schools and our church would be crowded with children from aged from five to 15. Every church had its own Anniversary and we would all go to everyone else's celebration. (JU94)

Although these were the major entertainments that many of the poorer children could hope for there was also a strong sense of each little area of the town looking after its own. Bearfield, for example, organized its own children's tea and sports day every summer, as the photograph on page 90, taken around 1934, shows. Phyl Powney, now Mrs. Huntley, who appears in the photograph as a 10 year-old, describes what would happen:

They used to have the sports every year, with a committee, men used to run the sports and the ladies used to do the teas. And after the sports we used to sit down and have our teas. I can always remember the slab cake, it was a lovely Madeira cake and it had a special taste. It was for the children. You always had skittles there and guessing the number of beans in a bottle. (PH93)

The men would mark out the field for the 100 yards, one race for the girls and a separate 100 yards race for the boys. There were all the traditional races such as the egg and spoon race, the sack race and the 3 legged race. It was organised by a committee of those adults who lived directly around Bearfield, but "interlopers" were rigorously kept out. As everyone knew each other, people from other areas of the town, however nearby, were recognised and excluded. As one "outsider" puts it:

> It was just for "the top of the hill". People down in town and over the other side, the Trowbridge Road side they were foreigners. They could come and watch it from afar – but they weren't allowed to sit down and have any nosh or partake in any of the races. (DH2/93)

On the other hand, John Ludlow, born in 1928 and living in Ashley Road, was on his own home patch.

> I always looked forward to it. Everyone would put something into it – someone would make a jelly, or a few paste sandwiches or a cake. As you went into the gate there was always this big lump of coal which Mr. Bird, the coalman, used to donate. You tried to guess the weight and if you were the nearest then it was yours. Bob Amor who lived at the bottom of my garden, his mother won it once, she thought she'd won the pools, this huge lump of coal about 4 feet across and 4 feet high. They used to have competitions like count the peas in the jar and guess the weight of the cake. They always used to have the Salvation Army or the Bratton Band in. I still like brass band music, I used to sit there under a tree all afternoon and watch the races. It was really nice, everyone was there and cheerful. If you weren't local you couldn't go, anyone in Wine street for example wasn't allowed in. Well, you knew who was who in those days. (JL97)

Overall the picture which emerges from the 1920s and 1930s is of a town with separate little communities within it. Although such distinctions would not be apparent to outsiders, inhabitants could draw clear boundaries between their little areas. Young Phyl Powney and her friends in Bearfield were not particularly interested in other parts of Bradford:

> They used to have some sports in the Victory Field by the canal, but we never used to go that way...it was the other side of the river, we seldom went to town...you had a couple of little shops you'd go to – one in Bearfield Buildings, number 2, you'd go in there and you'd get everything you needed – and then there was the Co-op.[5] (PH93)

One way in which these allegiances might change would be through the movement of a family from one dwelling to another – though frequently these moves were a matter of a few streets only. Jack Stafford's family has lived in

Bearfield annual children's tea around 1934. All these children lived in the immediate vicinity of Bearfield itself.

different houses but always near to Sladesbrook Mill since 1871. It was rare for a family to move from one side of the river to the other – domestic change was unlikely to be so drastic. The Bainton family, which has also been in the town for generations, is another example:

Most people were renting their houses. My mother always rented.. In my mother's early days you could rent a house for 2s.0d (10p) or 2s.6d (12.5p)...My mother started married life at Coppice Hill – up on the left – you went along a passage up a little way. Three children were born there. Then they came to live in a little cottage down a garden down Crown Court and three more were born there and then I was born there along in that other cottage (in Woolley Street) where we lived. Of course you didn't always have your piece of garden outside your house. The boundaries weren't very clear I expect often when a house changed hands little pieces of ground moved a bit, I'm sure they did. There was a row of cottages opposite and their gardens always used to be most funny angles. Well how did all that come about? (EW89)

As present day householders marvel at the odd arrangement of their garden plots, Mrs. Wilkins' question still goes unanswered.

Houses could change their shapes as well, thus accounting for the number of "flying freeholds" which exist in Bradford today. Since landlords often owned several cottages in a row, they could shift the rooms about as and when the needs of tenants changed. They might alter the rents accordingly, but they usually came out a little better in pocket for it. Here is Sid Stone describing what happened in some cottages towards the top of Whitehill:

There was number 30, that was built over the top of 31's kitchen. You'd go into 31, straight into their kitchen, then into the living room and up two flights of stairs to the bedroom and the attic bedroom. To get into number 30 you'd use a door in the little side lane. Now in number 32 there used to be an old dealer called Charlie Sartain. He'd deal in anything, horses, furniture, anything that came along. He used to live on his own in there. In 1939 we moved into 33. After we'd got in, the landlord said do you want more room? We said yes, so he said he'd have a word with Charlie next door. So he says to Charlie 'you only use one room, don't you,' and Charlie says, 'Oh, yes, I don't want no more room than that.' So the landlord says, 'Well, how about if I block your stairs off and leave you with one room and reduce your rent. Then I can put some of your place into 33 so they've got two extra bedrooms.' 'Are you going to reduce my rent,' says Charlie, 'well, that's alright.' So the landlord put some of 32 into 33, but of course our rent went up considerably.' (SS97)

The complete row of cottages was demolished as unsafe after the Second World War.

Some of the oldest parts of the town were, not surprisingly, the most run down. As Mrs. Wilkins has said: 'Tory's lovely now – it wasn't very good years ago...all those houses built into the bank were ever so damp. The salt in the kitchens was always wet.' Though most individual families laboured hard to keep their homes and their children clean and respectable, there is much evidence that some areas both south and north of the river were generally to be avoided unless you lived there. Sid Stone was a young lad living north of the town in the 1930s and had to make his way to school:

I went to Christchurch and then to Trinity School. Bradford was very rough. You had to be a tough boy, just because if you didn't live there you'd get a hiding. If you walked along the top of Tory and Middle Rank you got a hiding; if you walked down Wine Street you got a hiding; if you walked down Whitehill you got a hiding; so you had to walk down Masons Lane. They're on about violence today. They forget what is was like here fifty or sixty years ago.

Bradford's been a very very rough town, especially Tory and Middle Rank. Newtown was passable. Around Wine Street, Wine Street Terrace and Budbury you had to watch yourself though – when the old houses were there. As for Whitehill, there were some very rough families there who used to sling anything they didn't want out into the road. If they'd seen you coming and you walked past the upstairs window a lot of water would come out on top of you – well, you hoped it was water. (SS97)

As a boy, Dick Huntley would walk in with his father from Winsley to visit family members in Newtown and other parts of Bradford. Memories of that journey in the early 1930s are still fresh in his mind:

The old houses in Wine Street were tenements one on top of the other and Wine Street was the roughest quarter of the lot.

I can remember my father telling me that he was born in Newtown and then went living in Winsley and he used to say that when he was young Wine Street was virtually a no go area for people other than those who lived there. He was in the First World War so it was about 1910-14 perhaps. It didn't never used to bother him because he was such a big chap. I think it was a case that if they could see anybody that they could pick on they ruled the roost... you weren't allowed to go up and down Wine Street. They were rough and they were under the impression that you were encroaching on their territory, their patch.

It was still a rough quarter in the 1930s but I never came across anything as bad as he had. But then again you could more or less say that we were ruffians too. If I was with my father there was no problem. And in later years when I was at Trinity School I could walk up and down there because I was capable of looking after myself as well. But if there was anybody a little bit on the snooty side or anything, well, they would have let them know that they weren't wanted up there. We were very nearly on a par with them; we were so desperately poor that we had nothing and they knew that we had nothing so we had nothing to bother about going up and down. (DH2/97)

The local newspapers would carry reports of quarrels between neighbours, wider "affrays" or accounts of both sexes being brought before the local magistrates for being drunk and disorderly. It is hardly surprising that prudent Bradfordians kept to their own home patch - although some would venture further afield:

St. Margaret's Hill, called Morgan's Hill, there were lots of poor cottages there – that was a very poor part. Wine Street, Tory, Middle Rank are very upper class now. When the new Junior Fitzmaurice school was built, you only went there until you were eight and then you went up to Trinity. Then you took the scholarship from Trinity if you went to the Grammar School. So I went to Trinity for three years. We used to dare each other to go along from Newtown, up Well Path, run along Tory and down Conigre. It was so rough and dirty that it was a dare - and you ran all the way because the children were so rough. When you ran along there were always people sitting outside, because the rooms were quite small inside. And the children that came to school from that part of the town, well, they had usually had one pair of shoes with the bottoms falling off and their clothes were very poor.

Apart from the bigger houses up by St. Mary Tory the rest were falling down, lots of them. (JU96)

This reference to the two groups of larger houses by the church is interesting for these houses had some much more distinguished occupants. Small as the houses are, there seems to have been something of a feeling around that it was slightly bohemian and interesting to own one of these houses. Dione Moulton knew them well:

In the 1930s it was rather the in thing to take one of those pretty cottages in the two groups of bigger houses leading to St. Mary Tory. They are tiny, but artistic people thought it was fun to be up there. You could come up the Well Path and not go through any of the slummy places. Lady Tothill, who owned The Chantry, had one of them as a weekend cottage for the family. (DH1/97)

Not many people now know that Lady Bowes-Lyon owned the bow-fronted end house of the second group of houses almost opposite the pillar box in the wall on Tory. Reg Hayter, born in Tory Place in 1925, can confirm this with confidence:

One morning in about 1937/8 I was going down to school and a lady asked me to go down to Penny's the local baker in Newtown for her and naturally I said yes. Then later she said would you mind getting my shopping for me whenever I want it and I said yes, of course. So I did it for her whenever she was here, and she paid me well. That's how I came to meet Lady Bowes-Lyon. It was her summer holiday home.

Then, skipping a good number of years, I met Queen Elizabeth, the Queen Mother on 16 July 1985. It was the 41st anniversary of MENCAP, which I've been involved with for nearly 30 years. We were invited to St. James Palace and I was very honoured to be one of those introduced to the Queen Mother.

She asked me where I came from and when I said Bradford on Avon, she was very interested because she remembered it from holiday visits. She asked about the Bowes-Lyon house on Tory, and was thrilled to bits to hear that it was still there after all those years. I was about second in line and the whole retinue behind me had to wait while we had this long conversation.

Of course when you came up the long Well Path to Tory it was like a frontier line there. That was the posh end, the whole of that area was called White Horse View. (RH97)

The rest of the Tory houses, sloping away down to Conigre certainly could not boast any such distinction.

Against such pictures from the past, we need to dwell upon the advantages shared by all the children in the town whatever their background. Everyone took for granted the rich variety of green spaces and quiet streets freely available for their games and pastimes. Young Jo Uncles could bowl her hoop – a fine iron one, made in the Uncles' foundry across the way – up and down the Trowbridge Road in perfect safety. Her brother, Nelson, and his teenage friends used to play cricket in the evenings in the garden at the side of their house with several fielders standing in the middle of the Trowbridge Road. Jack Stafford and his cronies could jump on their bikes and race off to Ashley and the Conkwell woods and stay there until hunger drove them home. Poor as John Ludlow was, his childhood was a busy and happy one:

There were loads of kiddies up round Ashley and we used to get an old sheet and we'd go up to Conkwell and we'd stay there three or four days in the holidays. We used to have a lovely time there. In those days the chickens used to run wild in farmers' grounds and we used to pick eggs out of the hedge or get a potato out of the ground and boil it in an old cocoa tin. We'd be about ten years old but people didn't worry because they knew we were safe – you couldn't do that nowadays. (JL97)

All accounts of childhood between the wars emphasise the freedom to wander in fields, by the river and along the canal and even further afield without fear of any interference. Edie Ratcliff and her Wine Street friends had a playground just outside their door:

There was a shop next door to the Seven Stars…a sweet shop, all home made stuff…We had to be home by 9 o'clock. No fear in those days of being murdered or taken, so we could stay out till 9 o'clock. Skipping ropes with a long rope across the road. We had hoops, hopscotch, marbles, bowls. My brothers had iron hoops and I had a wooden hoop. Then we had tops, they were lovely. You could run with a hoop all along Newtown, and all down town.

That was our playground at the bottom of Wine Street, the Wine Street children. We used to play there all day. No traffic would come along because there was just the horse-drawn traffic – no motor cars or that. The memory will never go – it was wonderful, it was. (EB93)

The fields between the Avon and the railway lines provided their summer holiday place...

All our holidays we spent down the Line fields – down Barton Farm by the railway...we always called it the Line fields, that was our holiday, every year, day in and day out. When we were six weeks from school, our mum would give us our dinner, we used to play down there as good as gold and we used to paddle in the little river. My sister used to work up in the Trowbridge Road, and if anyone was coming that might be her then I used to get under the bridge so she didn't see me. My mother didn't want me to paddle in the river, that was all wrong – but we used to love it. Then we used to come out and go home and have our tea and then we used to come out again until our supper at 9 o'clock. All the mothers used to come to get the children down there and used to have a laugh and a joke. And that was our summer holidays, we used to be down there all the time. (EB93)

The "round house", a popular swimming point for local people on the north bank of the river Avon at Belcombe. It fell into disrepair soon after 1945.

This view of the bottom of Silver Street was taken from Mervyn Uncles' shoe shop. It dates from before 1932 which was around the time when Edwards the pork butcher closed his shop. Knees shop is on the left hand side of the road. The arched front to the brick-faced building mentioned by Jack Stafford has been filled in. It was Couplands the grocers for a time and then became the International Stores. A sweet shop lies just below Edwards' shop. The building nearest the camera on the right, 35 Silver Street, was for many years in the hands of Stanley James Taylor, outfitter. It was demolished in the 1970s to form a courtyard to the gabled house behind it.

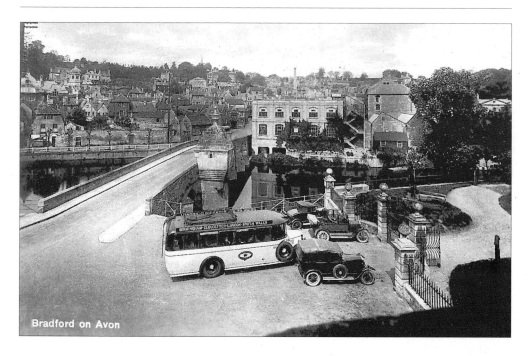

Bradford on Avon

Entrance to the public garden and swimming baths. Two of the original entrance pillars and the riverside railings still remain. The official car park for the town is outside the gates.

But although Bradford's inhabitants talk vividly about their individual small communities, the town paradoxically shared a unity in ways which we will never know. For example no one needed a clock. The noise of Spencer Moulton's factory hooter resounded through the town at least five times a day to announce changes of shift: 6 a.m. morning shift; 8 a.m. breakfast; 9 back to work; 1 p.m. dinner break; 2 p.m. back to work; 6 p.m. change of shift. When the hooter went there would be a wave of bicycles going up or down Trowbridge Road as the men hurried to and from work. Those living near the town bridge shared a further experience when each day's morning shift began:

> *Every morning before 6 o'clock except Sunday I would be woken up by the sound of crowds of men and women tramp, tramping down St. Margaret's Street on their way to clock in at Spencer Moulton. They wore heavy boots with nails in and the noise just came up from the street. (NC93)*

The fire station, housed in what is now St. Margaret's car park, was another focus of shared interest:

We had a maroon to warn the firemen that there was a fire. It was a maroon like they have for the lifeboats and it went up in the air with a tremendous bang, you could hear it all over town. The firemen were working at Spencer Moulton and all round the town – there were no permanent firemen, they were all maintained like they are now. Then they would race down to the fire station. One of the firemen lived opposite us. You'd see him come running out or going off on his bicycle. When the maroon went off everyone ran out to the door to see what was happening, then you'd hear the bell of the fire engine. Spencer Moulton had their own fire brigade as well. My next door neighbour was second in command, so that any small fire at Spencer Moulton they would deal with and only call the town fire brigade if they needed it. (JU96)

One day when we heard the bell on the fire engine we went out to the gate and the fire engine was driving up and down Trowbridge Road looking for a fire reported by someone in Tory. They discovered it was from Uncles' foundry where they were casting that day, and the flames from the furnace could be seen in Tory. (JU94)

Other familiar sounds all around the town, sounds which will never be heard again, came from the large shunting yard down by the station:

I can always remember this perpetual noise of shunting in what is now the station car park. They must have had their own shunting engine there. When you were in Trinity School you heard the shunting going on all day, no messing...the school was just above it, only just over the other side of the river. Waggons were being shunted round all the time. Of course everything was shifted by rail – Spencer Moulton used to transport all their stuff out by rail and they had carts and lorries which would take it from the factory to the station yard and it would be put into waggons. But it was mainly coal...there were several coal merchants in the town and they did have their own coal come in on the trucks and shunted into the loading bays where they used to sack it up and chuck it on their waggons.

They had this open shed in the shunting yard and at the end of the open shed they had a platform and there was this hand-cranked crane, quite a large one, it would lift a good old weight, I suppose if they had a big load come in by rail – if machinery for Spencer Moulton came in by rail then that crane would have been used to take it off the waggons to take it into the factory. (DH2/97).

In 1921, when there were 1,194 structurally separate houses in Bradford,[6] Mr. Doel, surveyor for the U.D.C., was dismayed to learn there were only 73 bathrooms in the town. This fact emerged in a discussion about water rates for the coming year; the reason was not only the obvious problem of piping water through limestone hillsides; it was also the high quarterly charges exacted by the water company. Even new houses were normally built without bathrooms. This was no disadvantage to young Edie Ratcliff, now Mrs. Edith Budds:

I was born at Wine Street in 1914, just when the war started, our house was brand new when we went into it. They've got railings around, just round the corner from where Wilkins brewery was. As you're going up, ours was No 50. We used to go to St. Mary Tory every Sunday, and it was lovely. As regards the brewery, I can see the furnace there now. It was horses and they had a bridge from this side of the brewery to the furnace, it's been pulled down now. We weren't really allowed to go into the brewery because they were working, but we were always there watching what was happening _ I can smell it now, it was wonderful.

Our houses were very modern, no bathroom but three nice bedrooms and a toilet inside, a living room and a sitting room, but not much garden. We had an allotment up the top where Budbury Tynings now are. That's why it's called Tynings now. There's one thing about Wine Street – they should never have pulled those lovely places down. It could have been made all modern like Barton Orchard is now. There are photographs with washing hanging across the street...It was wonderful, we were all one big happy family, all happy together. Every drop of water, no water indoors, you had to go right up the back of the house and get it from the tap up in the garden, no toilet indoors in those houses. But they could have been made modern...they all shared this one tap, it was hard work but they were all happy. (EB93)

A useful bathroom cupboard which could be kept in the bedroom or outhouse.

However Mrs. Rose Niblett, born in 1902, emphasises with some small but telling details the hard work of running a home:

> *I have lived on Whitehill for all my married life. There were five houses in our little row, but the bottom three were eventually condemned. The houses all had little tiny window squares. There were only two toilets for the five houses and they were up at the top of our rank on Whitehill itself. In 1929 when I was first married we lived over the other side of the road in a one up and one down. I knew the lady in the bottom house in this rank and when she died they said, "Why not get it" – so we did. It was 2s.6d a week. We had two bedrooms and a sitting room and kitchen and no bathroom.*
>
> *Everyone from the five houses in the rank came up for the water. We had one open tap which is still there. I lived down in the bottom house and as all the old people died so the young families came. There was a lady there with five children in a two up and two down getting all her water from the one shared tap. Then in another cottage another lady with another five children,. Then there was Mrs. Dando with another four, but next door to her the lady only had three children. They all had husbands. Every Friday morning all the women, all of us, we used to get down on our hands and knees and scrub all the stones in front of our houses right the way down. We all did our own portion. The whole path was as white as snow and looked beautiful. Then we took turns over scrubbing the lavatories. Bucket lavatories, someone used to come and empty them.*
>
> *On Sunday nights my husband used to fill two or three baths, the old fashioned zinc baths, so I shouldn't have to keep walking backwards and forwards up and down to the tap for washing on Mondays. We had a very small kitchen with a stone floor and a very low ceiling. Imagine doing the washing in an old-fashioned copper where you boiled everything up and only had candles to light you. (RN89)*

It is indeed almost impossible to imagine the back-aching intensity of such manual labour:

> *Think of the work people did – mother would get the coal and fill the copper with water, put the clothes in and boil them up. Then next to the copper was a big stand with a big mangle on it. She would take the heavy, steaming hot clothes out of the boiler and get them into the bath. Then she put them through the mangle and hung them out in the garden to dry. Sheets from the three beds meant another, separate wash. All heavy work. She washed on Monday, ironed on Tuesday. There was nowhere indoors to dry washing but we had a clothes horse so mother could put it on that by the fire. (JU96)*

Large families living in small rooms found drying clothes particularly trying in wet weather. There are various accounts of mothers sending all their children to bed on Mondays directly after their tea so that the entire living space could be used as a drying area.

Then there were all the other household chores:

> *It was all very hard manual work. When I was quite small we used to have just an ordinary hand-pushed carpet sweeper. In the Spring all the carpets were taken up one by one and put over the clothes line and beaten with walking sticks and a metal carpet beater to get the dust and dirt out. All the family had to lend a hand. It wasn't until I was at Grammar School in 1936 that we had a hoover: before that it was dustpan and brush and the carpet sweeper. You had to black lead the grate. I think mother did it every morning after she did the fire. We had a fancy iron fender, all sort of scrolled, round it as well. We always seemed to have a fire because all the cooking was done on the fire and in the side oven. We also had a small gas ring in the scullery. (JU96).*

A housewife might be scrupulously clean and still be defeated by the lack of proper sanitation around her. Bearfield was not well provided for:

> *We used to have a toilet down the garden, perhaps one between two or three families. They used to keep them beautifully clean. But Mrs. Hinton's toilet out the back was like a metal stand with a wooden seat on and in the middle of that was like a funnel. That funnel went straight down to the open sewer. It was always known that when you went out to use the toilet in the dark you always kicked it first because rats used to come up that sewer. (JL97)*

In the late 1920s electricity came to the Shambles and houses near to the town centre. But power had to be carefully allocated and so every household was allowed no more than three ceiling lights, which were installed at no cost to the occupant:

> *We had free electric light in the middle of the ceiling in the sitting room, one in the kitchen and one upstairs in mother and father's bedroom. You could say which rooms you wanted them in but you could only have three. I think we were quite excited because we'd only had gas lights downstairs. In the late 20s, I remember coming home of an evening when it would be pitch dark in the house. Father had to go in and light the gas and you had to wait outside until he'd lit it. Upstairs we used candles, and you went up with a candle stick. It was difficult reading in bed.*

I can remember we had an electric iron. When mother had it first she used to plug it in the ceiling light in the kitchen. She'd been used to putting the flat irons on the trivet against the fire to get them hot. When father brought the first electric iron she used it once or twice but she didn't like it. It wasn't very safe was it, having it in the light? (JU96)

Mrs. Cambourne spent her working life in her father's shop, Bryant's, in St. Margaret's Street. She has a great many memories of working and living in the centre of the town:

I can remember when the electric people here put in three lights free for everyone and that was all. We had paraffin lamps and I used to have to light the shop with them. We used to have Aladdin ones that you pumped up, had a mantle on them. We had a big one which hung in the shop window. It hung down and it had a spray coming out with 2 lights each side, and you lit them with methylated spirits and got them hot and then you pumped them up and then the mantle gradually lit like a gas mantle would. You see even after all the town had 3 lights each free the villages didn't have any electricity for a long time so you took the paraffin round for lighting, heating and cooking. (NC92)

The further the electricity cables ran from the Shambles, the dimmer the light produced in individual houses. The first cable up Whitehill was carried on overhead wooden poles (which are still in place at the end of the century, now mostly carrying telephone wires). To extend the system into Sladesbrook, Bath Road and all the northern side of town an underground electric cable was laid up to the top of Whitehill and another transformer put in place on the corner with New Road. This was a costly operation and Wessex Electricity Company had to ensure it would have sufficient customers for this newfangled source of power to justify the outlay.

Once the cable was in place, the company's salesmen went round knocking on everybody's doors to get them to have the electricity. As well as three free ceiling lights people were given just one wall socket with one two-pin plug, also free. The Electricity Company would get its financial return not only by the future sale of electrical power but also by persuading housewives (or their husbands) to buy an electric iron from them at the same time. Otherwise, what was the use of having the wall socket?[7] However this plug served little practical use in its early days. Women ironed on their kitchen tables, the flex on the iron was unlikely to reach from the wall socket to the table and so, if the electric iron was used at all, it would most probably be fixed into a double socket dangling from the ceiling fitment.

There were one or two advantages the hard-pressed housewife of the 1920s and 1930s had over her modern counterpart. Firstly, children of all ages would probably take themselves to school and secondly, it was usual for most goods to be delivered to the door. Items bought in one of the many shops in the town would be done up in brown paper parcels neatly tied with string while the customer watched and then, if required, brought up by the delivery boy or man. But it was normal to purchase food and other essentials simply by waiting for a knock on the door from the regular traders who came round:

> The baker came to the door with a basket full of bread and you chose which loaf you wanted. The milkman came round with a pail, they had the measures hanging over the side – half pint, pint, quart – and you took your jug to the door and they measured it out with the measure into your jug. Mr. Maggs, our milkman, had a little farm up the top of Regent's Place. Then the coalman came round and delivered the coal to the house, the fish man used to come, I'm almost sure he had a horse and cart, and the greengrocers, they came round as well. It would be oranges and bananas, that type of thing, because everyone had a garden or an allotment and you'd grow all your vegetables. We grew all our vegetables in the gardens, besides raspberries, strawberries, blackcurrants, redcurrants, several apple trees, a plum tree, gooseberries, rhubarb. We never had to buy jam. Logs for the fire were delivered from a farm. (JU93)

One of the shops at the forefront of the delivery trade was Bryant's. Mrs. Cambourne, born Lily Noreen Bryant, was 12 in 1923 when her father moved from his tiny shop at 2 Bearfield Buildings and opened his hardware business at 8 and 9 St. Margaret's Street. Mr. Bryant had been invalided out of the Army just before the end of the Great War. Now he put his considerable energies into building up a very successful business both in Bradford itself and throughout the outlying villages:

> After the Great War we had the proper travelling shop built by a firm in Freshford. It was still horse-drawn at this time. It was beautifully made with open racks to display the goods. The paintwork was green with gold outlining the shelves. Then later we had a Model T Ford which was also custom-made for transporting the hardware and paraffin. We then had two vans and between them they travelled weekly round the whole of Bradford, as well as to Westwood, Freshford, Limpley Stoke, nearly into Claverton and also to Winsley, Wingfield, Holt, and Bradford Leigh. (NC92)

On regular weekly rounds of outlying areas, the Bryant vans carried almost everything a householder might need. It was well organised and reliable:

It was quite an event when we went round with the van. We used to stop in the same place each time, for example when we got to Westwood we usually stopped just past the New Inn, where it was a bit wider. People used to come out and if they didn't buy anything they would walk round to see what we'd got. In the 1920s we were carrying cups, saucers, plates, chambers, anything...Matting, rugs, staples, tintacks to hammer into the walls and put things on them...packets of seeds, paraffin, soap, candles, starch (important thing in those days) string, balls of string. Anything that you wanted in that line, I'll bet we had it on there.

Then there were big heavy things like garden tools, buckets, baths, even long taper baths about 4 ft. long – that's all people had for bathing in, and you usually hung them outside the back door. Usually that kind of thing people would order one week and take it the next. We used to take a lot of orders. They might order a rug: they'd say I want a rug for the bedroom, will you bring me some to see. They'd ask about size and colour and we'd put up perhaps half-a-dozen on the van for them to have a look at. (NC92).

One of the most important services offered by Bryants was the delivery of paraffin. The domestic benefits of gas and electricity – especially outside of the town – were not yet fully available. Paraffin was used not only for lighting and heating but also, in many households, for cooking purposes as well:

We had a specially designed van, with a tank made to fit. It was a very flat tank, I suppose about a foot deep and two foot six wide, about four-feet long and it would carry about a hundred gallons of paraffin oil. In those days people only had one fireplace, usually it was a range type of fire in the living room: they'd have stone floors and no other heating in the house. Some of them hadn't very good cooking facilities at all so they used paraffin stoves. It was quite an improvement over cooking on a range with coal and wood. My mother had one, I can remember us having one because we'd had a range fitted when we moved to St. Margaret's Street. It never worked properly and mother had this Valor cooker-heater. It had three burners, it stood about three feet high, and had an oven on the top, with a proper door. It was surprising how quickly a paraffin cooker warmed up. My mother cooked for five of us and she did very well. (NC92)

Of course paraffin had to be kept carefully separate from groceries and other goods. But it had other advantages:

It's lovely for your hands, it used to keep your hands beautifully clean. I used to do all sorts of dirty jobs in those days when I went on the van, I used to wash my hands in paraffin when I got home and wash them again in something scented to take the smell off. (NC92)

Len Bryant standing beside Bryant's Travelling shop. This was especially adapted to carry paraffin and carefully designed to display goods easily and yet to ensure their safe keeping up and down local hills.

Friday evening was a particularly busy time in Bryant's shop:

I can remember there used to be a train came up from Avoncliff. There were about half a dozen quite elderly Avoncliff ladies who would come on it about fourish every Friday. Now we didn't go to Avoncliff, there weren't many houses to go down there for and it was a very awkward trip too. But they would come in and order things and then we would take them down, because we had a small van that delivered things that we didn't want to take a big van for. I used to look out of the window and think 'Ah, here they come, here's the train coming in'. And Friday evenings a lot of the Westwood people would come in and do their shopping – because they got paid Friday evenings.

The railway was a most significant part of the town, taken for granted as a reliable and constant transport system for both goods and people in ways we can now only envy. Coal in large quantities, iron for Lailey's forge, regular deliveries of goods for the shops. Spencer Moulton relied on the railway for supplies of coal as well as for transport of many of its finished products. For entertainment by the 1930s a very popular train to Bath was called the Woolworth's train because it ran at a cheaper price:

On Saturdays after five o'clock it was 9d (4.5p) return instead of 1s.3d (6.5p), there was a train came from London round the loop, you got on that one, it was a fast one and you always stood up because it was full of people from Melksham. All the shops were still open in them days until nine – or until eight o'clock easy. In Bradford they were, that's why they brought in all those laws to stop people overworking employees late at night. There was a fast train back at nine, a stopper at ten and then there was one at midnight. It didn't go very fast, it stopped everywhere including Avoncliff Halt. It didn't half rock about and everyone called it the Midnight Rocker. (JS96)

But there was no need to go out of the town for entertainment. Some of the younger girls, earning reasonable money at Spencer Moulton or the Sirdar Rubber Company, just enjoyed the postwar fashions – and perhaps brought a smile to the faces of some of the older inhabitants:

Can you imagine eight girls across St. Margaret's Street, walking arm in arm, with their fancy garters on, with rattles on them, the rattles were on their garters...even my Aunt Kate wore them. I wasn't allowed to mix with the flappers...short skirts and their garters were just showing...with rattles, little bells on them. (WB89)

It is quite difficult nowadays to picture such a remarkable sight in a nearly empty St. Margaret's Street, but other accounts support this description:

There was plenty of work for young girls around here, especially at Spencer Moulton. I didn't want to go down there...There were some girls called the flappers in the 1920s and they'd wear very short skirts and parade down St. Margaret's wearing garters with bells, yes fancy garters. My sisters wore fancy garters. My other sister she was all for fashion. My elder sister and myself weren't so much that way. (EW89)

Aunt Kate was not so shy:

My mother and Aunt Kate was out for a walk, and I think I'm right in saying it was Barton Farm, it was where a lot of people were, and they had to get over a stile. Poor Aunt Kate, she fell, and the thing she said was "Good job I had my fancy garters on." (WB89)

For more organised entertainment the Baths continued to serve its winter social function when its large interior space was reorganised and became available for all kinds of activities. Isabelle Carter loved it:

What I liked about living there was that in the winter the swimming bath was covered over with boards from about September to Easter for all kinds of social things. My sister and I had a lovely time because all the gentry used to come there for their birthdays and celebrations and big parties and would bring in their own caterers. Then there were dances and concerts on a wooden shaky stage and I enjoyed all that. My sister and I went to everything. (IC96)

Other more permanent leisure facilities gradually appeared. Silent films were shown in the main hall of the old Town Hall in the early 1920s. For the payment of three halfpennies (1p) customers could enjoy the worlds of Lilian Gish, Mary Pickford and Charlie Chaplin, enriched by the bravura of a lady pianist. This was superseded when the Territorial Drill Hall (once the dye house) in St. Margaret's was turned into The Alexander Picture Theatre. In that modern role it acquired a new entrance hall and served the town well. By the 1930s The Bradford on Avon Amateur Operatic and Dramatic Society was in full swing, with a spirited production each year: 1931 'Pearl, the Fishermaiden'; 1932 'Cupid & the Ogre'; 1933 'The Superior Sex'; 1934 'Count of Como'; 1935 'Slave in Araby'; 1936 'San Marino'; 1937 'Miss Hook of Holland'; and most ambitiously in 1938, 'No, No Nanette'.

At times people had money to spend on such entertainment, for although there were booms and slumps in the rubber trade, just as there had been in Bradford's clothmaking industry in earlier centuries. Spencer Moulton continued, overall, to expand. For example, it had had its own rubber plantations in Ceylon (later renamed Sri Lanka) as early as 1905. By now its plantations were in Malaysia as well. There was immense competition to get into Spencer Moulton and the usual way was by having family or friends already working there who would get you in. Henry Stevens went there in 1923 at the age of 14:

It wasn't an easy firm to get into because it paid good money. I can remember men waiting outside the King's Arms[8] to see if there was any work that day. I got in because a friend of my father's said he'd have me. I was supposed to go into the powerhouse. It generated electricity for the whole of the factory but it didn't pay like piecework. (HS94)

The foremen used to come and haggle a price, which is piecework really...we associate piecework with when we had the stop watch put on us. I suppose they always had to come back to the workforce to discover how long it took to make something because each job was different. The man came round with the stopwatch and you were professionally making it look as if you were going like the clappers but you weren't. If you took four minutes under his stopwatch; you'd have to be able to do it in three, if you wanted to earn good money. So if you had to rub it you'd do it, say six times, under the stop watch but when you weren't under the stop watch you'd rub it three times. We learnt all the tricks but equally the person that was doing the stop watch study was just as crafty as what we were. You had to be very careful – because they would go to someone else and time them doing the same job. So you would cut off your nose to spite your face because if someone was going to do it in half the time you were going to do it, then you'd look a right ninny. But most of them were very fair. If you'd do a good job and do it properly then they were fair enough. (DH93)

A Perfect Blue Flame. Easily Regulated as a Gas Stove.

A popular paraffin stove of the kind used throughout the country, especially in country districts. Almost the same design was still being made for years after the Second World War and continued to sell well.

They must have been fair – they even gave people a second chance:

> *I was on football bladders and they were coming along to time me. My mum was working there as well and she said don't go fast. And I went that slow that they had to come back and time me again. (LH97)*

It is abundantly clear that Spencer Moulton were not simply rubber manufacturers. They had a highly qualified workforce of chemists and engineers as well as skilled and intelligent workers on the shop floor. Items of all purposes and sizes, from very large to the minuscule were designed and made there. Different articles required different kinds of rubber and each would have its own demanding specifications for thickness, hardness, softness, pliability, colour and so on. Industrialists would bring their problems to Spencer Moulton who, as engineers in rubber, would solve them and produce a manufactured article of the highest quality. The Bradford workers knew their worth in the marketplace and always speak of their firm with great pride and affection. Making railway springs for train buffers was one of the major elements of the business. But piecework could produce its own demands:

> *We were on piecework for these springs. Come 12 o'clock some were still struggling, some would have done their stint, got their money and gone. They did so much and that was it. You had to see that to believe it. It was like a madhouse in there. A truck was loaded with these springs and they were packed in moulds, then it was pushed in that heater and the rubber was cured. When the moulds were ready to come out the men had to empty the truck. And that's when the fun used to start. When the truck came out you had to spray water over the moulds. They were so red hot you couldn't handle them and they weighed two or three hundredweight apiece. You took the bolt out and released all the moulds.. It was a free for all; if you could go faster than the bloke next door to you, you'd have five off of that truck and he'd only have two. You had to do so many, every man had to do so many. There were gangs in other parts of the factory, again like a madhouse: great brawny men with no shirts on. The piecework men went on and beat the system. (HS94)*

However the 1920s and 1930s were unstable times. There was a twelve-week national coal strike in 1921, for example, which brought Spencer Moulton to a halt for several weeks. The large stocks of coal necessary to run the steam engines ceased to arrive and the company had to stop production. Workers had to be laid off and received no wages. Similarly the General Strike of 1926, widespread national unrest and the Depression of the 1930s inevitably had a full impact on

local factories and business. There were times when nearby food industries –
such as the Nestlé factory at Staverton seemed a more secure employment. The
Bainton family, up in Woolley, was one family with two means of support:

> *Really we were fortunate because there were a lot out of work My father*
> *wasn't out of work – he was a fortunate man, a foreman over there at Staverton*
> *and never without a job. My sisters might have gone on short time when Nestlés*
> *wasn't so busy but I don't think they were ever out of work. Two of my brothers*
> *worked at Spencer Moulton. I think we were a fortunate family. In the depression*
> *there were a lot out of work. In our row of four houses the men in the other*
> *three were out of work, there was only my father working – that's only one little*
> *section of the town. (EW89)*

There were other means of employment of course; in the building trade, on
the railway, in the shops and within many services which the town provided.
Then there were the farms directly surrounding the town as well as the stone
quarries a little further out at Monkton Farleigh and Corsham. An industry
special to Bradford was that of commercial mushroom growing. This business,
which had been in Bradford from as far back as the 1870s, was carried out in
three disused stone quarries on the south side of the town. These were: Poulton,
by the canal bridge and which would find itself providing air raid shelter for
Fitzmaurice School in the Second World War; Jones, just off the right side of
Jones Hill and Bethel, the largest mushroom quarry of them all. This unusual
method of farming is described in much more detail in Chapter 6. The workers
were nearly all women and between the wars as many as 60 might be working
there. Otherwise domestic service might be the only answer:

> *If people didn't go into factories they went into service, those were the two*
> *things. My aunt's husband died young and she had no children and she went*
> *back to cook / housekeeping. In the early days you would start at the beginning*
> *and work your way up and perhaps some of the cooks weren't that nice to you*
> *if you were below them. My mother used to say she wouldn't like any of her*
> *children to do what her sister Em had done because she'd been worked too*
> *hard. My mother had a hard enough life bringing us all up but she didn't*
> *consider that as hard as my aunt's life. (EW89)*

By the end of the 1930s such work was not so easy to find locally. The grander
houses in the Trowbridge Road seemed to be managing with only daily staff and
the Georgian houses within the old town were no longer necessarily in family
occupation. There was however still an impressive ring of fine houses set in

their own grounds on the Bath side of town. The Hall had belonged to the Moulton family since the 1840s. Its south front had even been reproduced for the English pavilion at the Paris Exhibition of 1900 and it continued to be the most distinguished property in the town. The substantial gentlemen's residences known as Belcombe Court, Woolley Grange, Kingsfield Grange, Conigre House and North Leigh House were still lived in by families. But others were becoming too cumbersome for domestic use. Frankleigh House on the road to Bath had become a prep school in 1935, Leigh Park House (Lord Fitzmaurice's old home) was finally bought by the U.D.C. from Albert Davis in June 1936 for £1,500 as a hospital, convalescent and maternity home. By 1939 Berryfield House had long been empty. Then The Priory, a magnificent dwelling originally built in the fifteenth century and gloriously embellished in the eighteenth and which has been written about elsewhere[9] declined in significance and mostly disappeared in 1938. Many of those that remained would be serving new functions when the next war finally came.

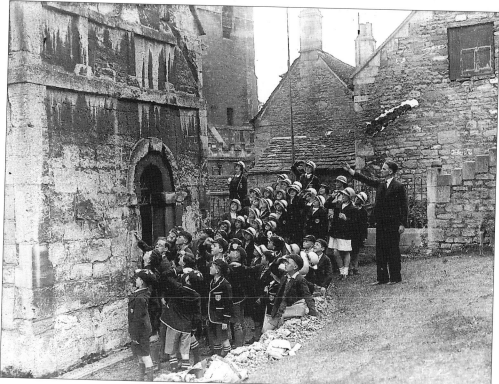

Children of St. Martin's School, Bayswater, London, examining the Saxon Church in June 1935 in the days when school trips to far-off places were much more unusual. They were brought down by their Headmaster, Mr. C.N. Moore, son of the late Mr. Tom Moore of Bradford.

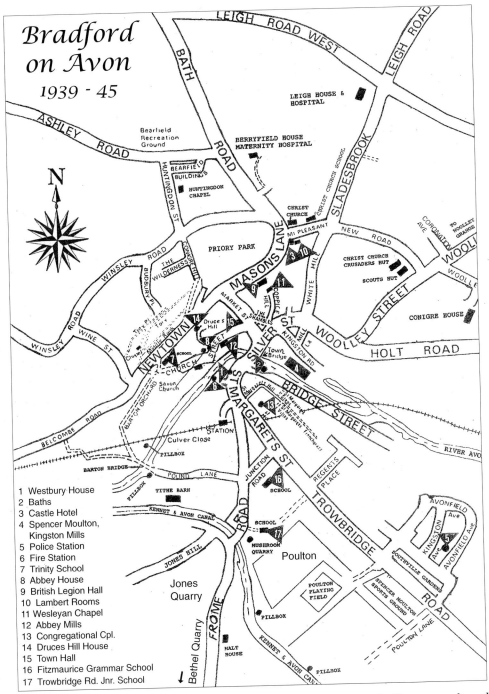

Bradford on Avon
1939 - 45

1. Westbury House
2. Baths
3. Castle Hotel
4. Spencer Moulton, Kingston Mills
5. Police Station
6. Fire Station
7. Trinity School
8. Abbey House
9. British Legion Hall
10. Lambert Rooms
11. Wesleyan Chapel
12. Abbey Mills
13. Congregational Cpl.
14. Druces Hill House
15. Town Hall
16. Fitzmaurice Grammar School
17. Trowbridge Rd. Jnr. School

Bradford 1939-45, with many open spaces which would be built upon after the war years. The figures refer to places used for wartime purposes which are listed in the bottom left hand corner.

CHAPTER FOUR
1939 - 1945
Bradford in the Second World War

Preparations for war ~ Evacuees ~ Spencer Moulton ~ Conscription and Call Up ~ Bradford's Fortifications and War Personnel ~ Local Bombing and the Air Crash ~ Soldiers in the Town ~ V.E. and V.J. Celebrations ~ Wartime use of Quarries in the Area ~ Influx of Workers for Secret Underground War Work

LIKE THE REST OF THE country, Bradford was firmly involved in the Second World War in ways unimaginable in 1914. Men and women went away to fight as before, but this time there was no reliance on local tribunals to keep up the numbers in the armed forces. Conscription began almost at the start of hostilities. The town had new demands upon it, demands never experienced before. In the First World War there was a sense of the town being reduced in size and energy as young men disappeared into the Army and Navy. But this time there was a huge influx of strangers, evacuee children who swamped the town's accommodation and its schools. Then there were also adults, people sent down from Spencer Moulton's Head Office in Westminster for office work in Bradford: office workers for Nestlé moved to their firm's factory at Staverton, and expectant mothers from the East End of London brought here to await the birth of their babies. All brought different ways and unfamiliar attitudes into the town.

Jack Mock is the son of Lance Corporal Herbert Nelson Mock of the 1st Wiltshire Regiment who was awarded the Distinguished Conduct Medal for gallantry in the Battle of the Somme in 1916. The family has lived in Bradford for generations and it seems very appropriate to give Jack, who was a schoolboy at the time, the opportunity to tell the story of his home town through the six years of the Second World War. His detailed diary of the war years has already been privately published.[1]

Jack Mock's account of the war, 1939 - 1945

Preparations for war

As early as January 1938, Bradford on Avon Urban District Council, under the chairmanship of Mr. A.E. Angell was shown various types of gas masks. This followed the passing, in 1937, of the Air Raid Precautions (A.R.P.) Act of Parliament. The act required that lighting restrictions be very severe. No normal street lighting, but only "aids to movement" were to be allowed: one or two shaded lights in places such as road junctions. Homes, shops and factories were to mask their windows and lights. Motor vehicle head lamps would also be shaded. The government stressed that the scheme should not interfere with industrial production. Air-raid wardens were an important feature of the scheme and volunteers from men more than 30 years of age were required.

Bradford was asked to provide 406 A.R.P. volunteers, which included air raid wardens, demolition squads, decontamination squads and ambulance drivers. The town's A.R.P. headquarters was Westbury House, near the town bridge, an ideal central position. First aid parties with posts at the town swimming baths, Bearfield Congregational Chapel and Christ Church were organised, with gas mask centres at Sladesbrook and St. Margaret's Street. Air raid signals were to be given by electric sirens at Westbury House and the Castle Hotel, at the top of Masons Lane and by steam siren at Kingston Mill, Spencer Moulton's premises. (In January 1940 a siren was installed at Bradford's police station in Avonfield Avenue.)

Mr. R.W. Trace, Clerk to the Urban District Council was appointed local food officer, and in October 1938, Mr. Rossiter, the town's chief fire officer, attended a council meeting, when they approved his emergency fire brigade scheme for the district.

At the Holy Trinity Church the Flemish window to the south was boarded up against bomb blast, the cost being met by gifts and the church wardens' account. Sandbags were placed around the outer walls of the Saxon Church for the same reason. Many households in the town were buying black-out material to cover their doors and windows, and they soon found that the price of the cloth rose from 2/6d (12.5p) to 3/11d (20p) per yard and the quality became noticeably inferior.

The tall chimney of Messrs. Geo. Spencer, Moulton was painted army style in a camouflage finish, to prevent easy identification from the air. Air Raid shelters were established at Church House, Church Street; 32, St. Margaret's Street; Christ Church Vicarage, Masons Lane; The Malt House, Frome Road; The Old Bear Inn, Silver Street; and The Three Horse Shoes Public House, Frome Road. (By June 1940 the shelters at Church House and the Three Horse

Shoes were declared unsafe.) Several shelters were built on the premises of Geo. Spencer, Moulton, one of which is still standing. It was built below the arches of the two-storey building, very close to the town bridge.

The town's Fire Brigade had just acquired a new Dennis fire engine at a cost of £876. The Brigade's H.Q. was situated in a building in front of St. Margaret's Hall, slightly to the rear of Westbury House. The Chief A.R.P. Wardens arranged for a census of the adult civilian inhabitants to see how many gas masks the U.D.C. would need for the entire population. Townsfolk were asked to attend either the Congregational schoolroom, St. Margaret's Street, Sladesbrook Temperance Hall or the Trinity Senior School, Newtown. A similar task was undertaken at the schools in the town and many still have vivid memories of being fitted for gas masks a little later on.

Thus the town prepared itself for the inevitable news of the 3 September 1939 that the country was at war with Germany.

Evacuation

Nationally, evacuation of urban centres was a major operation. During the four days from Friday 1 September to Monday 4 September 1939, almost one and a half million evacuees, including escorts and teachers arrived in reception areas and were carried from 72 stations by some 4,000 special trains to various "safe" areas of the country.

On 30 August, and in anticipation of this event, the Wiltshire County Council requisitioned Berryfield House, Bradford, to be used as a maternity hospital for expectant mothers. 75 arrived in the town by coach in the late afternoon of the 2nd September. During the four days of this initial evacuation, a further 746 evacuees came to the town, arriving by train at Trowbridge station and conveyed to Bradford by coach, hired from Messrs D.R. Keates. They were then distributed to three reception buildings: Fitzmaurice Grammar School, Junction Road; Trinity Senior School, Newtown and Christ Church Junior School, Mount Pleasant, where emergency rations, provided by the Ministry of Food were issued to each adult and child.

On 3 September it was found impossible to arrange billets for all the evacuees who had just arrived so Abbey House in Church Street was requisitioned for 40 women and children. The next day saw a further 30 persons billeted at Leigh House, also requisitioned for the same reason. Abbey House was released on 24 November to the military, when the Council took over 41, Trowbridge Road for the evacuees.

Classroom accommodation in the schools in the town was inevitably stretched to its limits with this sudden influx of pupils. For example, Christchurch School used the British Legion Hall in Masons Lane, the Lambert Rooms in Mount

Pleasant and the Crusaders' Hut in New Road for additional class space. I was just coming up to six when the war started. I had one brother who was 13 years older than me. I was about to start at the Trowbridge Road School, later called the Fitzmaurice Junior School. I was not consciously aware that there were evacuees at the time but I can remember there was a sudden influx of people I didn't know. We were living in Trowbridge Road, a small cottage more or less opposite the shop at the top of Poulton Lane. At that time my brother and I were still home until he went into the Forces in 1941. We only had two bedrooms so we did not have any evacuees billeted on us.

At school when the siren went we were all lined up in our crocodiles and we all trooped down to the nearby Poulton mushroom quarry, taking our gas masks and fold-up stools with us. It was very claustrophobic in there and we used to sing songs and hymns to pass the time. I remember the oil lamps hung around the walls for us to see where we were. The mushroom quarries were still working and we were basically just inside the main entrance and I gather the actual mushrooms were grown in offshoot rooms off the main entrance. Even now when I get near mushroom compost in bags, that smell brings back those memories. It was a little bit frightening.

One time I remember there was a dogfight with the Spitfires and enemy aircraft just above us. The teachers stood at the entrance to the mushroom quarry and several bullet shells came down just in front of them. Perhaps the German planes were coming back from bombing Bristol: I know that during the Bath bombing in April 1942 there were several dogfights in this area, as well as several bombs being off loaded.

I'm given to understand that the Fitzmaurice Grammar School had an agreement with Mr. Chrystal, Works Manager at Spencer Moulton. He arranged that a flag would be hoisted on top of Abbey Mill (which could be seen at the school) if there was a Red Alert. This would come via the Observer Corps when enemy aircraft were thought to be close to Bradford. Pupils who lived fairly close used to go home when the siren sounded, and would take with them any friends who lived too far away to do the same.

However, by April 1940 many of the evacuees had returned to their homes in the London area, because fear of any immediate bombing had subsided. By this time it seems that only 100 evacuees were still in Bradford. Mrs. Niblett had taken in one of these early evacuees:

First of all we had a little girl, same age as my daughter, so I treated them both the same. The little girl was one of six. One day her parents came, awfully scruffy I have to say. When I put the little girl to bed I gave her a hot water bottle. And her mother said "Oh she won't be treated like this when she gets home". And they came and took her away. Whether they thought I was treating her too well I don't know. (RN89)

Joyce Baumann remembers how London children brought their London ways with them:

I was living with my parents. I remember one little girl called Lucy who'd come down from London, she was a nice little girl but my mum was absolutely soft with her. I came home from work one day and. I found all of our pathway covered in big chalk marks where she'd been having kiddies in to play a sort of game of noughts and crosses. And I thought, oh my goodness – the people round here won't like this. (JB97)

On 13 June a further 326 unaccompanied children, 30 teachers and two helpers were received in the town and the authorities were forced to requisition Conigre House for use as a hostel, where an additional 74 children were billeted. A further 40 were transferred from Trowbridge and Warminster to the hostel. Local ladies helped out in all kinds of ways, including a weekly sewing circle which met there to darn the endless pile of evacuees' socks. Again Christchurch School was desperate for accommodation and this time the Huntingdon Street Schoolroom and the Wesleyan Chapel schoolroom in Coppice Hill were used.

The London blitz intensified, and on 7 September 1940 some 250 additional evacuees arrived in the town. As billeting became more difficult to arrange the Billeting Officer called on the Police for assistance in placing them in private homes. Later several residents were fined at the Bradford Magistrates court for refusing to comply with the billeting notices concerning their evacuee quotas.

In October 1940, the Clerk of Bradford's Urban District Council reported that:

...there were 1,100 persons billeted in the town under the evacuation scheme. The town's population was considerably increased by the large number of persons who have arrived, having made private arrangements, and others by reason of requirements of the Ministry. The population had increased from the mid-1938 figure of 4,749 to the October 1940 figure of 6,304. This has put a considerable strain upon the town's water supply and for the past two months the water has been cut off daily between the hours of 7 p.m. and 6 a.m. The Council felt that no further evacuees could be accepted in the town.

In spite of this, further groups were received in the town as the war drew on. The Council organised Christmas parties for them, sponsored by the London

County Council. (During January 1944 a party of evacuees were taken to the Bath Pantomime when dinner and tea were taken at the Bath Parkside British Restaurant.)

Mrs. Wilkins remembers this period very well:

I was married in 1938 and my son was born in 1941. There were shortages and poor food but we got by because most people had allotments. Woolley Grange was taken over by a handicapped school. After that went we had the expectant mothers for the Maternity Hospital at Berryfield. They'd come and stay at Woolley Grange when eight months pregnant and they'd have their babies and go back to London...I had to go in a private nursing home to have my son – they wouldn't have me because I was local. My son was born at Hilperton. They used to go in the public house sometimes, the men didn't like it, a group of eight very pregnant women converging on the pub. In The George it was chiefly men in the bar and when all these pregnant women used to come in and sit up at the bar, the men didn't think it was very nice to look at. But you seemed to get used to these things. (EW89)

Plenty of local people have memories of the expectant mothers sent down here from the East End of London for the final month of pregnancy. Some were billeted at The Hall where Mrs. John Moulton kept a firm but hospitable eye on them. Her granddaughter, Dione Hartnoll can recall with sympathy the efforts they had to make in walking up local hills. Not unnaturally they stayed together for company in their unfamiliar surroundings and thus took up a lot of narrow pavement when they explored the town.

Gradually the blitz eased and the evacuees returned to their homes. But a few remained in Bradford and still live in the town to this day. Jackie Farley (née Munn) recalls:

I often wonder what it would be like living in Bexhill, but Bradford is a lovely place – I'm glad I stayed.

John Higgins, who was billeted with the Wicheard family in Wine Street, commented:

I do feel I was very lucky coming to Bradford and living with the Wicheards, who made me feel one of the family. I have lived, married and brought up my family in the town. I tried, and I think succeeded, in becoming a Bradfordian.

However, in August 1940 it is obvious that one young lad did not think too well of Bradford. Thomas Whittaker aged four was an evacuee living at 41 Trowbridge Road with his mother, brothers and sisters. He went missing. After an extensive search by police in the area, a message came through that Tommie had been found in Newport, Monmouthshire. He is believed to have travelled there by train!

I think the last word on evacuation should go to George Leonard Carey, our present Archbishop of Canterbury, who as a young boy was evacuated to Bradford with his mother, brother and sisters. He kindly wrote to me in 1996 and part of his story reads:

Mr. Musselwhite was the Billeting Officer who took Mother and the four of us into the loving care of the Musselwhite family who lived at No 4 Sladesbrook. At a later date we were evacuated to Warminster; it occupies no place in our memories whatsoever! Bradford on Avon remains as the happiest period of our childhood because of the way in which the community embraced us and made us feel so much at home. I am quite sure that the way in which Mr. Musselwhite and the Congregation at Christ Church received us was a very significant step in my Christian journey.

War Weapons Week, April 1941. The Committee stands on the steps of Westbury House, the Urban District Council offices. From left to right: Mr H.W. Slade, Mr. W.H. Burgess, Mr. C.W. Shepherd (Hon. Sec.), Mr. J.M. Chrystal (Chairman), Mr. W.H. Brown (Sec. of Entertainments sub-committee), Mr. J Glass (Hon. Treasurer) and Mr. H.E. Moore (Publicity).

Messrs George Spencer Moulton & Co. Ltd.
Kingston Mills, Bradford on Avon, 1939-1945

Spencer Moulton was destined to play a vital role in the Battle of Britain, and assist the armada of boats which flung an allied army on to the shores of France, and aided the development of scientific inventions which staggered the world in the second devastating war. Mr. J.M. Chrystal, the Works Manager, led the production of millions of articles and appliances which helped to provide our forces in all quarters of the world with armaments for the final crushing defeat of Hitler.

As war loomed, the Company's management held conferences with Government representatives and other industrial leaders. Machinery was quickly modified for new production methods. Speed was important and when war was declared the company was ready to play its part in the war effort. At this time, there was no indication that raw rubber supplies would be interfered with, but gradually supplies of natural rubber decreased following loss of plantations in Malaya.

Unique and previously acquired knowledge of the use of special types of rubber mixtures and synthetics such as neoprene was of the greatest value. Spencer Moulton were to some extent pioneers in certain synthetic applications, under the direction of Dr. S. Pickles, the Company's Chief Chemist. Within a few months of the outbreak of war, well over 50 armament firms throughout the country engaged on munitions and the relevant Ministries were being supplied with vital rubber parts, accessories and apparatus. But often Spencer Moulton was the only firm which was able to meet the stringent specifications laid down by the Ministries for a variety of production items.

Out of a pre-war total number of approximately 750 employees, 183 men and 14 women joined H.M. Forces during the war years. Some stayed on as they were in a reserved occupation. As these employees left for the services and production increased, the women of the town were called upon to help fill the gaps, which they did with willing hands. Because of this and with the help of their highly skilled workers and technical staff, the company was able to cope with all production requirements.

Some departments in the factory worked seven days a week in order to meet schedules. One example of the hours worked and wages earned is my father's wage sheet for 12 December 1941:

Long Hose Department. Clock No. 366, H.N. Mock. Hours worked 55.

Piece Work	£5 : 5 : 0d
Day Wages	1 : 9d
War Bonus	2 : 2d
	£5 : 8 : 11d
Less Insurance	1 : 9d
Total	£5 : 7 : 2d

During the days when Spitfires and Hurricanes were fighting the Battle of Britain and when our bombers were battering German cities, the company was playing no small part in keeping our planes flying and enabling aircraft production to increase. Henry Stevens, who had joined Spencer Moulton in 1924, was on Special Developments during the war, staying there as part of the reserved occupation allocation. One of the projects he worked on was to create a device which would stop birds getting into the engine of the plane:

We developed a little guard which was made of piano wire and had rubber surrounding it and which was very strong. Design draftsmen and engineers would have a chat with me and ask if we could come up with some possible answer to a specific problem. For any rubber article a mould has to be made. A steel mould costs a lot of money so they never spent until they'd got it right. Spencer Moulton had a suggestion box and I used to be paid for all the ideas I put into that, well paid.

I would be working there in the middle of the night and Dr. Pickles would come in. He'd have just had a call from Bristol Aeroplanes, could they do something about some important part on a plane. He'd try to set it up, get it going and invariably I got involved. I knew what he was after and I'd do my best to get it out. I were pretty good at it. Rubber's a funny material, but over the years, if you spend a long time on the quality of curing compounds you build up a picture of what you can do and I used to love it. (HS93)

Many parts were manufactured which kept the Crusader, Cromwell and Valentine tanks mobile. Essential parts for the escort ships of the Arctic convoys and the Battle of the Atlantic are further examples of the operations in which the Bradford firm was involved. There were few branches of the armament and munitions drive into which the products of Spencer Moulton did not eventually find their way.[2] Spencer Moulton continued to produce the many items which kept the railways of Britain and other railway systems throughout the allied countries in operation.

In the early months of the war, when air raid warnings were sounded, all employees rushed to the specially constructed shelters within the factory premises. Later, as production was so important to the war effort and the early fear of bombing subsided, when the sirens sounded in the town, work continued, unless a Red Alert was received via the Royal Observer Corps station at Budbury, when a bell system in the factory indicated that it was necessary to go to the shelters.

Fire watching was organised on a rota basis. The roofs of Abbey Mills and the "New Lamb" building were used as observation posts.

The following tale came to light recently: two employees, who had been fire-watching somewhere within the factory, were taking their well earned sleep, though still on the premises. Eventually one awoke and decided to go home. He picked up a pair of shoes, put them on and went home, leaving his pal still asleep. Later his friend awoke from his slumbers and found his shoes had gone. Those left were not his ! He managed to get them on and hobbled to his pal's house to exchange them for his own. He got no reply to his knocking. The shoes were eventually restored to their rightful owners, and all was well.

The family atmosphere which had always been part of the firm was emphasised by the stresses of war. One lady recalls her experiences there through these years:

> We had to work hard, sometimes seven days a week. There were many good times with laughter and singing which could be heard throughout the factory. A real family feeling which helped to get us through the war time problems. We felt we were "doing our bit" for the war effort.

Highly secret work also went on in other rubber factories as well. Joyce Baumann cycled from Bradford to Melksham every day:

> My job was the inspection of the gas-masks. Then 12 of us were put in a room on our own with a girl called Nora in charge of us. We were working on inflatable rubber boats that had been made in the factory. We had to make sure there were no bubbles on the canvas that had been put on the boats which had to pass our inspection before they could go out. So we were the last ones to touch them. We didn't know it at the time but those boats were for the D-Day invasion on the 6 June 1944.. My brother must have gone over in one of those boats. He wasn't lost in the landings because I had a birthday card from him after that date. But he was missing, presumed killed, on the 9 or 10 July when they were fighting around Caen. He was 19. (JB97)

Unfortunately there were casualties amongst the employees who served in the Armed Forces. A plaque erected on the front of Kingston House, Kingston Road, Bradford, shows the names of the 11 men who gave their lives.

Conscription/Call Up

Prior to the declaration of war on 3 September 1939, the Government established the National Registration Act, which was a register of all persons in the U.K., and building on this the National Service Act required all males between 18 and 41 to serve in the armed forces. The Armed Forces Act made any Territorial soldier liable for overseas posting. On 31 August 1939 the army and R.A.F. reservists were called up and the navy was mobilised. A number of Bradford Territorials and Reservists were called up.

Joe Lucas was a young lad, living in Budbury Place at the outbreak of war. He recalls: 'Father had long Army service and was still a reservist with the Somerset Light Infantry. On the day war was declared, he came home from work, packed a few belongings and set off down the hill to the station – It was almost a year before he came home on leave.'

By January 1940, two million 19 to 27 year old men were conscripted nationally. Over a year later, on 17 March 1941, Ernest Bevin, the Minister of Labour, announced a massive mobilisation plan for women, which included registration of 20 and 21 year-olds to fill jobs in industry, farming and auxiliary services.

During the First World War a high percentage of Bradford men had enrolled into the Wiltshire Regiment and completed their basic training at Devizes. The Second World War saw men being conscripted into many other regiments, corps, R.A.F. and the navy. For instance, my own brother Charlie, who was called up on 16 October 1941, only 11 days after his 21st birthday, was enlisted into the Royal Artillery.

December 1941 saw the registration of women rise to 40 years of age for both single and married women. All single females between 20 and 30 were called up. This was to put quite a strain on the female residents of Bradford, who were urgently required in local industry.

The town had its inevitable share of casualties and bereavements during the war. One tragic story is that of Mrs W.E. Sadd of 42 Frome Road, Bradford, who received, by the same post, news that two of her sons lost their lives on active service. Private Eric Sadd was killed in action in Burma and was 21 years-old. Private Ronald Sadd, of the Somerset Light Infantry, died of wounds in North West Europe, and was 28 years-old.

The names of those who fell during the war can be found on the War Memorial in Westbury House Gardens.

Bradford's War Fortifications

Early in June 1940, with the German army occupying the French Channel coast, it was thought that the west of England was open to attack by the enemy, from both the north and south. It was considered unlikely but possible that the Germans could occupy Ireland, leaving the Bristol Channel open to an attempt to land on the Somerset coast, as well as attack on the south coast from France. The loss of the south-west would have opened the way to the industrial Midlands and London.

It was proposed that lines of forts would be erected as strategic barriers against invasion. These lines, called Stop Lines, included pillboxes and anti-tank obstacles. There were several designs of pillboxes, constructed to take different types of anti tank guns. One, the six-pounder design, had huge apertures in front to give a wide range of fire, thus making the pillbox vulnerable to hand grenade attack. One Stop Line went due south from the Bristol Channel across Somerset and Dorset to the English Channel. The other Stop Line came along the south side of the Bristol Channel, through North Wiltshire and then swept round further eastward and down to the south coast. This latter line was to include the Bradford on Avon stretches of the Kennet and Avon Canal and the River Avon. The scheme was placed before the Army Chiefs of Staff and Winston Churchill and approved on 25 June. The huge task was given to the Works Branch of the Royal Engineers and Civilian Contractors.

In Bradford two pillboxes were constructed near the canal towpath, between the Frome Road lock and the Beehive Inn canal bridge, Trowbridge Road. One is still in existence, approximately 200 yards from the lock; another, closer to the Frome Road lock, was demolished in early 1970s, prior to the building of the estate adjacent to Moulton Drive. Because of the thickness of concrete it was necessary to use explosives to dismantle this pillbox. Local residents were warned of the impending explosion. The house of Mr. Sartain in Rowden Lane, which runs parallel to the canal, was damaged by the blast. Another pillbox still standing can be seen by the River Avon at Barton Farm, close to the Pack Horse Bridge. Joe Lucas gives us more details:

> In addition to the pillbox by the Pack Horse Bridge, just to the north of this box, within a triangle formed by the river, Barton Orchard and the railway line, was a second pillbox, just off the river bank. Long since demolished, I don't think a trace remains. The interesting fact was that it had a red pantiled roof to disguise it as a cottage. Quite effective, apart from the tiles broken by myself and others climbing over it! The tiles were supported by cement and timbered joists – but I don't think it had a chimney stack.

Avoncliff has a pillbox still standing, which can be viewed from the aqueduct. Another was situated between the Avoncliff and Turleigh roads. Others are still standing along both canal and river banks in the Bradford area.

At various spots along the railway track in the town, anti-tank cone obstacles (called pimples) were constructed. A number can still be seen by the side of the railway line, between Bradford railway station and the Barton Farm railway crossing. Mysterious constructions appeared on some roads which could be turned into extra obstructions if it ever became necessary. Jack Stafford describes one built near to him.

> *They had tank traps in the roads everywhere, there was one at the top of Whitehill near my land. They'd dig a hole in the road, four feet deep and four feet wide, fill it up with concrete and leave holes in it to a peculiar shape like a letter U upside down. Then the construction could be dropped in there quickly. But they weren't there permanently. There was a piece of wood over the holes so you could go down the hill in the normal manner. (JS97)*

Near Bradford town bridge, a group of welded steel girders and concrete blocks were in position ready to form a barrier across the road in case of invasion. I well remember climbing on these when I was a small lad.

In addition to this, algae was encouraged to grow on the canal to form a green/brown camouflage and as mentioned elsewhere the factory chimney at the Spencer Moulton works was also painted for the same reason. Further afield the Westbury White Horse was covered to avoid easy recognition from the air.

Wartime Pillbox on the Kennet & Avon Canal between Frome Road lock and the Beehive canal bridge. Photographed in 1996 by Jack Mock.

Bradford's Local Defence Volunteers (L.D.V.)/Home Guard

Within a couple of days of Mr. Eden's broadcast on 17 May 1940, which called for volunteers from men between 15 and 65 years to come forward and offer their services to defend their country, 85 men had come forward and given their names at Bradford Police Station. A few days later, under the supervision of the Armed Forces from Tidworth, 20 rifles, 200 rounds of ammunition, 40 caps and 30 overalls were delivered to the Police Station for use by the L.D.V.

Bradford's H Company, 4th Wiltshire Home Guard, under the command of Major J.M. Chrystal had been formed. (The L.D.V. were renamed Home Guard in July 1940). The Company's headquarters was at 9, Kingston Road, where the quartermaster was Mr. E.W. (Eddy) Inkpen and Harry Hayter was one of his keenest volunteers.

The long-distance rifle range, situated near the canal swing bridge, was in constant use. Several former Home Guards relate the story of an incident during practice at the range. Apparently it was not only the local wildlife which was disturbed from the hedgerows, but also the occasional black American soldier, accompanied by his girlfriend! Part of the guard duties of the Company included a patrol from Bradford railway station, along the track to Avoncliff station, where a base was established in the Old Pump house near the railway line. On one such patrol, a noise was heard in the bushes, and after the required verbal warning was made and no reply received, a bullet was fired in the direction of the noise. Later it was found that a cow belonging to Farmer Chard, also a member of the Home Guard, had been killed.

Royal Observer Corps

This Corps was established in Bradford in January 1938 and George Tiley recalls: The Bradford Post was set up at Budbury Ridge on farmland then owned by Miss Godwin and later owned by Mr. Flood. Mr. Pyemont was Chief Observer. Special telephone lines were established to enable the Observers to communicate

Opposite above: A simulated A.R.P. exercise in April 1940, with a "victim" needing attention on the Market Street side of the town bridge. As part of the overall exercise, the Baths were fitted out as a First Aid post and casualty clearing station, a house in Bath Road having been supposedly hit by an High Explosive bomb. Further incidents were devised in St. Margaret's Street which was rendered impassable and in Culver Close where cows reported as killed. All the town's resources, including veterinary services, were used in the exercise.

Opposite below: A part of Wine Street in April 1940. The rescue squad has been called to the old maltings where several people are supposedly trapped on the first floor of this building.

Another simulated exercise in 1940. The Wiltshire Times *reported: 'One of the biggest incidents was at the Priory where a bomb had been dropped in the grounds, demolishing the buildings, causing fires and bursting water and gas mains and seriously injuring several people. Auxiliary motor pumps were used to deliver water from the back of the Swan Hotel to the Priory; doctors and other A.R.P. services were needed and everything appeared to be done in a correct manner.' (WT 20.4.40)*

The devastated area in the foreground has nothing to do with bomb damage, real or simulated. The scene is at the top of Market Street, the first floor of the Thatched Cottage in Masons Lane is in the top right-hand corner. The Priory having recently been sold, most of its high battlemented wall which went round the property from the entrance gates to the wall of The Priory itself in Market Street has already been demolished. This was to provide a pedestrian pavement for the first time and to improve the very poor visibility for traffic at this narrow junction with Newtown and Masons Lane. The original gates and doorway entrance to the Priory still remain in this photograph but were also demolished later.

with Bristol H.Q. and the posts at Bratton and Devizes. The Corps were the "Eyes and Ears" of the Royal Air Force, essential for the effective working of the air raid warning system.

Originally known as The Observer Corps, their valuable work was recognized by the granting of the title Royal in April 1941. Their work involved identifying and tracking all aircraft, friendly or hostile. The posts were situated on high ground and on tops of buildings, with a wide field of vision. All posts were linked by telephone to an operations room. On 10 May 1945 the Corps "stood down" from their duties.

The Royal Observer Corps at their post in Budbury Ridge in 1957/8. Although a later group of men, the building behind shows the Post used by the Corps throughout the Second World War.

Joe Lucas recalls:

At Budbury Place and from the area of the seat (still there) overlooking Bradford and Trowbridge there was a marvellous view of the sky, and we prided ourselves in being experts at aircraft recognition, especially anything new. At the far side of the field to the east of Budbury Place lay the Royal Observer Corps Post, surrounded by sandbags and with a tripod and telescope in the centre. One of the Observers was a Mr. Say, from Winsley. Activities from the airfield at Keevil were easily seen from Budbury, where the sky was always busy with aircraft movements.

Scouts

Bradford's scouts, under Scoutmaster Alec Wiltshire, had their headquarters in a hut in New Road, now part of the Saxon Garage. During the war years the troop played their part in the war effort. In September 1940 Scouts Arthur Huntley and Ken Long received letters from the Governors of Winsley

Sanatorium, thanking them for their services rendered by attending the hospital for Air Raid Precaution telephone call duty, both day and night shifts. May 1940 saw the scouts involved in a message service between the Royal Observer Corps Post at Budbury and Abbey House, Church Street, where the Royal Artillery were in residence. Fire watching on the Christ Church buildings also saw the Scouts undertaking the weekend patrols, where they used the spare room at the Lambert Rooms as a base.

Following the Government's emergency call to collect waste paper, Scoutmaster Wiltshire organised the collection of paper throughout the town. This involved long, arduous and dirty work for the troop. In April 1942 it was announced that the troop reluctantly had to stop collection as the Council had taken over the task. In all, the Scouts collected 67 tons three hundredweight of paper, with a value of £161. The Nursing Association and the Red Cross Penny a Week Fund, amongst others, benefited by their efforts.

During the war years the 1st. Bradford on Avon Scout Troop went on 17 Camps, in various parts of the area. In these times it was necessary for the Police to sanction such activities by issuing a permit. Following one such application, Alec Wiltshire the Scoutmaster received a reply on 12 July 1942, from the Chief Constable at Police H.Q., Devizes, stating that he (Alec Wiltshire) did not now require a permit to camp at Murhill. Unfortunately the request for a permit on the site at Manor Farm, Monkton Farleigh could not be allowed, as this site was situated within a camping restricted area. Obviously too close to the Monkton Farleigh mines, where many tons of explosives were stored.

Local Bombing
The nearest airfield was Melksham and there were other major airfields at Colerne, Keevil, Hullavington and Boscombe. The Headquarters of Fighter Command for the South West was at Rudloe Manor, near Corsham and, as the Luftwaffe bombed strategic targets further west, there were air battles between the two. As folk became more used to air raids there was less rushing to shelters and more staying indoors when the sirens went. But the weekend of 25 and 26 April 1942 brought enemy action close to home, Jack Stafford was watching:

The German bombers had a peculiar drone because of the type of engine, they used to go over every night. When they went to bomb Cardiff, they came over here; when Avonmouth used to catch it, they came over here. I was here when they raided Bath. We saw this great glow in the sky and at first we thought it was Bristol because Bristol was being bombed every night. (JS97)

This unexpected bombing of Bath, was part of Hitler's "Baedeker Blitz". The

A wartime wedding. In June 1941 Miss Frances Lilian Duck married for the first time at the age of 60. Her husband, fresh from church, is Charlie Davis, a well known member of the family of greengrocers and fishmongers of Bradford on Avon and Trowbridge. Charlie's brother, Albert, who had died the previous year, was the most significant member of the family. Starting from humble beginnings on Tory, Albert Davis rose by hard work and shrewd dealing to become a very significant person in Bradford. Beginning from other premises he eventually opened shops in The Shambles and Market Street, partly supplied from his greenhouses and gardens in Newtown and Masons Lane. In the late 1930s he had amassed enough money to buy firstly Leigh Park House on the death of Lord Fitzmaurice and then, having sold that property to the U.D.C., to purchase much of the land which until 1937 belonged to The Priory. Albert Davis was frequently in the news, either for his eccentric exploits or for his generosity in giving money to local good causes.

Red Cross nurses on parade outside Leigh Park House which was made into a hospital. Lily Holbrook, who is one of the nurses, recalls that they had just scrubbed out the interior of the building to make it ready for an influx of patients.

R.A.F. had bombed Lubeck, and later Rostock, strategic German targets which were also beautiful old cities. Hitler, incensed at this destruction, decided on retaliation and, it seems, consulted his Baedeker Guidebook for appropriate targets. He selected five 3-star historic English towns – Exeter, Bath, Norwich, York and Canterbury – and sent in his bombers. Bath had experienced isolated bombing before, mostly bombs being offloaded by German pilots off course. But nothing prepared the city for these two days of consistent and devastating attack. Many Bath people lost their homes. The Circus received three hits, the Royal Crescent one and the Assembly rooms were almost entirely demolished. The area around the river was devastated, although, rather like St. Paul's in the London Blitz, the Abbey remained unscathed. Deaths of Bath men, women and children totalled 417 and hundreds more were injured. Over 130 high explosive bombs fell on central Bath and a map, recording each hit has now been made.[3] Because of the enormous number of incendiaries dropped, it has proved impossible to chart them in a similar way. Bath, a tourism city, no longer makes much of this tragic piece of its domestic history.

Many fled from the city in panic, not knowing how long bombing would continue. The War Office had moved many of its personnel to Bath, its nerve centre being the Empire Hotel. Now, as a temporary measure, some staff were

The Home Guard in 1943 on parade in Church Street, the end of The Swan and then the Old Bank House, just behind them.

hurriedly moved to The Hall in Bradford. From 26 April to 1 May the Trowbridge Road Junior School, Bradford, and the Town Hall, Bradford, were opened as rest centres for a large number of refugees from Bath who had lost their homes through the severe raids. Meals were served by the British Restaurant[4] in the Congregational Schoolroom (now the United Reform Church), St. Margaret's Street. Later in the war a letter was received from the Mayor of Bath thanking the town for its assistance during the troubled times of the city.

By 1942 emergency services in the town were fully operational, a natural progression from the more *ad hoc* arrangements of 1939. Mrs. Noreen Cambourne who had taken out her driving licence at the age of 17 in 1928 had been one of the first to volunteer for ambulance driving. The family business, Bryants, had a vehicle which could be used in the early days as a substitute ambulance:

Miss Hopkins arranged the ambulance transport, she was one of the first lady drivers in the town. We used to go one night a week down to the first aid post which was the old swimming baths. We didn't have a proper ambulance so we used our Ford V8 shooting brake and I would drive it. We had to put the stretcher on the floor and I think the poor patients must have suffered every bump in the road – it must have been agony. Then they sent us an ambulance, a big old Chrysler which took four stretchers, in two double decks. It was an old wooden thing. It was awful to drive because the accelerator and the clutch were on the opposite side to normal. If you forgot, you wouldn't go in the right direction. (NC92)

During the Bath bombings, and in the early hours of daylight on 27 April, a German bomber was being chased by British fighters away from Bath and across Bradford towards Trowbridge. As it reached the area near Bradford cemetery, Holt Road, it jettisoned two 500 pound bombs, causing little damage, although windows were blown out up the New Road and as far as Sladesbrook Mill. Naturally plenty of people went to have a look:

The bomb was just down the Holt Road past the cemetery. The hole was about 60 feet across and about ten feet deep and round the hole in places it was solid clay – the explosion had thrown out great lumps about four feet high, up in the air and dropped them all around. (JS97)

When reaching the canal, close to the Beehive Inn, Trowbridge Road, a further two 500 pound bombs were offloaded. These had a wider effect:

The banks of the canal were destroyed. The dredger on the canal, the Iron Duke, just lay there, dead on the mud, and fish were spread about all over the place for several fields away. Our cottage on Whitehill shook with all the bomb blast. It had to be shored up just before the end of the war. (SS97)

Six further bombs fell at Inwoods, Farleigh Wick on land owned by Major Whitehead, one of the craters being 63 feet across. Two 500 pounders fell at Turleigh, while a large incendiary bomb container was jettisoned on Mizen's Farm, South Wraxall. In all cases no casualties were reported. During this period there were dogfights between some of our few R.A.F. fighters and the German bombers as they flew towards the south coast. Bradford saw machine gun bullets fall in the streets and on the Town Hall, some being collected by souvenir hunters.

Air Crash
During the evening of Sunday 26 March 1944 a Halifax bomber from a station at Tolthorpe, Yorkshire flew low across the skies of Bradford. Coming from the Trowbridge direction it had smoke billowing from its engines, it was obviously in trouble. The pilot, Brian Hall of the Royal Canadian Air Force, realised he was losing height rapidly. By remaining in the plane, he unselfishly sacrificed his own life and saved the lives of residents of the Christ Church area by bringing

the machine down at Priory Park, not far from Christ Church. Upon striking the ground the craft burst into flames, ammunition exploded and the noise was heard over a wide area. One of the first on the scene was Scoutmaster Alec Wiltshire who lived close by in the Wilderness. He managed to climb the gates of the park, when he and others tried to rescue the tail gunner, who was unfortunately dead.

Members of the Town Fire Brigade were quickly there as well, first trying the hydrant outside the Rising Sun public house, where they found the water pressure too low. It was then necessary to pump water up from the static water tank situated in Priory House gardens and then from the river in the centre of town.

One crew member, Craig Reid the only survivor of the crash, baled out at Upton Scudamore and was not injured. Other bodies were recovered around Bradford.

Betty Taylor (née Hart) recalls:

> *After the crash, I cried to my father, fearing all the crew were dead. He tried to comfort me, saying they were safe as they had all baled out by parachute. Of course they were too low for the chutes to open. One airman crashed through an outside toilet of a house in Tory.*

Lily Holbrook, who was a new Red Cross volunteer immediately reported for duty at the Swimming Baths in Bridge Street. She found herself helping to clean the bodies of the pilot and rear gunner who had been unable to bale out of the aircraft:

> *It was my first experience of that sort of thing and I was a bag of nerves. But the others said it was one of the things we'd have to get used to. They were such lovely looking boys. I've never forgotten their faces. (LH 97)*

Fifty years later, in 1994, a plaque in memory of the three British and three Canadian airmen who died in the crash was unveiled in Westbury House gardens and Craig Reid came over from Canada to be a very special guest at the ceremony. A Hercules aircraft from R.A.F. Lyneham flew over the town centre as a tribute to the servicemen, while young air cadets from the town's detached flight formed a guard of honour.

Dig for Victory
One of the great battle cries in the country was "Dig for Victory" – Britain had to be self-sufficient and every piece of ground was required to be turned over to

cultivation. Workers in industry and the like needed more calories, and due to the shortage of some foods, many people made up the gap by cultivating their allotments. Nationwide the number of allotment users rose from 815,000 in 1939 to 1.5 million in 1943.

There were several places in Bradford where allotments were in use during the war. Mr. Middleton, the popular war time Radio Gardener, during one of his Sunday afternoon broadcasts stated that onions and potatoes were munitions of war as surely as bullets and shells.

Approximately 15 such plots were at Poulton Lane, off the Trowbridge Road, where several policemen and postmen as well as men who worked at the local rubber factory, were seen regularly tending their vegetables. A similar number of plots were cultivated in the Woolley/Sladesbrook area. The *Wiltshire Times* of 13 April 1940 carried the following announcement: "Under the Dig for Victory campaign, allotments are to be let at the Tyning, Winsley Road, and applicants are to apply to Mr. W.E. Knott, Winsley Road, Bradford on Avon."

Railings and Gates

In March 1942 the Government announced that iron railings and gates were to be removed, to be turned into weapons. The Bradford Town Council issued a schedule which included amongst others 47 and 48 St. Margaret Street, 230 Winsley Road and 29 Church Street. During April there were several protests made by residents against having their railings removed.

By May 1943 railings had been taken in Trowbridge Road and Councillor Benjamin, at a Council meeting, stated that he was afraid that straying cattle in this road were causing havoc, people's gardens were getting in a terrible state. August 1943 saw workmen removing the iron railings from the Parish Church and Vicarage and even from the graves in the churchyard. The only exception was a small length left for the sake of the public safety near the Chantry entrance. The railings outside the Liberal Club in the town were also saved for safety reasons.

American Soldiers in Town

August 1942 saw the first American troops in the West Country. The G.I.'s (Government Issue) swiftly spread themselves around the country. The main camp in the Bradford area was at Upper Westwood. In order to avoid possible conflict between black and white G.I.'s, the American authorities arranged for the black soldiers to spend their leisure time in Bradford and the whites in Trowbridge. It was the first time that many townsfolk had seen a non-white person.

A lady who lived in Wine Street when she was a girl remembers on one particular trip to town walking in Church Street near Abbey House and being confronted by a group of black troops. She was completely taken aback, it was the first time she had seen a black person. One old Bradfordian referring to the black G.I.'s remarked: 'I like them Yanks, but 'oo be they white chaps they'm brought along wi' 'em?'

Druces Hill House, Church Street, Bradford was used as a troop canteen, run by volunteers from the church. The Bradford Crusaders Boys Club gave parties for the G.I.'s where games and food were enjoyed by all. Impromptu concerts followed where the visitors sang lovely spirituals. The Americans were seen regularly swimming by the River Avon, and unfortunately one young black soldier, Pte. Johnson, drowned while bathing with his comrades.

Regular dances were held at the old Town Hall and there was an awkward scene at a dance at the hall on 9 June 1945 when a quarrel developed between various black American Army soldiers and other black members of the R.A.F. from Jamaica. An early quarrel led to a fight between the two parties. U.S. Army Police intervened. Knives were drawn in the melée. Bradford Police Sergt. Cullimore and Special War Police Sergt. Benjamin attended and later reinforcements were sent for, and Inspector Howell and P.C.s Sutton and Leslie helped. A Jamaican airman was carried away on a stretcher and taken to hospital.

Following a number of such incidents, the police and other authorities banned dances at the Town Hall.

Victory Europe (V.E.) and Victory Japan (V.J.) Day Celebrations

On 8 May 1945, V.E. celebrations were held in the town. Flags and bunting were displayed on businesses and houses, and in the centre of town festoons of flags stretched across the streets. The town bridge and river were illuminated with hundreds of gaily coloured lanterns, which in the dark produced a fairyland scene as the flickering lights reflected in the water. The lanterns were small honey jars with night light candles and were strung across the river on wire loops to allow for lighting. Westbury House grounds and the War Memorial were floodlit. Spencer Moulton's buildings were also decorated and floodlit. The Scouts, who had played a very full part in the town's war efforts, led a torchlight procession to Jones Hill, where a bonfire was lit, burning a guy of Hitler. Victory street parties were later held in various locations in the area. On 10 May 1945 the Royal Observer Corps stood down from its duties.

Victory over Japan saw similar celebrations, held on 16. August 1945. There was dancing at the Town Baths car park and Messrs Billy Smart's Fair and roundabouts were in Culver Close. Thanksgiving services were held in the churches and chapels throughout the town.

The war was over.

Wartime Secrets

Jack Mock's detailed description of life in Bradford through the war years shows a town pursuing, in a relatively quiet way, its efforts to help win the war. The biggest upheavals of the period were taking place just around the edges of the town. The labyrinth of stone quarries in the area was ideal for wartime use and were swiftly brought into use, involving some townsfolk either directly or indirectly in totally new experiences. For example, the Bethel Quarry in the Frome Road was taken over at the beginning of the war by the Ministry of Defence. Reg Hayter spent some time there until he was called up:

> *Its particular use was as an Admiralty store. For example depth charges to go onto submarines were kept there – although they didn't have their detonators in place when we stored them. I was allowed to drive the small lorry in and out of the quarry, unloading and loading from the big lorry outside. My father was the caretaker for the Fitzmaurice Grammar School. In his previous Army days in India he had been a Regimental Sergeant Major so he now became the store manager. It was an important transit point and goods were always being moved in and out to places like Liverpool or Southampton. (RH97)*

The Royal Enfield Motor Cycle Company, which came to Bridge Street during the war, was already making use of a quarry in Westwood. This was turned into an underground factory engaged on war work for the British armament industry - precision engineering being its particular strength. A more tranquil use was found for another part of the same quarry. A special air conditioned section housed the Egyptian antiquities from the British Museum.

Bradford railway station was busier than ever. Normal freight such as malt from Bailey's Malt House (which stood where The Maltings were later built) had always been shifted by rail. Now there was a constant fleet of some 10 to 12 lorries distributing heavy deliveries of raw materials to other requisitioned quarries in the vicinity. Young Reg Hayter worked on these as well:

> *The lorries were allocated by the British War Transport Commission for the area. Without a word of a lie we were shifting 72 tons of cement at a time up to Monkton Farleigh from Bradford railway station as well as moving cement from Holt and Corsham. There were four lines of shunting track in Bradford station yard and a built in crane – trucks, vans, lorries. It never stopped. (RH97)*

Many people know of the secret underground city that developed in the abandoned stone quarries at Monkton Farleigh as an ammunition depôt. It had a massive air conditioning system, a huge powerhouse to provide electricity and an arterial system of conveyors and narrow gauge railways. A tunnel over a mile long connected it with the main line railway. At its peak it held over 165,000 tons of high explosive. The vast number of personnel needed to organise and service this subterranean military establishment, most of whom had to be fed and housed in the immediate vicinity can be left to the imagination.

Another lesser known but equally mighty range of underground operations was created at Corsham, on the Copenacre stone mine site and, closer to Bradford, off the B3109 in what is now called R.A.F. Rudloe Manor above the Wadswick area. To build the secret munitions factory, a vast workforce had to be assembled. It is said that at the height of operations, some 25,000 people were employed there on its day and night shifts. Jack Stafford was one of them:

> *The last three months before I was called up in 1942 I worked on the shafts over near Corsham. There were men billeted in Bradford and for 30 miles around as far as Salisbury. There were those waiting to be called up and men who were too old to fight. Then there were thousands of Southern Irishmen working there – they were theoretically neutral but they weren't at all friendly. We were brought in every day and had to be taken back afterwards. I'd go outside my house just after seven and get on one of the coaches. Before we got halfway to Corsham we would be in a convoy with coaches coming from all directions. The worst part was when we got to the Bath to Melksham Road, they'd be in a queue bumper to bumper coming up from Bath. There was no right of way then for anyone coming from the right, so we had trouble trying to dodge into this continual column. There were thousands and thousands of us there, and everyone making a terrific wage. I got a lot more there than I did off the business.*
>
> *There were rows and rows of great long huts for checking in and checking out with every so far a little window with someone checking. We'd get to this big locker place and find someone had broken in. I took a lot of tools the first day and all the men laughed at me. They told me to take them home, just keep a few of them. I had a secret bottom in my box with valuable tools hidden underneath. Occasionally they got robbed, but I was fortunate, I didn't.*
>
> *A man would come round in the day at any time to check each separate little gang and make sure no one had gone off. Some of these crafty Irish men were coming in for double time on Sunday and having time off in the week. So they put their foot down to stop that. If you had a day off in the week you couldn't work on Sunday. One checker who went round told me one day, "My life's in danger when I've got to go round where those Irishmen are." (JS97)*

In this vast secret underground world, there was a continual need to move the old stone spoil, discarded by the early quarrymen up to the surface and to get raw materials in. Jack was employed by the building firm of Sir Alfred MacAlpine, working on the construction of some of the huge shafts which made all this possible:

> *They needed drains, pipes and cables down there to service munition factories. Then they would put in reinforced concrete floors, with a trap door every so often for access. So they had to get these huge heaps of loose rubble out. We worked on the slope shaft which had a rubber conveyor belt at a 45 degree angle right up into a great gantry. And all these rocks they were clearing out from down below would be going up the conveyor belt and crashing down into the tipper trucks underneath waiting on railway lines. The noise was terrible. There were four tanker type goods engines which hauled the tipper trucks onto a huge dump which got wider and wider like a railway cutting about 50 feet deep. Every time they tipped another lot over the edge, all these navvies with their crowbars moved the railway line over bodily, sleepers and all, so the next lot could be dumped down the slope. (JS97)*

There were ventilator shafts with propellers inside to pump up stale air and another shaft 24 feet x 12 feet, made to that size to take the crates coming over from America, full of lathes and other machinery with which to manufacture the armaments. The British Small Arms Company (B.S.A.) was part of this vast underground city, turning out gun barrels for Spitfire aircraft. In his dinner hour Jack would wander about down below, sometimes hearing the rumbles from the Box tunnel nearby and observing the steady activity. Ranks of machines were set to drill with delicate precision through six-feet bars of solid steel: the girls watched the machines, removing the fine coils of steel as they came away from the machines, jagged debris which would tear hands to pieces if carelessly touched. Oil poured constantly over the machines and through the barrels to keep the metal cool. The heat and smell were overpowering:

> *There were air vents that filtered the air in the parts that were finished but none in the part under construction. The lovely yellow Bath stone would go black. There were all these diesel trucks on the narrow lines underground, moving stuff about and puffing smoke. You had to jump out of the way, they didn't care about you. A man sat on there with a row of trucks behind him, perhaps piled five-feet high. Every now and again one would come off the line. Then you'd hear a lot of swearing and that. Everyone was on a lot of piece work. Working on this shaft we used to get black on our lungs – if you'd spit you'd get black. (JS97)*

It is no wonder that there had to be a huge number of new personnel housed both in Bradford and its environs. Noreen Cambourne, used to driving the Bryant's van on weekly rounds of the district recalls the "village" built up at Westwood as part of this influx:

> At Westwood we usually stopped just past the New Inn, where it was a bit wider. During the war when all these extra workers were housed there a lot of Irishmen, big and burly, would come out to the van as soon as we got there. Soap was short, it was on coupons, and they would keep begging me for some soap or some matches even, or a battery – in the war people would stand on their head for a battery. (NC97)

The roads were clearly crowded, not only with army vehicles from Salisbury Plain and local naval establishments but also with the steady movement of people and raw materials from Bradford to these secret places. Jack's detailed descriptions of making the shafts, which had to be bombproof and whose walls were at least five-feet thick, of the numbers of buildings above ground and the need for living quarters as well as all the servicing arrangements for this vast army of workers make it clear that an innocent looking town was being built above ground and a purposeful industrial city was busy below the surface.

What remains nearly sixty years later? The Monkton Farleigh Mine, with a small museum explaining its wartime past was open in the late 1980s, though now it is closed. The M.O.D. has remained at Copenacre and still retains the Rudloe site which Jack knew so well. From the B3109, a vent for the Box tunnel on the right near the double mini-roundabout helps to mark the area which once teemed with people. The serried ranks of wooden huts have gone but the shafts of reinforced concrete, now made secure, must still be there, being too substantial to be easily removed. It is fortunate that there are still people around with vivid memories who can help to record a past which otherwise might soon become unknown to most of us.

Bradford Station, shunting yard and coalyard in the 1950s. The crane was fixed and hand operated. The rail track directly beside the crane is cut at a lower level for ease of loading and therefore is out of sight in this photograph.

CHAPTER FIVE

1946 - 1964
Continuity & Change;
Decay & Regeneration

Continuing Pre-War and Country Ways: Barton Farm ~ Growth of Town: New Council Estates within Town Boundaries ~ Demolition of Old Houses and Threats of Redevelopment ~ Tory & Middle Rank Preservation Scheme ~ Industries in the town:Spencer Moulton becomes Avon Rubber Company in 1956 ~ Moulton Developments Ltd, 1962 & the Moulton Bicycle Introduced in 1962 ~ Alterations at St. Margaret's ~ New School ~ Floods

IN 1946 BRADFORD SLOWLY BEGAN TO RETURN to civilian life. The evacuees had gone and men and women in the armed services were gradually demobbed and came back to the town. Fred Fielding, who had been serving in Germany, was given his release papers in 1947:

As I recall we landed at Harwich, were fed and very soon put on a train for York. The journey there took most of the day and we were taken by army lorry to a transit camp for the night. After another check of identities and more processing of paperwork we walked into a large hall full of civilian clothing: rows of suits, sports coats, trousers, shirts, ties, socks, hats and underwear. We were met by civilians who measured us for correct sizes, helped us select and treated us like customers in a shop. I chose a blue suit with a stripe, a light blue shirt and black shoes, with a raincoat and Trilby hat (the Trilby hat was not my style but my father was pleased). It was then all packed into a large cardboard box and we were given civilian ration coupons and a railway travel warrant. So with six weeks leave pending final discharge I walked out into civilian life. Outside were a couple of men offering to buy our suits or our complete boxes of clothes. An army private's pay being only 3s.0d. (15p) a day some must have been very tempted. Anywhere in the country if you saw a soldier carrying a large brown cardboard box you would know he had just been discharged. (FF97)

National Service became compulsory in 1947, firstly for 18 months and by 1950 for two years, a system continued until 1960. Young Bradford men found themselves taken out of the town billeted in unfamiliar places. Sometimes they served in other parts of the world, perhaps even fighting in Korea or Kenya, certainly learning new skills and inevitably returning to Bradford affected by their experiences.

In many respects the town itself seemed to be continuing in its pre-war ways, with just a few advances due to the recent hostilities. For example firemen were now summoned for duty by the siren in Westbury Gardens which had sounded the All Clear after an enemy air raid and which replaced their old maroon signal in use since the 1930s. But Tory still provided the same grandstand view of all that went on in the town:

The children used to look out of the bedroom window when the siren went and out came the fire engine It was red and it was gold and the firemen came running along at a tremendous pace. I was always full of admiration at the speed with which they arrived. Then the firemen would climb round the sides of the engine with their helmets on; and off it would go. It was the most exciting thing. The fire station was just down by what is now St. Margaret's car park. Lots of town noises come up onto Tory. People used to say it must be lovely and quiet up there with no road. Of course it's not true at all. We had the sound of the steam train engines, we had the shunting from the trucks, we had the fire engine and the noises of traffic coming up the Market Street – not to mention the church bells. (UB97)

Apart from its industrial centre on either side of the river the town was still very rural. In the latter part of the nineteenth century Joseph Chard walked all the way from Binegar, near Shepton Mallet, to Bradford in order to lease the Barton Farm, its farmhouse and its fields from Sir Charles Hobhouse. It was to remain in the occupation of the Chard family for well over seventy years until it became the Country Park. Although Joseph's son, Ernest "Joe" Chard, had been obliged to plough up some of his fields during the recent war, the farm had always been mainly a dairy farm and it returned to full milk production as soon as possible. Farmer Chard also had 75 acres of his own land, mostly in the fields behind The Beehive on the Trowbridge Road. Thus his herd of cows continued to amble twice a day up Pound Lane, into Junction Road and all the way along the Trowbridge Road to the canal bridge to graze in these fields and then back for milking. It was just the same procedure as it had been for the last 70 years or so. Naturally Mrs. Lywood, born Hilary Chard, can describe this for us:

The cows had to be taken along the main road and it didn't stop until my father more or less retired in about 1973. It had been a particular hazard during the war when they had to be fetched in the dark. They had to have someone in front of them and someone behind them with lights because there were no street lights. And during the war a lot of railings were taken down in the front gardens in Trowbridge Road and of course the cows tended to go in the gardens. And a lot of the railings weren't put back. (HL97)

Not surprisingly householders also remember this daily occurrence in some detail:

The cows went up and down Trowbridge Road twice a day, it was quite a large herd. I can remember you had to wait quite a time for them to go by. I suppose there would be 20 or 30 if not more. They seemed to stretch out a long way. Jim Trott used to drive them and he used to try to keep them over to one side...the trouble was they walked on the pavements and the result was not very nice. Very often, you had to go out and wash the pavement down. People took it for granted and the traffic just waited, well there wasn't much traffic really. I always remember that day when Jim Trott had some heifers, they were young ones, and there were about a dozen or more and I remember them going into the garden further up the Trowbridge Road and they ran all over that garden. I know they went up one of these pathways between the houses and knocked the garden wall down. There are a lot of little pathways off this road. (JU93)

Chris Penny remembers this event particularly well – it was his wall.

The cattle grazed at times in Culver Close, an open space now given over to tennis and cricket. Between the Victory Field and the Tithe Barn lay the field for Barton Farm's straw ricks; farm implements were kept in the Tithe Barn. What is now the public car park was the kitchen garden with fruit trees and nut trees. The children's play area in the Country Park which seems aptly named Nursery Field derives that name from its older use as the field where all the young calves were reared. The cowsheds, known as "the skillins"[1] were turned into a row of workshops and tearooms after the farm became Barton Farm Country Park in 1971. However it had always been something of an open space for Bradford since the Chard family generously shared their fields. There are many stories of Bradfordians playing along by the canal as children, of families enjoying summer picnics in the farm fields and of swimming or fishing in the Avon. Hilary Chard, although an only child, had plenty of company:

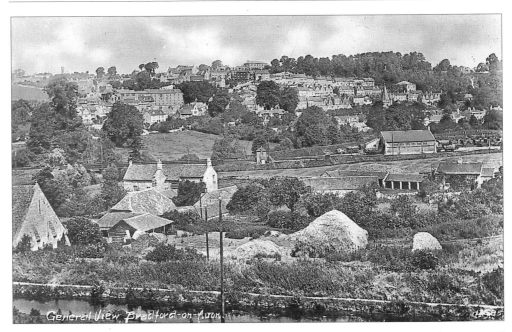

Rural Bradford. A view taken from Jones' Hill with the canal in the foreground and a side of the Tithe Barn on the left. This shows Barton Farm with its outbuildings and straw ricks as a working farm. The 'skillins' are clearly in the middle right. Behind is the railway with shunting yard, engine shed and signal box.

When we were at the farm our front door always used to be open wide from morning to night in the summer. We had a lovely stone tiled floor in the hall there, different colours in squares, and that was always polished to the hilt and you often got people just stepping inside just to have a look at it. (HL97)

Up until the war, and beyond, the farmyard behind the big house had traditionally been the setting twice a year for an age-old Christian custom:

We used to have a service down here at Harvest and Rogation Sunday and then they used to walk in procession from Holy Trinity and Christ Church. The clergy used to go up to the top of the granary barn steps to take the service and everyone else used to stand in the yard. Rogation Sunday was when they blessed the crops at the start of the year's sowing. (HL97)

The north side of the town was equally rural. There was a farm on the corner of Ashley Road and Bath Road. Freddie Green used to take the milk round from the farm. He used to get two pails of milk on the handlebars of his bicycle and ride round from door to door with a measure and measure the milk out into household jugs. Then there was Teddy Rudman, known to everyone as the Midnight Milkman. He kept his country ways until he died in the 1950s:

> *Teddy Rudman kept his cows on the slopes up around Sandy Leaze and Grove Leaze. He lived in the Winsley Road and delivered milk twice a day out of a churn. He was walking round with that both before and after the last war. He didn't do anything down in the town; it was all on the top of the hill. He'd start taking milk round about 11 o'clock, that was his first morning round He used to run round with a churn on two wheels and his feet were splayed out sideways, you might say at a quarter to three, and everybody used to take the mickey out of him. But he was ever such a nice chap really. He'd come round somewhere about 7 or 8 o'clock at night or much later with his afternoon delivery of milk. They all knew Teddy Rudman, the Midnight Milkman, and they knew he'd be there sometime. (SS97)*

John Ludlow, used to help him in his later years:

> *Teddy was always down on his uppers. He had very bad feet and children used to make fun of him, but he was a lovely chap. He used to have cows on the big sloping field next to Wine Street on the Winsley side. If he ran out of milk he used to walk down there, milk the cows and come back. As he got older and he couldn't do the cows he used to go to Trowbridge and bring back a churn of milk on the bus from the United Dairies near the railways. I'd help him lift the churn off the bus on the Winsley Road. (JL97)*

After the war John came back to Ashley Road, which had seen little change:

> *There was no gas or electric in the house. Before the war, when they wanted the electric put in they had to have a certain number of people in the street to say yes. Now there was one lady up there, I always remember her name, it was Bessie Bull, and she refused. So we never did get the electric or the gas put in. Even when I got married in 1952 there was still no electric or gas in the house. We cooked on the coal fire with a small oven on one side and on the opposite side there was a tank of water with a tap. Of course with the fire burning under it, it was boiling away all the time and we had to keep topping it up. We used to have a damper up in the flu and you'd be amazed how you could control the temperature. It would cook a beautiful cake. (JL97)*

But there were more modern areas in the town. After the Great War the

UDC had moved fairly quickly to provide some "homes fit for heroes to live in". Its first council housing scheme had been underway by 1921. This was a development on the Trowbridge Road still known as "The Square", more houses later being built along the main road. The average cost of £962 for each council house was a huge sum of money at the time. By 1939 Bradford had 117 council dwellings. But everywhere the urgent demand for new housing for young couples after the Second World War was enormous. After all, to be blunt about it, so many more young men had survived this time.

The Town and Country Planning Act of 1947 which replaced the earlier one of 1932 was far more stringent than its predecessor. This major Act transformed the casual attitudes of the past and was the beginning of a new approach to planning. Its purpose was to guide and control housing development throughout England and consequently the powers of the Minister of Housing and Local Government were immense. Some areas deemed suitable for development could now be compulsorily purchased. Other land around towns was now protected under a Green Belt policy; strong regulations came into force which had to be met before permission for building would be granted. Central Government was now required to compile lists of buildings of special architectural or historical interest throughout the country. But since the value of protecting an entire townscape was not yet recognised Bradford did not figure on Wiltshire's list, which focused on the many individual grand houses in the county.

In order to qualify for council housing, a would-be tenant and his/her family had to amass the appropriate number of points. Length of time on the waiting list, overcrowding, lack of proper sanitation, the poor state of the building currently occupied and any health problems within the family living there were all significant factors in a successful application. Each name on the waiting list would be that of the head of the household only. Thus a much larger number of individual names lie unobserved behind the quoted figures.

Far more people, especially newly married couples, qualified than could be accommodated. Answering their needs was made even more difficult by the shortage of trained labour and building materials. In January 1947 the Ministry of Health's exhibition, "Design of Houses", which was travelling the country, was put on in Bradford with the co-operation of the U.D.C. The Chairman of the U.D.C, boxed in by planning regulations and restrictions and besieged by inhabitants demanding homes, made his position clear:

> *You either get bouquets thrown at you or rotten eggs. It depends on the person. There were something like four to five hundred on the waiting list who would regard the exhibition as a form of organised cruelty. After the 1914-18 war they did not do sufficient planning but on the contrary produced the houses.*

The lack of planning was responsible for such as the ribbon development of the Winsley Road... He thought they would see the reason for planning if they visited the prefab houses at Budbury Circle – which he thought admirable. (WT11.1.47)

But even plans for the erection of temporary prefabs at Budbury Circle, intended to be a quick start to the housing programme, had not gone through without considerable difficulty. Mr. Guy Underwood, who had a solicitor's business in Bath, was a prominent local resident with a gift for stirring up controversy in the town. As an elected Town Councillor with strong and independent opinions on every town matter, he was a thorn in the Council's side for many years. Mr. Underwood had begun excavating the ancient earthwork at Budbury, somewhat unscientifically, in 1945. Now he roundly declared the ground should not be built on. The U.D.C. altered its plans and reduced the number of prefabs, but Mr. Underwood continued his campaign. This prompted a letter in the *Wiltshire Times* in October 1945 signed "One of Bradford's Homeless" and saying:

Perhaps Mr. Underwood would prefer to people Bradford with an exclusive colony of Temple Worshippers who could make their offerings at the Budbury Temple each day with Mr. Underwood as High Priest.

Mr. Underwood could only raise £500 from the public to fund his campaign and so by 1947 ten temporary prefabs had been erected at Budbury Circle and all were occupied. Plans for building a council estate at Churches had been approved back in August 1939, but inevitably put aside during the war. Now more housing was being erected or was proposed: Churches – 42 permanent; Priory Park – 42 permanent; Ashley Rd. – 20 aluminium; New Road – 50 permanent and 5 OAP dwellings. Another 70 permanent prefabricated two-storey houses were also proposed for the Avonfield area.

All kinds of alien materials were being used in Wiltshire to provide permanent houses which could be erected at speed. Aluminium houses were to be assembled in Trowbridge and Swedish timber ones at Staverton and Hilperton. Such constructions, which included a non-traditional one called a "Cornish Unit", were not popular and local councils had a habit of accepting them and trying to replace them with traditionally built houses at a later planning stage. This ploy did not work. Wiltshire County Council had negotiated a governmental deal wherein these assembled houses (which did not need skilled craftsmen) were over and above the allocations granted for houses in more traditional materials. Therefore it could not allow such switchovers. By 1952 the county had achieved the erection of an extra 2,114 houses through this policy – a bonus on the number of traditional houses within its allocation.

By the end of 1949 Bradford UDC had built 68 permanent postwar houses and had 30 temporary prefabs in occupation: the waiting list was 230. Three years later the permanent houses had grown to 159 and the waiting list shrunk to 150. The council estates of Churches, Priory Park (started in 1952) and Budbury Tyning (1954) not only answered a pressing need and gave families a chance to move out of old damp properties. They also altered old Bradford for ever as green and open spaces within the town which had previously separated little hamlets such as Bearfield and upper Woolley Street from the centre now disappeared:

> *When I lived in Tory Place, Churches was being built. Ashley was separate, a village on its own with one or two houses straggling up from the Bath Road and a small prefab estate at Budbury Close. If you walked on to the Winsley Road and walked to the corner where Churches and the Elmfield estate meet, that basically was the edge of Bradford: it was all fields beyond that and Elmfield wasn't built then. I would walk from Christchurch school through what is now Priory Close and it was fields all the way. The New Road stopped at the Saxon garage and turned right and that was the main road, going down through Woolley. Kingsfield was all fields. There was nothing between the Saxon Garage and the Holt Road except a big house, Kingsfield Grange, just gardens and orchards. So it's changed completely, totally changed. It was a much more smaller town and in 30 years it's more than doubled in size. (TW97)*

The *Wiltshire Times* frequently reports arguments in Bradford's UDC meetings. One of the most articulate councillors was, predictably, Guy Underwood. He pointed out that permanent prefabs cost £1,400-£1,500 each, which was 25% more than a traditional house. He also fought hard and continuously to save buildings which most of the U.D.C. wanted to demolish. Numbers 30, 31, 32 and 33 Whitehill were to have been pulled down in 1939 but had been left, still occupied throughout the war. These are the cottages described by Sid Stone in Chapter 3. In August 1947 Guy Underwood protested at:

> *....the scandalous inclusion of a number of houses in Whitehill and Wine Street in a Clearance Order having regard to the serious shortage of houses...these old houses which could be renovated and made habitable were in keeping with the old world tradition of the town and ought to be preserved. One of the town's biggest assets was its old buildings. (Laughter). (WT 9.8.47)*

Back came Mr. Eacott's response:

31 was damp and unsafe, water was continually oozing through the back of one room and the upstairs room where all the family slept, (2 adults and 2 children) was damp. A deplorable state, I'd rather live in a shed. The Council would give them to anyone who would have them. (WT 9.8.47)

The Clearance Order went ahead. For many more years, as Bradford's old buildings either fell or were pulled down, Guy Underwood continued to campaign vigorously against Clearance Orders. He had been doing so back in 1939 when swathes of houses in St. Margaret's Street and Wine Street as well as Whitehill were only reprieved because of the war. In 1952 he was still arguing that 12 and 13 Whitehill "... are not slums, they are simply good houses in a bad state of repair." At the same Council meeting 10, 11 and 14 Whitehill together with 8 and 9 Wine Street faced the same fate.

According to Mr. Bowyer:

"These houses are absolutely finished, rubbishy, worn out. The only thing is to carry out our moral obligation."

Mr. Underwood replied: "I have restored a lot of old houses far worse than these you wish to demolish and when they are properly repaired they are twice as good as the houses are nowadays. (WT 6.2.52)

During his years of living in Belcombe, Guy Underwood had indeed bought some crumbling properties around the town, including several small cottages on Tory from which he made two slightly larger houses with adjoining courtyards. A later owner of number 21 Tory considered his alterations were good by 1930 standards. But it seems that he did not always finish the restoration projects he had in mind. So perhaps it is not surprising that the U.D.C. found excuses to ignore comments which we would, with hindsight, consider absolutely justified.

These post-war years were so full of restrictions that many people wondered whether Great Britain and her allies had actually won the war. All forms of fuel economy had to be practised and were enforced. When the U.D.C. met in Westbury House in the severe February weather of 1947 members not only wore their overcoats but even wrapped up their legs for extra warmth. In May 1947 a resident in Southville Gardens was charged with unlawful use of electricity for heating his greenhouse. He was one of the leading carnation growers in the country and in 1945 had received the premium prize for all England with his exhibition blooms. But regulations said you could only heat a greenhouse to grow vegetables. He was found guilty and fined £10 with costs.

Bradford fashions in 1949. The Carnival Queen candidates in the Town Hall yard in Market Street, a space which is now a private parking area. This particular series of carnivals, which was organised by the then strong Bradford branch of the British Legion ran from 1949 to 1952.

It was a time for austerity. New goods and services were mostly on allocation. Any couple marrying in 1947 would be given enough coupons to be allowed to go out and buy a very limited amount of new "Utility" furniture. One such couple chose to use all their coupons on the marital bedroom and bought a double bed, a full-size wardrobe, a man's wardrobe and a dressing table. All their other furniture had to be acquired second-hand. The allocation of curtain coupons was just enough for this bride to buy enough new material to make a romantic bedspread for their new Utility double bed. The Government allowed her coupons to buy three double sheets. But the bride showed initiative: "But I got another pair on the black market and a friend whose fiancé had been killed in the war sold me another pair. So I was lucky: I had seven sheets." New tablecloths were unobtainable but she happened to be in the right place when a large departmental store in Gloucester was selling second-hand hotel linen so she joined the long queue and got some. "There were holes in the tablecloths but you could make them up into smaller ones. Otherwise we used old sugar bags and put braid round them and they were our table cloths." "Making Do" was a great watchword both during and after the war.

The usual drinking crowd. Frank "Dodger" Mayell, publican of the Rising Sun, Winsley Road, standing holding a bottle and glass in the centre of a group of his customers in the 1950s. He lived to be 100 years old and was still landlord when he reached his centenary.

To get authorisation to buy a new car, it was necessary to be classed as an "essential service" user. Such grading was hard to get. Consequently the prices of second-hand cars, just like furniture, rocketed out of all proportion to value or serviceability.

Ordinary life was no easier. Each area of the country had a Food Control Committee and the majority of essential foodstuffs, including meat, eggs, sugar, butter and margarine remained on ration. In 1946 bread, cakes and flour were also put on ration – which had not been the case all through the war. Bread rationing – intended to be a temporary measure – lasted for two years. The ferocious winter of 1947-8 destroyed the country's potato crop and the government was obliged to introduce controlled distribution of the little stock that remained. Each person was allocated 3 pounds of potatoes per week. The nation's plight was so dire that food parcels were being sent from Australia to help hungry families in Britain. In December 1947 the Nestlé factory in Staverton was the official distribution centre for Bradford and the surrounding area. As late as 1952 the weekly tea ration was still 2 ounces per person per week – just as it had been throughout the war itself. Ration books were still being issued and in use as late as 1954.

But it was the question of housing which remained the most constant problem throughout the 1950s. The Census returns for 1951 show that 20% of Bradford households still had to share piped water or had none at all and 15% shared or had no indoor W.C.. A few households had some shared bathroom facilities but nearly 48% of households still had no fixed bath. The population of the town had increased by 18% since the last Census of 1931.[2] Should old buildings be knocked down and replaced by new ones? Dr. Jean Murray, Medical Officer for Health for the U.D.C., put the dilemma so clearly in her annual report for 1953 that it is worth reproducing this in some detail:

PRESERVING THE PICTURESQUE: WHILST COMPLYING WITH MODERN LEGISLATION

It is agreed by all who know it, that Bradford on Avon is one of the most interesting small towns in the country, from the very fact that its known history goes back to settled Saxon days...that it has been built of enduring stone on rock foundations on its steep hillside; and that this site, plus continuity of habitation has given the town an individuality possessed by no other. The difficulties of applying the Housing Acts without destroying its enchantment (appreciated especially by knowledgeable visitors who do not have to live in the old houses) seem insufferable.

Were it not for the stone terraces grouped round the Saxon Church, Parish Church with Norman remains, and Pilgrim's Chapel on the heights of Tory, which seem to have grown out of the rock, there would be no Bradford on Avon. But these terraces consist of houses which have been built on narrow shelves dug out of the rock, piled up one room above another to three or four storeys in height – with the rock and earth behind them up to second to fourth storeys (each house one room per storey). Some have a small garden opposite the house across the only access path; some have an access path behind, which allows for a back door in the top flat.

Some of the houses have been brought into line with modern requirements by their owner-occupiers, in that room has been found for W.C.s and bathrooms. A few with "amenities" are now let to tenants who, like the owner-occupiers, consider that the magnificent situation more than cancels out the difficulties endured. But the tenants of some of the others and the unfortunate persons responsible for the delivery of coal, removal of house refuse and such, find that picturesqueness entails a great deal of hard work and effort to keep up with modern standards of cleanliness and general living.

From the officials' and Council's viewpoint, the tenants' complaints, while entirely justified, raise many problems. "A roof is letting in rain". In brick and slate towns, a replacement of a few slates is frequently all that is needed. In our old houses, huge ancient stone tiles pegged down by oak pegs to the original rafters may have slipped – or broken – and while the owner finds that his builder advises that the rafters are dangerous, he is faced with the problem of re-roofing completely a cottage that brings in a rent of a few shillings a week.

It is not realised by those outside the work that, once a complaint is made to the Sanitary Inspector and he has inspected a house, he has to list all defects for the owner's consideration. If the defects were such that repairs could not be carried out at a reasonable expense, a statutory notice for repairs could not be issued, and unless the owner were willing to spend this unreasonable figure there is no alternative but to close the house.

The new Act in process of consideration may help in many cases, but again in a town the size of Bradford, with so many problems to be faced, the amount of money that the town can afford to spend on old property has to be considered. We are only a little town, with a small rateable value. It has always seemed regrettable to me that such places, which are part of the essential England, should be dependent only on what the Council with its limited spending capacity can do. The case of Lavenham in Suffolk always comes to mind as an example of what can be done by what might be termed "outside" co-operation. (WT25.12.54)

Supportive evidence comes from the many sale advertisements in the local newspapers. For example, in 1954:

Bradford on Avon: close to centre, stone-built dwelling house with living room, bedroom, attic room, outhouse and all mains offered ready for occupation at £450 only (to include adjacent five-room dwelling as let to produce £22.2s.0d (£22.10p) per annum gross). Suit couple. Offers invited, as must be sold (WT 6.11.54)

Other typical examples from 1960 include:

Bradford on Avon: 3 stone built cottages for demolition. Tons of excellent building stone, walling stone, etc. 2 years given to demolish and remove. Apply Tilley & Culverwell, Trowbridge. (WT 26.2.60)

For restoration and improvement, Bradford on Avon "old world" double fronted stone built Cottage Residence, 2 living rooms, 2 beds, bathroom, etc.

Left: The bottom of Silver Street in the 1950s, not long before Knees on the right hand side was pulled down. This demolition allowed Silver Street to be widened at this point while the rest of the site was left empty to provide more visibility for motorists. The Co-op on the left hand side survived until the beginning of the 1990s. A Spencer Moulton lorry is crossing the bridge.

Demolition of old buildings around St. Margaret's Hall to make way for a new car park and approach to the hall in 1960. This work revealed a totally new view of Holy Trinity church and of Tory. Westbury House on the right was still the council offices of the U.D.C. Note the central ground floor window which matches the two on either side. This window was replced by a doorway and pillared entrance wall when the building was sold after 1974 and converted into private flats.

Demolition work in progress on the premises in Silver Street formerly occupied by Mr H. Willson, Chemist. The space thus gained would become a new entrance to the Spencer Moulton factory. The Lamb building is on the right.

The blessing by the Bishop of Clifton of the new Roman Catholic church at its opening in the former Town Hall in June 1955. There had not been a Roman Catholic Church in Bradford for centuries. The Bishop took the first Mass in the new church, which was formerly the courtroom and public hall of the building.

and all mains. At present under closing order, £150 only (WT 9.9.60)

One mile from centre. 2 substantial stone-built dwelling houses, each with 2 living rooms, 2 beds. etc. main elec. and drainage, main water available and good garden. At present under closing orders. £300 the two. (WT 23.9.60)

Mr. and Mrs. Niblett had lived in the same rank of cottages off Whitehill since the 1930s:

Then in 1954 we bought this house 21 Whitehill, the top house in the rank. Mr. Slade was the agent who came to collect our rent of 2s.6d. (12.5p) a week . We had water coming in at the back of the cottage and we said we must have something done about it. The owner died and his nephew who lived in Canada said "Why don't you buy it."... My husband said "What would you want?" The man said "Make me an offer and so we said £50 and the man said "Done.". It was a terrible winter around that Christmas but we put up with it...and as we saved so we had a little bit done to it at a time. The first thing we did was to have the water put in. It was marvellous to have a flush toilet. And you can imagine how beautiful it was to turn the tap on and watch the water come out in your own house. (RN93)

Eventually the three bottom cottages were condemned and pulled down: Nothing replaced them and so Mr. and Mrs. Niblett benefited:

Of course we've also got a piece of ground down at the end of the rank where our cottage used to be. We shared the ground down there with our neighbour and we paid £2. 10s.0d. (£2.50) for it when he died. It was all legally done through a solicitor (RN93)

A newly built "Bradstone elevation" 3-bedroom semi-detached house on the Priory Park estate cost £3,250 in 1960, whereas plenty of dilapidated cottages were advertised at prices around £300 or £500. But building societies would not give mortgages on such risky old buildings and would only agree to lend capital on new or reliable properties. A huge influx of money would be required to save the town.

Bradford's plight, so eloquently described by Dr. Murray became serious enough to attract public concern well beyond Bradford. Back in 1945 the Society for the Protection of Ancient Buildings had prepared a thorough report on the "Adaptation and Reconditioning of the old buildings of Bradford on Avon" and recommended the saving of a picturesque early nineteenth century terrace of houses in Wine Street Nothing was done to implement this report. Tensions mounted. A local resident, Dawn McLeod, had alerted no less a figure than John Betjeman who wrote a powerful article in the *Daily Telegraph* about threats to the town. But the Wine Street houses were demolished in the Spring of 1958. It seemed inevitable that much of Tory and Middle Rank was about to suffer the same fate.

Mr. and Mrs. Boulding were among the first incomers to the town to appreciate the beauty of the hillside: They bought their house on Tory through Mr. Hillier, the town's estate agent, even though the then Vicar of Christ Church had told them not to buy in Bradford which he regarded as a sink of iniquity!

My husband got a job teaching in Trowbridge High School. We had a flat in Trowbridge for about 18 months while we were looking round for a house. Then I came over to Bradford on one brilliant October day in 1951. The colours of the leaves were absolutely lovely against that grey stone – beautiful. I saw this cottage which was built flat into the rock. It was totally unsuitable because it was nothing but stairs. At the top of the house was the back door on the third floor which opened straight out onto a pathway so that when you turned and looked at the house from the back it looked like a one storey cabin.

Inside there were two lots of corkscrew stairs with three little stairs in the middle in the dividing bit. The bathroom was built out up the first set of stairs and then there were two or three little stairs on the left. Then there was a hallway and two rooms, one small and one large. Then another flight of corkscrew stairs up to two more rooms. The garden was on three levels with stone steps which were remarkably uneven, the terraces on each level were about seven or eight feet in width and I had a baby of 18 months old. So it was totally unsuitable. But once I brought my husband over to see it there was no stopping him, he had to have it, he absolutely loved it. And so we moved in and settled in and stayed there 35 years.

When we came most of the cottages let at about 2s 6d (25p) a week and there was no water in the houses, each cottage had one tap and a privy down in its garden. We had the remains of our privy down two or three extremely uneven stone steps and round to the left. There was no sharing of privies, so I suppose it was a bit updated in a way. As far as I remember there was a flush in each one of them. But by the time we reached Tory the house had an indoor bathroom built over the courtyard where there had previously been a separate cottage. So I never had to bother with the one in the garden. (UB97)

Everyone who lived on Tory in its earlier days speaks of the camaraderie among the neighbours. Ursula Boulding was readily accepted into life on "the hill":

Largely speaking they were real old cottagers there and the way they accepted us was quite delightful. I can remember old Mrs. Tucker who inhabited the biggest house in the lowest part of Tory and lived there with her two daughters. She was a very old lady and they used to put her basket chair out on the front, on the pathway on a sunny day and she would sit there and watch the world go by. Of course the place was full of young children who would run up and down and all the cottagers had their front doors open. Consequently everybody looked after everybody else's child. I never had any worry about my youngest who by the time he was two was riding in a kiddicar or running up and down because everybody looked after him as they did everybody else.

My next door neighbour but one was extremely sweet to me. When my three children went to school and I was back at work, teaching, she always had her front door open for them when they came back from school. The kettle was on the hob and she'd make them some tea until I got back. I remember she used to come and automatically scrub my front doorstep for me. She said, I know you haven't been brought up to do things like that so I'll do it for you. (UB97)

Other Bradfordians felt that Mrs Boulding should have found a different home:

I think in those days people thought it was an unsuitable place for us to live. I can remember you didn't have to carry your shopping – it was all brought up to you. The order was taken, the baker came, the grocer came, the greengrocer came and the butcher came – they all came. So you didn't have to worry about things like that. But the chaps who brought the food used to say this is not a suitable place, you ought to have a nice council house.

It was very happy. I can remember the Coronation of Elizabeth II in June 1953. We had a party and there were trestle tables all the way down the lower part of Tory. Everybody brought contributions, whatever we could find because in those days the rationing was still on and it wasn't easy to produce anything. We did what we could. Bradford decorated itself with jampots which were painted in colours. We put little night lights in them and lit them up at night so it was extremely pretty. We had some on the walls of Tory and there were lights all across the town bridge down below. From Tory you could see everything.

Then there was the threat from the council to pull down the cottages at the lower end of Tory and build blocks of flats. That's when we took action. People got together. We composed letters to the council to say how it would absolutely ruin the backcloth of Bradford. In Tory I don't think the cottagers minded much because they were going to be rehoused. They were going to have running water inside the houses and so on. Most of them were taken up to Churches where they built new houses for them and I think they felt this was a great improvement. (UB97)

Sid Stone certainly thought it was time for change:

I spoke out against renovating Tory and Middle Rank: We know they are period houses and a link with the past and let us save the link with the past. Make them into a museum but don't ask people to live in them. I've lived in these old houses all my life and there's nothing you can do with them, literally nothing. (SS97)

St. Margaret's Street, showing the narrow entrance to St. Margaret's Hill (Morgan's Hill) on the right. The concrete lamp post was in place by 1949. The houses below the ornamental ironwork of the entrance to the Congregational Church were compulsorily purchased in 1963 as part of the extensive redevelopment of St. Margaret's Hill and now, in part, provide an empty space for car parking.

Diana Newman certainly saw the value of rehousing many of the tenants on Tory:

> In order to live in a house in an area like Tory you've got to have a love for that sort of building and a desire to put something into it. I don't think it's a terribly useful place for a family with not too much money and so it was a good thing to be able to rehouse people. Wet back walls, very crowded, not at all pleasant. Then again in Middle Rank a lot of people were in the same position. (DN97)

The continuing destruction of the heart of the old town again reached national press coverage in 1957. Many of the town's residents were increasingly determined to save Bradford and prepared to take firm action on this issue. Diana Newman was one such person:

> We went up to Tory Place in 1953, we were living in the Trowbridge Road, we didn't think we could afford a house, we were really looking for something to rent. Then we saw this advertised and my husband was interested because it had a lot of apple trees and he couldn't think where it was. And we went to see it and then in just over a month we'd bought it and we were in – there was only a lane down to it from the Winsley Road.
>
> I was asked if I would stand for the Council in 1960. I took up the opportunity because living in Tory Place and walking down through Tory, Middle Rank, Newtown, Church Street was so very depressing. Barton Orchard was horrible – an empty shell.
>
> I dreaded the thought of pulling those houses down in Tory and Middle Rank because that, more than any other, would have completely ruined Bradford. You might be sorry about some old cottages coming down in St. Margaret's Hill but they didn't show up so much as the ones up on the hill. I couldn't see anything else being built there because it was so steep no one could imagine what kind of buildings would be going up in place of them. That was my thought at the time. The council certainly came round to wanting to do something about it and in fact was doing something about it. (DN97)

The Bradford on Avon Preservation Society, with Lord Methuen as its President, had also been formed in 1959 to help to meet the threat, its inaugural meeting at The Swan receiving unexpected evidence that buildings need careful attention.

> I think I'm right in saying that a leg came through the ceiling at that first

*meeting because there were builders up there and the building, The Swan, was
very decrepit at the time. If anything was wanted to prove something should be
done, that would seem to be it. (UB97)*

The Preservation Society constantly publicised Bradford's problems at both
local and national level and established a working liaison with the Wiltshire
County Council Planning Office. Leading members of the Historic Buildings
Council for England as well as the Civic Trust came to Bradford to investigate
and to speak out against any more destruction. In May 1960 there was a week's
exhibition of drawings of the town by students of the Department of Architecture
at Kingston on Thames School of Art together with talks on the history and
preservation of Bradford from outside authorities. Such serious attention from
so many quarters had considerable impact. The Trowbridge-based *Wiltshire
Times* commented, somewhat loftily:

> *A preview of the exhibition given to a Wiltshire Times reporter this week
> proves that Bradford has certainly shown itself worthy of study. (WT 20.5.60)*

The U.D.C. had already recognised that it must come to a serious policy
decision on the future of Bradford's townscape. Now it had to decide between
three possibilities:

> *To purchase the properties and improve them (the Tory houses) to modern
> standards, preserving the façades of the buildings and the backcloth picture of
> the town;*
> *To clear the whole area and replace with new buildings constructed in stone
> or stone-faced concrete blocks;*
> *To clear the whole area and plant with trees, shrubs, etc. (U.D.C. document
> 26.6.63)*

It was the gathering together of financial resources far beyond the pockets of
the town itself which provided the significant breakthrough and enabled the
U.D.C. to take positive action. Contributions came in from Wiltshire County
Council, the Civic Trust, the Society for the Protection of Ancient Buildings, and
other national bodies. On Tory, numbers 1 to 10 and a block nearer St. Mary
Tory could now be compulsorily purchased. Proposals, counter proposals and
yet more plans proliferated while houses on the hillside continued to disintegrate.
It took years of hard work by the U.D.C. and many others before the restoration
of the entire area was successfully completed. Builders' original tenders for the
project proved far too expensive. More money had to be wrenched out of public

funds; residents had to be moved out whereupon the empty houses attracted the rough element of the town, as one despairing letter in the newspaper indicates:

> *Dear Sir, I write as the occupant of a house on Tory (there are still some of us!) who objects to walking to his house through a litter of broken glass and smashed tiles... (WT 2.3.62)*

But at last the official opening by Lord Euston, Chairman of the Society for the Protection of Ancient Buildings, of phase 1, the U.D.C.'s Tory Preservation Scheme, took place on 26 June 1963.

But even before the opening of phase 1, interest in living in numbers 1-10 Tory was intense – as the Preservation Society pointed out in a public letter:

> *Many outsiders are now enquiring as to the possibility of obtaining a small period house in Bradford and the Society hopes this trend will not escape the notice of the local council. (WT 16.3.62)*

However the U.D.C. were to become well aware of this for themselves, needing no such prodding from elsewhere. After the two advertisements to find tenants for the renovated Tory dwellings:

> *...ultimately over eighty applications were received from persons residing in various parts of England from as far afield as London and Torquay. The interest in these units of accommodation was phenomenal and out of the eighty applications the Council could have let these units several times over. (U.D.C. document 26.6.63)*

This extensive restoration project was truly a turning point for the town:

> *Doing those houses up in Tory, numbers 1-10 and then numbers 23 and 24 at the other end meant that everybody in between realised that it was worth spending money on their properties. Nowadays it's marvellous to look back on it and think that once the Council put money into Tory, private people who needed to feel it was safe to put their money into property followed suit. (DN97)*

Phase Two of the U.D.C. redevelopment was Middle Rank. The intention was to buy the entire line of houses by compulsory order. Absentee landlords were ready to comply, but the owner of one house situated in the centre was not prepared to agree. He had bought the house two years previously:

When my parents bought this house in 1961, many of the houses were owned by landlords who had let them deteriorate. They were lovely but it was an inconvenient place to live and not everybody saw the beauty of living in a place like this. We wanted to move back to this side of town and possibly we bought this particular house because it was so cheap. People were still living here, only one or two were empty but they weren't in very good nick. Next door to us there was nothing, just a façade up to first floor, all the rest had fallen in. And there was another one exactly the same further along, just at the top of the steps. I think originally the houses in Middle Rank went further along up the steps at the end, you can still see some retaining walls.

My father offered the owner £500 cash and he nearly snatched my father's hand off because he didn't think he'd get that much because no one wanted to live up here.

About a couple of years later the council put a compulsory purchase order on all the houses along Middle Rank. It was some time after they had completed the ones on Tory. But because we had an inside toilet and bathroom they couldn't buy this one and make a clean sweep of the whole lot. So they only bought part of the rank. A private builder bought the three cottages next to this house and made them into one. The houses the U.D.C. compulsorily purchased are all built straight into the hillside. But from number 7 down towards Conigre the houses have always been privately owned because they have all got backyards and therefore there has been room to build facilities on at the back. What is now the kitchen here was then the kitchen, bathroom and toilet. (TW97)

Nowadays these rows of much loved, well-tended cottages appear to stand serene on their sunny hillside, untouched by time, past acrimony almost forgotten. It is a long story, but well worth the retelling. How many people are aware of the years of passionate and partisan debate within the town followed by the detailed work needed to preserve Tory and Middle Rank?

Another significant house, Orpins in Church Street, also received much needed attention. This house, originally part of the vicar's glebe[3] is owned by the church and administered by a charitable Trust. In 1960 the vicar revealed:

Orpins has been occupied for many years contrary to the terms of the Trust. Now vacant, it will be necessary to consider the repair of the house which over the years has got into a very bad condition. As is so often the case with these old properties, the income from rent has been small and quite inadequate to cover the cost of keeping the property in proper repair. ...the Trustees in these circumstances are faced with a well-nigh insoluble problem. (WT 8.4.60)

View of Middle Rank before rebuilding.

The rebuilding of part of Middle Rank in the later 1960s. The old houses which the U.D.C. did not buy lie further along the path, the spire of Christ Church showing clearly in the background. There was some considerable controversy over the use of simulated Bath stone for the rebuilding of both Tory and of Middle Rank houses. (Photo reproduced by kind permssion of Bath Chronicle)

But in 1962 some of Church Street received the careful restoration it deserved. Orpins, by then in danger of demolition, was saved. Repairs and modernisation were expected to cost £1,499. In a reversal of some of its earlier attitudes, the UDC now found itself ready to make grant of £400 towards the cost.

The struggle to save other parts of the town was a long and complicated one: nor was it a story of total success. In 1963 the cottages owned by the Congregational Church in St. Margaret's Street and the caretaker's cottage in St. Margaret's Hill (Morgan's Hill) where there is now a small car park – were compulsorily purchased by the Town Council for £450 and demolished to make a wider road for the new St. Margaret's Court. The deeds went back to 1710 but it is thought that they were built earlier than that. Unhappily the demolition of other ancient houses on St. Margaret's Hill could not be prevented. Weighty opposition to such destruction came from Lord Euston of the Society for the Preservation of Ancient Buildings (SPAB), James Lees-Milne, Architectural Adviser to the National Trust and Lord Methuen who raised the matter in the House of Lords. Bradford was emphatically not on the way to becoming another Lavenham. Alan Newman, Vicar of Christ Church, viewed his surroundings quite differently:

I sometimes wonder what our visitors honestly think of this "quaint little old fashioned town" with its air of lethargy, its many ugly and shabby buildings, its mucky river and its foul canal, its high quota of litterbugs, its exhibition of rusty corrugated iron. (Parish Magazine, 1962)

Bradford was a working town and its industrial backbone remained very evident. A range of factories continued in production in the Greenland Mills: Enfield Cycles; Dotesios Printers; Weir Electric and Rex Rubber. Agaric, the mushroom farm in the old quarries, still sent its daily output by train all over the country. Most importantly the rubber works, with its five-and-a-half acre factory site and its offices at Abbey Mill, continued in full operation. The policy of the Company was "Nothing but the best must leave the factory" and this policy, not unnaturally, brought world wide recommendations for Spencer Moulton products. Carbon black was an essential ingredient in the manufacture of rubber. Soot from the coal fired boilers poured out of the tall factory chimneys and fell constantly all over the town. It had even been necessary at times to use shovels to remove it from the roof of The Hall just down wind from the main factory buildings. In dry summers, heavy granules of black dust blew along nearby streets and over the town bridge. The firm's paternalistic attitude, so evident in Mr. John Moulton's time in the early part of the century, was still in place when Jack Mock joined the firm straight from school in August 1949:

A view of the central part of Whitehill, taken from Ivy Terrace in 1959 and showing in the foreground some of the allotments which were an essential part of Bradford domestic life until very recently. A row of detached houses was built there in the late 1960s. On the further side of the road, a set of four properties had previously existed in the open area. The lowest two had been tenement buildings some three storeys high and were regarded as real slums. There had been one tap and one privy for all four houses.

I went to Spencer Moulton because my dad was there. I was in the accounts department at Abbey Mills. In those years before my National Service I was a junior member of the Accounts Dept. I've still got my first wage slip. It's just a little slip of paper about two-and-a half-inches long and an inch wide. Friday afternoons I used to have a list of things I had to do, one of which was to take wads of cash into the Swan Hotel to pay the bills for the Spencer Moulton people who used to come down from London Head Office and stay there. I was trusted with all this money though I didn't think about it at the time. But the main thing was taking these brown envelopes with cash to some of the firm's pensioners who lived in the vicinity. They had to open up the packet in front of me, make sure it was the correct amount and sign the receipt which I had to take back. So I knew exactly what they got. I think pensions from years at work was a comparatively new thing to them at the time so it was good. But it was only a small amount. My father worked there for 50 years but he had a very small pension. (JM97)

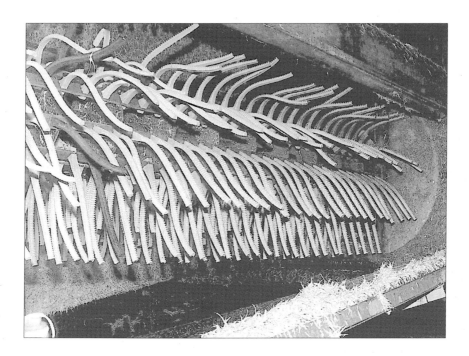

Above: a feather plucker machine with "fingers" made by Avon Rubber.

Right: Loading a lorry with railway springs at Abbey Mill in Church Street. Making products for railway systems across the world was always a major part of the rubber industry in Bradford.

Spencer Moulton was still the major industry in the town, boys being glad to leave Trinity School and start earning money there as soon after their fifteenth birthday as possible. The diversity of its products remained as wide as ever, ranging from washers for aerosols to cooling hoses for motor cars. Railway springs of all shapes and sizes continued to be at the heart of the firm's trading and were sent throughout the country and all over the world. Even after the war the firm continued to produce tank tracks for the army, sensing elements for anti-personnel mines and inflatable boats for both private and military use. Such specialist equipment as firemen's axes was also made there, rubber handles being necessary to prevent a fireman being electrocuted should he chop through a live electric wire. Their more unusual products included "feather pluckers". These were long finger-like items, about nine inches long made with two types of rubber. One end of each feather plucker was rather more stiff than the other. They were fitted to machines which then plucked chickens and turkeys – no doubt an innovation in the new industrial farming techniques being devised after the war.

However in spite of considerable reorganisation and updating Spencer Moulton was obliged to sell out to Avon Rubber of Melksham in 1956. Avon Rubber kept the two enterprises running separately for a considerable time and so the Bradford workforce found little change in their working practices. The new owners asked Alex Moulton – later Dr. Alex Moulton – to remain with them. But he decided to break away on his own. In the same year a totally new enterprise emerged under the Moulton name. The creation of Moulton Developments in the Stables of The Hall put the town on the national map in an entirely new way:

> In recent years it has been the effort to preserve the heritage of the past that has brought Bradford on Avon into the national limelight... readers of national newspapers must have thought that the picturesque town was almost solely concerned with the beauty of its past and hardly at all with the present and the future.
>
> This of course is not a true picture...last week the nation at large was able to read how a Bradford man, working with his team of Bradford boys in the lovely old house which is one of Bradford's finest legacies from the past, had invented and perfected something which is right up to date, if anything ever was – a system of suspension that offers a new kind of comfort to users of the vehicle of the twentieth century – the motor car. (WT 24.8.62)

Dr. Alex Moulton had invented a Hydrolastic suspension system for motor cars in which rubber hermetically containing fluid provided the suspension

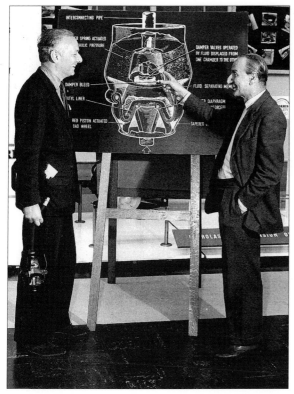

Dr. Alex Moulton (left) and Sir Alec Issigonis at the launch of the Morris 1100 in 1962 in front of a diagram of the Hydrolastic vehicle suspension system.

instead of the conventional metal springs and dampers. This brilliant innovative method was central to the design of the B.M.C. Morris 1100 which was launched in 1962 followed by the Mini and the 1800,[4] and his name is consequently closely associated with that of the British car designer, Issigonis. The invention has been central to car design ever since, being used in a range of Rover cars and chosen for the new MGF car which went into production in 1997.

Dr. Moulton is well-known as the inventor of the Moulton bicycle, a project which first started in Bradford in 1957 and went on public display in London in 1962. Again Dr. Moulton's primary interest was in the suspension system. The prime intention was to make a bicycle for adults more pleasing to have and to use than the conventional model. It had small wheels with high pressure tyres, and suspension for both wheels, with an open unisex frame. Many variations of his original design have followed, receiving national and international acclaim since those early days. Still at the forefront of modern thinking, the R.A.C. is now promoting the Moulton bicycle as part of its approach to traffic problems in the twenty-first century. Currently the most expensive models are made in the Stables at the Hall and are exported to Japan. Further developments are to be expected.

The year 1962 saw other developments. The new Trinity School off Ashley Road was opened and would eventually have a considerable effect on the development of the town. The consequent closure of the old school in Newtown meant more empty buildings on the hillside until the Ropewalk retirement apartments appeared in their place many years later.

Another innovation in the same year was one which inhabitants have been grateful for ever since. This was the construction of the pedestrian footbridge

Mr E.H. Darby, Headmaster of Trinity Scool in Newtown cutting the first sod of the new Trinity School which later became St. Laurence School on the then outskirts of the town in June 1960. Staff and some pupils watch the ceremony.

Trinity School building now deserted in 1963, its pupils having transferred to the new site in 1961. Part of Newtown can be seen on the left. The main school premises continued in use as a Youth Centre as well as for play group sessions and other social activities over a number of years. This much gabled building was eventually replaced by the retirement apartments of the Ropewalk. After considerable controversy the new development recreated some of the architectural motifs of the original school within its modern design.

Two massive cranes placed on opposite sides of the river Avon were at work on a Wednesday morning in October 1962, engaged in lowering into position two sections of the pre-stressed concrete footbridge between St. Margaret's Hall and Church Street. Each section weighed nearly ten tons and it took about seven hours to place the two curved sides accurately on their resting pads. The centre section arrived later in the same week. The bridge was made for the U.D.C. by Messrs. Bryco. Ltd. of Taunton and the steps, ramps and the finishing of the abutments were accomplished by U.D.C. workmen.

across the river Avon from St. Margaret's Street to Church Street. The project had been around in U.D.C. thinking since the previous century – being mooted as an appropriate town scheme to commemorate the various coronations and jubilees. Always there was some pressing reason to put it aside. But now there was agreement to build a bridge designed by Bob Cherry, his original specification being changed to give the structure a greater curve to bring it well above the flood levels so familiar to the town. All the work had to be done from the Church

Street side of the river because access on the southern side was almost impossible. A little later that area too, now St. Margaret's car park, was redeveloped. The Fire station was re-sited near the railway station where it was officially opened on 6 January 1965. The Quaker Meeting House was demolished and a maze of varied buildings of all ages disappeared, leaving the space we see today. The most significant building, once a dye house, then the Drill Hall, then the Alexander Cinema until 1959, became St. Margaret's Hall. With the new pedestrian bridge across the river, suddenly the two sides of the town came closer together.

Whatever else changed in Bradford there was always the same likelihood of floods, especially during the winter months. The most devastating inundation is still recorded in Westbury Gardens on the stone arch in the river wall. The mark is above head-height and the date is 1882. The floods in 1884 nearly matched it and throughout all later accounts of the town's affairs reports of serious flooding in the centre of the town are a constant feature. It was such a normal occurrence that people took disruption for granted. There was always a simple, if illegal, way to get past the floods around the bridge. If north of the river, you walked down Barton Orchard to the footpath over the railway line and then walked along the railway line to the station. Southerners reversed the process:

> *My husband taught in Trowbridge and when there were floods in the 1950s he used to walk to the station along the railway line. A lot of people did that. You didn't bother about the trains, you just walked at the side of the track. It wouldn't be allowed now. But lots of things were allowed then that aren't allowed now. (UB97)*

Bridge Street had always been regularly flooded and the waters would also rise into the Bullpit and beyond, sometimes even into Church Street. Normally there would be several hours warning before the River Avon, supplemented by waters from the river Biss from Trowbridge, actually rose up into the streets. Spencer Moulton, on their riverside site, had always had emergency measures well worked out and would get the workforce to manhandle all the heavy machinery above the expected flood levels. Avon Rubber did the same. For normal domestic needs there were enough shops either side of the river and if it was necessary to cross the bridge, there was the age-old custom of getting a lift across. Earlier in the century a wagon charged 2d a ride: now a high lorry or an Army duck could provide the transport.

It was pointed out that Bradford's problem was made worse by the town bridge itself, which created a strong barrier to the river when in flood and caused the waters to flow over its banks. The solution, it was claimed, was to demolish the bridge! This is one piece of vandalism which did not find much enthusiastic support. Because the river was augmented at Limpley Stoke by the waters of the river Frome, Bath also flooded frequently. An extensive flood prevention scheme for the entire Avon was under consideration when the worst floods of the twentieth century in the area occurred in December 1960. It had rained heavily and unceasingly for two days and Bradford, taking the full impact of the combined waters of the Avon and the Biss, was the worst hit town. Extracts from newspaper reports fill in the details:

The river rose 14ft. 7ins above its normal summer level, and the results in the town centre were devastating. Most people said that they had never seen anything like it in their lives. Some people were warned on Saturday evening that the river was rising but they were not to know that it would reach the height it did. It came up over 4 ft. in an hour on Sunday and by 11 a.m. roads through the centre were impassable. Five feet of water flowed into the centuries old building of The Three Gables restaurant, and most other places had between 4ft. 6 and 5 ft. Bridge Street was badly affected and some of the houses were flooded to a depth of 3 ft.

Everywhere the story of loss of stocks is the same. Spokesmen for various shops and business premises on both sides of the river bridge said that on Saturday they had raised their stocks on trestles to about 4 ft. or removed them upstairs but by Sunday the same stock had been washed off the trestles and was floating round the shops. Some plate glass windows were smashed with the force of the water, and some stock floated out into the river.

Also affected was the Swan Hotel where floodwater reached the cellars and entirely cut off entrance to them. Messrs. George Spencer Moulton & Co. Ltd. production was affected for a time on Tuesday when lack of steam prevented work on the presses. The floodwater poured into the works to levels never previously recorded. The telephone switchboard failed at the factory, and post office workers installed a new one, working all day on Monday to complete the work.

On Tuesday every shop in the town looked as though it had been given a mud bath, with grit and grime clinging to every bit of stock caught by the sudden torrent and furniture ripped from screw and hinge holds.

Private cars in the yard of Mr. C. H. S. Bowyer (i.e. the Bullpit) were saved from the flood, although one was submerged before Mr. Bowyer was able to reach it. He said this week he had had absolutely no warning. When he and his family woke on Sunday morning the water had risen so high that it was almost impossible to see the vehicles at the far end of his building yard. Also partly submerged was Mr. Bowyer's lorry which had water up to floorboard level. By knocking down a garden wall and driving 5 of the 7 vehicles up his garden path and parking them in a narrow courtyard at the rear of the house, Mr. Bowyer was able to avert much more serious damage.

Despite the severity of the floods, not once was Bradford completely divided. This was due to the unprecedented generosity of a local businessman who loaned an almost new diesel lorry and supplied free transport across the river throughout Sunday and Monday. The man wishes to remain anonymous. In consequence of his help and the loan of the vehicle, Trinity Secondary School meals were transported as well as mail, milk, bread, newspapers and hundreds of people.

At Bradford the water just extended round the corner by the Swan Hotel; Barton Bridge was invisible; Mr. Chard had 4 feet of water in at Barton Farm; water reached Holy Trinity church door and water seeped close to the chancel. (Reports from papers December 1960)

The Chard family seemed to take this flood in their stride:

We'd have a flood every other year perhaps but 1960 was a really bad one. It lasted two or three days perhaps. That flood came into the farmhouse and it was too deep to just wear boots. If you wanted to get from the kitchen to the stairs you had to have two chairs, stand on one chair and swing the other one round in front of you and get onto that one and swing the first one round again. (HL97)

Such devastation along the Avon valley and in Bath accelerated the long awaited flood prevention schemes. The next severe floods came in 1963 and it was agreed that without the measures newly in place the results might have been worse than 1960 or even than the great flood of 1882. Some progress had been made.

The town itself was also continuing to change. Encouraged by the work on Tory and Middle Rank, some owners of dilapidated houses began to see that their properties could also have a renewal of life. Dr. Davies, the U.D.C. Medical Officer for Health, had already noted the beginning of this trend when, in early 1965, he produced his Annual Report on Bradford for 1964:

One feature worthy of note...relates to the large number of old houses in the town which have been bought and reconditioned privately. I feel sure this trend will be emphasised when the Housing Act programme is revised at the end of 1965.

Dr. Davies was absolutely right. The recommendations of the 1965 Housing Act were taken up with great enthusiasm in Bradford and were to form the basis for practical and detailed restoration of much of the heart of the town. The next twenty years would prove to be one of the most active periods in the town's architectural history.

Barton Farm, towards the left of the photograph, under flood. This taken from the railway crossing on the north side of Barton Farm fields. The right foreground shows the Rowing Club building. On the far left are the town's gasworks between the Frome Road and the canal. Although North Sea gas took over from town gas production later, the gas holder was not demolished for many years.

Right: Dr. Alex Moulton carries an AM bicycle which separates into two peices. He was awarded the 1997 Sir Misha Black Memorial Medal for design education.

Left: The revolutionary 1983 AM bicycle, demonstrated by its designer, at The Hall, Bradford on Avon, in 1983. The essential ergonomic dimensions are identical to those of a full-size conventional machine, but the small wheels make the Moulton more compact, despite a slightly larger wheelbase for stability.

CHAPTER SIX

1965 - 1985
Opening up to a Wider World

Changing Attitudes to Conservation ~ The Town Scheme ~ The Preservation Trust ~ Historic Buildings in the Town ~ Opening up of M4 and Local Roads ~ Influx of Newcomers ~ Local Reorganisation in 1974: UDC's Loss of Autonomy ~ Avon Rubber ~ Changes in the Town's Industry Patterns

IN 1965 THE COUNCIL FOR British Archaeology, a small but influential body, included Bradford in its list of 51 towns which were considered to be so special that ultimate responsibility for them should be at national level. The Historic Buildings Council was also very concerned at proposals to demolish yet more of Bradford's ancient buildings, many of which were not listed. Fortunately at this point national and local forces came together to create a coherent policy on ways of preserving buildings at risk of demolition:

> *When I think of my early council Minutes, we were always talking about Closing Orders and demolition orders and so on. Then it changed and these orders were being rescinded because places had been done up. It was marvellous. We did lose some – I think we had to lose some – some were no good to keep and some were too far gone. But when the U.D.C. put demolition orders on properties we mostly hoped it would activate someone into doing something. I can clearly remember Barton Orchard, which was only a shell in the 1960s. Another councillor suggested a demolition order was put on it – then it was advertised in the Sunday Times for £1,000 and it sold almost straight away. (DN97)*

These comments by Diana Newman who became the chairman of the Housing Committee of the U.D.C. in 1966 illustrate the gradual changes in public attitudes to conservation which began to emerge in the mid-1960s when concern for Bradford's old buildings came into happy partnership with new sources for substantial funding. Partly through government impetus, the Bradford on Avon Town Scheme was inaugurated in June 1966 to cover approximately four hundred buildings in the centre of the town. Here Bradford was at the forefront of national thinking. The first ever such joint funding Town Scheme had been inaugurated in Bath in 1954, a pioneer initiative set up to deal with the urgent need to regenerate Bath after the severe bombing from the Baedecker Raids of 1942. Bradford was one of the earliest to follow Bath's lead and certainly the first one in Wiltshire. Without such practical and positive work, Bradford would not look anything like it does today. It has now continued to operate for well over thirty years.

Cottages about to be demolished on St. Margaret's Hill in 1965. Their derelict state is very evident. They were replaced by a new complex of retirement flats, as St. Margaret's Court. The road itself was considerably widened as part of the U.D.C. scheme. The neighbouring property on the right, of which a small section can be seen, was in more recent years the home of Mr. and Mrs. Harold Fassnidge. In 1965 this house fronted directly onto the pavement; as a result of the U.D.C. scheme it acquired a small front garden.

Part of the roof and wall of Hall's Almshouses in St. Margaret's Street can just be discerned through the gap at the bottom of the hill.

The Town Scheme is administered by an amalgamation of interested public groups. At the outset the three funding bodies were the Wiltshire County Council (which took the leading role in planning matters) Bradford UDC and the Historic Buildings Council. Two other non-funding bodies were also represented, namely the Wiltshire Historic Buildings Trust and the Bradford on Avon Preservation Trust. When the scheme began, the annual income produced by its funding was about £4,000. The basis of the Town Scheme has been that its Committee should work with the owner of the property under restoration on a 50/50 basis, i.e. the owner would put up 50% of the money and the Town Scheme would then match it. Colin Johns, the County Architectural Adviser in charge of Bradford's Town Scheme from 1974 for twenty years emphasises the massive injections of money this created within the town:

> *From 1967 or so the £4,000 per annum crept up. In 1993, twenty-six years later, English Heritage decided to withdraw from funding in Bradford because in their view Bradford no longer had priority – there were other areas that had a greater need. Bradford had become the victim of its own success. But probably at the peak the funding would have been £30,00 or £40,000 a year. Remember that the owners had to match it pound for pound so the Town Scheme funding was only half the money spent on a property Sometimes we gave less than half because the rules of the scheme meant that you didn't get a Town Scheme grant for anything you were doing which was classified as "improvement". You only got the grant for the building structure – the walls, the roof, the architectural decoration, anything related to keeping the building standing. But you didn't get any money towards a new kitchen or bathroom or sanitary fittings. You could get that kind of money from Housing and the U.D.C. in the normal way. After 1974 West Wilts District Council provided the same sort of funding. (CJ97)*

The first Town Scheme project began in 1966 when a group of humble but significantly placed cottages in Church Street was restored. As this epitomises other major work which followed, it seems worth quoting from Colin Johns' 1991 report (4646E) to W.C.C. in some detail:

> *The first project to be grant aided through the Town Scheme was 9-13 Church Cottages, Church Street. These five houses, though joined together, were each built at different dates, and the difference in style, evolved within a continuous tradition, is combined in a group of considerable interest and scenic value. The earliest building, no. 10, is dated 1697 and was apparently built over part of the Saxon burial ground.*

Beyond the provision of outside conveniences at each end of the group, two indoor taps and one standpipe, the buildings remained virtually in their original condition. The properties were in the hands of the Church, but, by reason of low controlled rents and other restrictions, they had deteriorated by 1960 to a condition which led inevitably to a Closing Order. Following an article and illustration in the Daily Telegraph *the whole property was sold and the new owner set about preparing a rescue scheme. The new owner found the costs of repair far greater than had been anticipated, and at one stage the newly-formed Wiltshire Historic Buildings Trust considered taking on the restoration scheme.*

Eventually grant aid was approved and the work of rehabilitation started in July 1966, being completed in April 1967. There is no doubt that grant aid was vital in securing the repair of these buildings. The successful restoration of Church Cottages was a tribute to the cause of the Town Scheme and it served as a showpiece for future work by the Joint Committee. (CJ91)

THE

CHINA HEN

for

Antique
Furniture
China
Glass
Pottery, etc.

5 WOOLLEY STREET

Bradford-on-Avon 3369

Early Closing Wednesday

We have two Showrooms at this address and one in THE BARN, WHITE HILL for larger pieces of Furniture

VISITORS CORDIALLY WELCOMED

The Preservation Society, which had been so active in earlier debates about the town's future, found in 1962 that there were irreconcilable differences among members as to its future policy. One faction was determined to play an active role in the restoration of buildings and this group, which included Elizabeth Stephenson and Katherine MacKean, formed itself into the Bradford on Avon Preservation Trust. Inaugurated as a Limited Company and Registered Charity, it has steadily involved itself ever since

Advertisement in the town's official guide for the antique shop run by Elizabeth Stephenson and Katherine MacKean, two of the founders of the Preservation Trust.

in the preservation of significant buildings in the town as well as being concerned with local planning matters. Since 1975 it has also played an important role in the landscaping and protection of open spaces in and around the town.

Priory Barn in Newtown, dating from about 1470, became its first project in 1964. It had been bought in a totally ruinous state by Elizabeth Stephenson, who then presented it to the Trust for restoration. It took five years to raise enough funds for the purpose, and townsfolk contributed generously to the appeal. After Lord Methuen opened the part of the building which is now a meeting hall, the remainder of the building was converted into Priory Barn Cottage and sold on a 21-year lease. Another generous gift came in 1970 when Lynchetts, 15 Woolley Street, a distinguished eighteenth and nineteenth century house with a large garden rising up into the hillside above it, was given to the Trust by Mrs. Olga Walker. Four years later, after extensive renovation, this house was sold on a long lease for some £20,000. By this means the Trust achieved a significant amount of working capital which enabled it to take on yet another substantial project. Thus Silver Street House in Silver Street was bought, restored and eventually converted into six flats. This building was opened in 1978 by the Duke of Grafton.

The decaying terrace of four eighteenth century shops at 5 to 8 Market Street, now known as Pippett Buildings, had long been a prominent and depressing symbol of the neglect Bradford's buildings had suffered through so many years. Now, with the money realised on the leasehold sale of the Silver Street House flats, the Preservation Trust was able to buy Pippet Buildings and restore them to their former status. The total cost of this project was £212,000. The amount of voluntary work required to cope with such an ambitious undertaking was, inevitably, prodigious. As with all the Trust's projects, it involved continuous fund raising, coping with the complex and time-consuming business of gathering in grants as well as working with architects and builders to achieve a worthy result. Work was completed in 1982 and the buildings opened by Alec Clifton-Taylor, the eminent architectural historian, later in the same year. By 1983 all four shops and all four flats were sold. Comparison of photographs of these buildings before and after restoration demonstrate the dramatic change thus brought about in the very heart of Bradford. The scheme won a Civic Trust award in 1984.

The Town Scheme ensured that other buildings in the centre of town were getting attention throughout these twenty years. Between 1966 and 1985 over sixty grants were given towards the repair, or part repair, of historic buildings. The first ones to receive aid included 44 St. Margaret's Street , The Liberal Club in St. Margaret's Street and 28 Whitehill. A grant was made towards the Priory Barn restoration. Later beneficiaries were Canterbury House, 10 Silver Street

Pippet Buildings, Market Street, before and after restoration.

completed in 1976; 4 Middle Rank completed in 1978; the Old Baptist Chapel completed in 1980; 7 and 8 The Shambles completed in 1983; 29 Silver Street completed in 1980 and 11 Silver Street, where work began in 1985. All repairs had to be carried out under very close supervision from the architects of the County Council and the Historic Buildings Council for England. Such detailed investigation of inner structures of Bradford's buildings by the experts who were called in to assess restoration work frequently produced new evidence on the antiquity of the centre of the town. Here is part of Colin John's report on 11 Silver Street, which at the time of his investigation had long been established as a dairy. It is now an antique shop:

> *Inspection revealed that it was not a single building but three interlocking structures, the oldest of which dates from the fifteenth century. Hidden behind the front block of the building is a small building with a three-bay hardwood roof, all with pegged joints and curved wind braces. Carpentry repairs were required to this part of the roof structure, although the plan of the building makes access to the upper part of the rear section difficult.*
> *Cost £20,965..... grant £9,857*

Not all requests for Town Scheme funding could be accepted. There was an interesting application from Avon Rubber for financial help in removing the camouflage from its Lamb Factory building which had been painted during the last war to disguise the outline. This application had to be refused.

One of the innovative principles in the Town Scheme was that humble town buildings are as important to a town's heritage as larger, more magnificent ones traditionally seen as worthy of preservation. A private member's Bill, which became the Civic Amenities Act, went through Parliament in 1967. This was the first promotion of what we now know as Conservation Areas: at last the contribution which every building makes to a total townscape was recognised. Colin Johns emphasises the difference this made to Bradford:

> *Right up to the designation of the Conservation Area, much of Bradford was outside local authority control and it was not until the passing of the Town and Country Planning (Amendment) Act of 1972 that demolition in Conservation Areas was brought under local authority control. Until that date if you owned a cottage and you wanted to demolish it and it wasn't actually listed, you were free to do so. Later on, in the early 1970s, when Bradford's historic buildings were resurveyed a lot of buildings were added to the list and became subject to control. (CJ97)*

It must not be assumed from this brief description of changes in attitude towards town regeneration that old Bradford was being transformed at dramatic speed. Change was gradual. But it was losing the aspect of neglect which Peggy Cussins describes on her first visit to the town:

> *My husband was in the Navy and we lived in Weymouth. We came through Bradford in 1959 and I thought it was wonderful. We were looking for a house for £1,000 because I had a little legacy. When the estate agents gave me information about houses, Bradford was never mentioned. I think then there were all these houses that hadn't yet been converted and put up for sale, there were so many tumbledown places. We went on to Bath and we found a little house there. Later on I had reason and opportunity to come back to Bradford with a business partner. We opened a shop, Terracotta, and I've been here and loved it ever since. (PC97)*

In spite of uncertainties in the country's industrial and economic climate, Bradford continued to survive.

> *Avon Rubber was very much a going concern. There was far more*

employment in Bradford in those days than there is now. We could tell what
state the whole country was in by looking out of the window at night. If the
lights were on in Avon Rubber we knew everything was going well. And when
the lights were out at night we knew things throughout the country were not
going so well (UB97)

There was also employment in one flourishing industry unique to Bradford -
a mushroom business just off the Frome Road. Mushrooms had been grown
commercially in Bradford since the 1870s, disused quarries providing ideal
conditions. Agaric, bought by Darlington, a subsidiary of Heinz, in 1970, was
started as far back as 1914 by Mr. Baumann. In the First World War manure for
the mushroom compost was collected from the cavalry stables on Salisbury Plain
and brought over during the hours of darkness. Between the wars enough
mushrooms were cultivated in the dank, dark tunnels of Jones, Poulton and
Bethel Quarries to supply the Cunard liners on their regular crossings to America
with fresh and reliable supplies. Mushrooms could be picked early in the day,
sent by rail to Bristol or London and eaten on board ship, or in hotels and
restaurants, the same evening. By the 1960s, their son, Dink, and his wife Joyce
were giving their lives to running this extensive operation:

I had 40 pickers and we had about 20 part timers, mostly from Fitzmaurice
Grammar school. As long as they were over the age of 16 we were allowed to
employ them. We worked every day and I can assure you we worked Christmas
Day as well. As the mushrooms grew, so you had to pick them. We would go in
at eight o'clock (6-10 on Saturdays and Sundays), stop at 12, started again at
one and work on until five. Now that freezing has come in, they've got a different
way of doing it.

In the early days the mushrooms were grown in grave-like mounds on the
ground; now they're grown in specially made wooden troughs. You had the big
fans at the doors and then they had tubing with holes in it into the quarries,
because mushrooms have to have air. The air was turned around about four
times in a day. You were in the dark of course. They have electricity in there
now but in the old days we had carbide lamps which you held in one hand,
along with your trug and then you picked with the other hand. We used to
make tea in the quarry and if one of the directors came by or Mr. Cottrell, the
Mayor of Bath who used to come round as well, when we were making a cup of
tea with a primus stove, we'd just blow it out and keep quiet and they would
walk past us, they couldn't see us.

It was a good life, a very special world nobody else was in. I don't think the
girls had much social life outside and this was social because you could talk

all the time. There were falls in the quarries where the stone had fallen down, and one of the fellows got up on one of the falls and stuck a pair of Wellington boots upside down so it looked as if someone was stuck there and of course when any new person who went into the quarry for instance, he'd say "that's somebody who couldn't get out". We had a lot of fun in there.

My husband used to go and get the manure from the racing stables at places like Lambourne and Marlborough in two lorries. He'd bring it back to the yard and then it was washed and turned and piled up into great big graves. They'd leave it and then they would wash it and turn it again before it came into the quarries. It didn't really smell, because it was washed. There are new houses now in what used to be our yard. (JB97)

A group of mushroom pickers at work in the Bethel mushroom quarry during the days when the mushrooms were grown in "grave-like mounds". In later years they were grown in troughs at a less backaching level for the pickers. Because this photograph was taken by flashlight, it gives a misleading impression of the amount of light available in the quarry in those days. They worked in much darker conditions, illumination coming from the carbide lamp which each picker held in the same hand with which they carried the trug. Mrs. Joyce Baumann is on the far right. Her husband (Dink) is second from the left.

Like other small towns throughout the country, Bradford still had good range of shops for daily needs, its varied industries and a good railway service. But it was not yet on a wide estate agents' network and it has to be said that various people fresh to the town in the 1960s, were inclined to feel that time had passed it by.

Geoffrey Saxty, came here in the mid 1970s when he was thinking of joining Hilliers, the town's estate agent:

> *My father knew Mr. Hillier... I drove into the town and I thought it was the most undeveloped town I'd seen in West Wiltshire. I was fortunate enough to go round thereafter to all the different towns – Warminster, Westbury, Calne, Trowbridge, Chippenham and see them all. But Bradford seemed to be quietly tucked away, nothing actually happened here, nothing took place; everybody went to work and everybody went home. Then, much later, someone said, "Oh Bradford, what a nice place," and we began to see an influx of people, it was almost like discovering a new town. While Milton Keynes was built, Bradford was discovered. (GS97)*

Some of the earliest incomers to the town were those attracted to the newly converted period dwellings in Tory and Middle Rank:

> *When they did 1-10 Tory it changed the mix of people enormously. It began to attract professional people – nurses and schoolteachers. Original families had to be rehoused, many of them in Churches, the new council estate, and I'm sure they were pleased.*
>
> *Mrs. Tucker was so old and so happy on Tory that she stayed there. After a while she died and her daughters left and then that house was completely redone inside and a family took over. Down at the Conigre end it tended to be mostly single professional women who came in. We had two nurses down there and for a long time our local traffic policewoman had one of the flats. Some of them were privately owned and some were council. Ruby Seton, an artist, had one of the houses, Miss Sergeant who was a teacher at Trowbridge had another. We had very nice neighbours, an architect. Then up in the corner cottage we had a couple of school secretaries and further along the row another architect. Next door was my friend who is a social worker. In the later 1960s and 1970s we were becoming more or less professional people. It was an enormous change; basically the old indigenous cottagers moved out and the middle class moved in. (UB97)*

More of the green areas within the town began to disappear as pockets of land were sold off for housing. For example, semi-detached 3-bedroom houses on the new estate in Church Acre, previously orchard and quarry land between Bearfield Buildings and Winsley Road, were advertised in 1969 for between £3,800 and £4,600. They commanded this relatively high price because, unlike Bradford's old buildings, they could be offered with a 95% mortgage. During the same period, new housing was beginning to appear around the edges of old Bradford. Geoffrey Saxty, who has remained the estate agent in the town he fell in love with, summarises its dramatic expansion over the twenty years:

Mr. Butler owned a house and land along Winsley Road and that's where they built Downs View – constructed in 1965. Then came the development on Church Acre, off Huntingdon Street. If you then go slightly further afield over to Berryfields and Leigh Park, you see more development from 1966 to 1969. There are thirteen different styles of house on the Berryfield estate. We saw this line of development from Downs View to Church Acre to Leigh Park and so the whole of the top of the town changed shape. Where a lot of the building in earlier centuries had been on hillside land, we were now constructing estates on the top of the escarpment, creating modern houses to accommodate the families which were moving into the area.

After that, expansion took place to the southern side of town and English & Continental started to build what we now know as Southway Park. That was begun in 1976 and basically progressed as a series of cleverly constructed cul-de-sacs containing family homes. Fitzmaurice Close was the first and from there Thorner took over the development. Then it was finished off in the early '80s by Barretts. (GS97)

Another major housing development was taking shape on Grove Leaze and Sandy Leaze, once the pasture land for the cows of the Midnight Milkman. In January 1973 plans for twelve houses were approved, each house to have a double garage. Bradford was beginning to appeal to a different kind of homeowner. Where did this new influx come from?

At that particular time the Ministry of Defence had many of its personnel in the locality. When one man moved, three moved. One came out of Bath, someone came up from Plymouth and then someone came down from Rosyth. In those days there was a positive cycle in the M.O.D.. You could see them go from Bath to Plymouth, Chatham or Rosyth; or else Rosyth, Chatham and then down to Plymouth and back up again. I've sold houses for gentlemen who went on that cycle and who finally ended up in the newly built houses of Bradford on Avon. (GS97)

Commercial development in the locality also brought new people into Bradford. As work began on industrial units around Trowbridge, those at managerial level looked for family homes within easy driving distance but not too close to work. Bradford suited them very well. With the later development of the White Horse Business Park this trend continued still further.

So far it seemed that most newcomers to the town had arrived because their employment was in the area. Others arrived almost by chance, often when they were on their way to explore Bath. But new patterns of movement were beginning to emerge. In the mid 1960s, after years of speculation and wrangling, the route of the motorway, the M4 from London to Bristol across Wiltshire, was finally resolved. This 140-mile link between London and Newport, Monmouthshire, via the new Severn Bridge, was expected to be completed by 1971. For over six years the local newspapers continued to report gradual progress as contracts were agreed and completed on the several sections of the M4 through Wiltshire. An interchange, (now Junction 17, but then unnumbered) was planned on the A429 at Stanton St. Quintin. Then in late 1969 came the announcement that a service station on the M4 would be built close by at Leigh Delamere. The *Wiltshire Times*, as unaware as everyone else of what motorway travel would eventually be like, waxed poetic in its vision of the future:

Opposite: Floods in the town: The flood prevention schemes of the early 1960s could not save the town from later freak weather conditions.

Opposite above: Torrential rain through much of the West Country in mid-July 1968 brought serious flooding into the town. In the foreground in St. Margaret's car park is the Public Library portakabin opened on 7 June 1966 when Alderman G. Ward of the County Library Museums Committee ceremonially invited Councillor H. Grant Baker, Chairman of the U.D.C., to borrow a book. This temporary structure, which allowed for a bookstock of 15,000 volumes, continued in use until the new Library was built on the old Swimming Bath site by the river. The new Swimming Bath was opened in its riverside site off St. Margaret's Street in 1971.

Opposite below: The flood in the town centre in 1980 which does not compare with floods earlier in the century when the entire bridge might be under water. Note the industrial drums which have floated downriver. The force of water would suck these under the bridge and then toss them high into the air when they emerged on the other side. Observers say that the noise when this happened was tremendous. St. Margaret's Court retirement flats, recently built, appear in the top left-hand area.

The natural beauty of the area has been fully taken into account in the design and layout of the site...one of the highlights of the service area will be the picnic area, landscaped to make eating there as quiet and as picturesque as in any woodland glade. (WT 10.10.69)

Although it took some years before it became obvious, the M4 and other improved roads began to have an effect upon the town. People who had spent their lives in south-east England and were now looking to retire to peaceful countryside found the West Country offered what they needed – with the advantage that London was now within easy driving distance. House prices were also considerably lower than those nearer to London. Such purchasers who had sold their previous homes could buy old properties without the need of a mortgage and thus Bradford began to experience new kinds of inhabitants – those who arrived not by accident of birth or for employment but because they deliberately chose to settle in Bradford.

The new ease of access and the relative cheapness of old Bradford property also encouraged other kinds of purchasers – those looking for a second home, a part-time rural retreat:

The M4 brought the Londoners. The difference was noticeable almost immediately because they were coming down and buying up the cottages for weekend use. A lot of people didn't like that, they wanted residents. I think it was in the late 70s and 80s that people got really bothered. It was a great period for second homes. I don't think people have second homes in quite that way now. At that time you could buy a second home so cheaply that people could do it: now a second home here would cost you a lot of money. Prices rocketed. We bought our cottage on Tory for £2,250 in 1951 and I sold it for £55,000 in 1985. A year later I was told it was sold again for £90,000. It kept changing hands. Two Londoners bought it from me and then the next year they sold it to another Londoner. (UB97)

People coming in from the Home Counties saw Bradford with a fresh eye. With the energy that a change of home can produce and often with extra money from the sale of their previous properties, some of them set about altering what they found. "People come to Bradford, like it and immediately want to change it" is a constant cry against the incomers. But sometimes such confident "interference" can bring about good results. In the 1950s the Wesleyan Chapel in Coppice Hill, a dramatic building of 1818, was becoming so unsafe that the Wesleyan Methodists who worshipped there had to move into their schoolroom nearby which was converted into a small chapel. By 1973 the Wesleyan Chapel was in danger of vanishing for ever. Peter and Claire Guest, who bought the property immediately above it when they moved out of London, found themselves looking down on the ruin.

> *We are both conservation minded and thought it (the derelict Wesleyan Chapel) added something to the whole hillside, but something had to be done quickly. We bought it and thought of making it an open air theatre and working it in with the Bath Festival, but the parking facilities were not available. Then we decided on a swimming pool because it was so sheltered and very private. (WT 8.4.82)*

Thus the Wesleyan Chapel's splendid façade in Coppice Hill was carefully preserved and is once more a significant part of the townscape, especially when seen from the south side of town. Visitors have no idea that a swimming pool is concealed behind its distinguished exterior. Having saved a bit of old Bradford, Mr. and Mrs. Guest moved on to Buckingham.

Another important building in the town which received over 14 years of dedicated love and restoration from a couple who had come to Bradford from Gerrards Cross was Church House in Church Street. During the war, this splendid building, later described by Pevsner as "stately Georgian", had been taken over by the UDC and eventually turned into five separate flats for evacuees. In the ownership of Guy Underwood, the house was a wreck in 1959 when the Reverend Gordon Green and his wife first saw it and felt it must be saved. Here are some extracts from

The Wesleyan Chapel at the top of Coppice Hill in its heyday. The chapel's schoolroom which became their place of worship is on the right

Gordon Green's own account of the awesome task they set themselves. Before they made an offer for the property, they naturally inspected the interior. The grand entrance hall, the kitchen, in fact every room in the house was in a state of total dereliction:

> *We hardly dare go down into the cellars but eventually plucked up courage. What a sight met our eyes! Hanging from the ceilings of the cellars were literally thousands of grapelike things which we later learned were the homes of spiders. Spiders webs were everywhere and it was a business getting through the various rooms, the windows of the cellar under the main hall were broken and weeds had grown through. The floors had been buried in tons of rubbish and earth, most disconcerting. It had not been occupied for well over five years and had been the playground of vandals. But there was something about the house which drew us to it. (GG97)*

The interior hall of Church House in Church Street after the Reverend Gordon Green and his family had renovated the entire building.

So they bought the house and poured their energies and their private money into its restoration. During the lengthy renovations secret doors to ancient parts of the house came to light and several wells were revealed, usually because things and sometimes people had suddenly disappeared down unexpected holes.

They even discovered a hidden stairway going down to the cellars which led to a passage under the bank next door. Their hard work brought interesting evidence of the many different ways in which the house had been used in its long life. For example the bolts on the chambermaid's bedroom in the attic had been placed on the outside of her door so that she could not get out once the bolts were closed. The wing of the house which had been used as the original bank (which went bankrupt in 1841) still contained an ancient safe, unopened for 150 years. Inside this safe which required the expert skill of the "official safe-breaker for the Dutch government" before it would open, they found another safe, older still, which contained deeds and documents relating to the earliest years of the house, as far back as 1632. Sadly these were loaned to a lady who never returned them and all this history is now lost.

Gordon Green's account demonstrates how he and his family worked hard for Bradford, though not with any particular financial success. He opened up a little wrought iron firm on the premises, which turned into Wiltshire Crafts. The family began a restaurant in one wing and provided a coffee bar to keep the young people off the streets and give them somewhere to go. This met with some local opposition. In 1972 it was time to sell:

> *Time was running out for me, so we decided to sell up and move to a small house. The house agents thought we would get at least £40,000 for it, but when the day came it had been snowing and few turned up at the auction with the result that it was withdrawn. Later I sold it for £25,000. It was then sold later for about £54,000 and later still for over £200,000 I understand. Obviously I sold too soon. Life at Church House for 14 years was good but hard work. I am proud to have saved what was a derelict wreck of a place. May subsequent owners of the house put as much love and care into Church House as I and my family did in rescuing it from what may well have been a sad end. (GG97)*

There has always been a wide range of churches, going back to the late eighteenth century and the growth of nonconformist worship. This active part of Bradford life has continued through the twentieth century. After the Reverend Stella Sivyour came to be minister at the Congregational church in 1964, she suggested that the Free Church Federal Council should approach Holy Trinity, Christ Church, the Catholic Church and the Quakers with a view to setting up a series of meetings where the churches could discuss their origins and different forms of worship. From this developed the Bradford Council of Churches, the beginning of ecumenical worship in the town. This is now called Bradford Area Churches Together. United services are held with all the various Churches taking part. In the winter they provide hot meals on Sundays for the homeless and a

Kids Club in the holidays.

In 1972 the Congregational Church in St. Margaret's Street became the United Reformed Church with the union of the Congregational and Presbyterian Churches in England. Two years later the Methodists left their little chapel in Coppice Hill and began to hold joint services in the United Reformed Church. In 1976 the two churches decided to work, worship and witness together as one church and finally on 1 January 1981 they became the United Church. Their building benefited from the Town Scheme when it was found that the church roof needed retiling. As the church is in the Conservation Area, permission was needed before any work could be done. Renovation and improvements were estimated at £32,000. This was an enormous amount for the church members to find but with many original fund raising schemes, and a substantial grant from the Town Scheme, this was achieved.

Continuing increase in traffic through the town encouraged the County Council and the U.D.C. in their own road widening schemes. For example Ashley Road, previously a little country lane, was widened, after many delays, in the early 1970s, the increasing traffic to St. Laurence School making this a priority. Its junction with the Bath Road was also improved by the County Council. The narrow entrance of Winsley Road into Bath Road had proved to be a particular hazard. To answer the problem, a new junction was created by cutting through the grounds of Brunswick House. Winsley Road as far as The Rising Sun was also widened – the eighteenth century row of cottages on the north side of the road losing half their front gardens in the process. The original entrance to Winsley Road is now a *cul-de-sac* called Church Lane and it seems almost unbelievable that until the 1970s double-decker buses had to negotiate this bottleneck in what was then a two way street. More of Winsley Road from Huntingdon Street to the U.D.C. boundary with Winsley was also nearly doubled in width. Springfield was yet another new road, speeding up the traffic and opening up the possibilities of building on Kingsfield Grange land. Bradford roads began to take on the appearance they have today.

Pedestrians were also having trouble: no longer was it possible to saunter down the centre of St. Margaret's Street or Market Street. How different it was from the 1930s! In those days the bottom of Market Street between The Shambles and the bridge roundabout was called Horse Street. Romance had blossomed between the butcher, Bert Scrine, whose double-fronted shop was on The Swan's side of this narrow space, and Edie Baxter, the lady in the Co-op cake shop which was then directly opposite. This interesting state of affairs must have enlivened many shoppers' daily routine, and no doubt in those far-off days their courtship could be conducted in some tranquillity even in business hours. When they married, they set up a restaurant and tearoom in The Three Gables, a rare

The Co-op on the corner of Church Lane and the Bath Road stands forlornly empty after its long and busy life. The Slade family had run their grocery business in these premises for many years, keeping the upstairs as their living quarters. In the early 1920s the entrance to the shop was on the curved side of the building, the original filled-in doorway still being evident in this photograph. Mr. Slade sold the business to the Co-op and it remained in their possession until demolished. The Bath Road was then widened, using some of the available space, the two houses on the other side of Church Lane also losing some garden for the same purpose. The entrance to Church Lane is now pedestrian only.

move for Bradfordians from one side of the river to the other.

Jack Stafford also recalls working in Horse Street somewhere between 1930 and 1933 on the side walls of the building at the foot of Market Street:

> *We were working for Frank Andrews, painting the top windows of what was then the Post Office building in Horse Street. To get to the top gables we had two long ladders tied together and to get the right angle the ladder was about two feet out into the roadway with a man standing on the bottom rung. Only one car at a time could get past. But then there was nothing much coming past anyway. That little shop in the side wall of The Swan was a quite a busy butchers at the time. You wouldn't have called it the wrong side of the road in those days. No traffic problem at all. (JS97)*

But by 1969 the pace of life had undoubtedly changed. The *Wiltshire Times* announced:

> *The U.D.C. has placed about a dozen kerbstones from the corner of the vehicle scarred Swan Hotel up Market Street. The effect has greater visibility for pedestrians going from Church Street to the Shambles. (WT 11.2.69)*

Cars were certainly becoming part of ordinary life. Some of the steepest parts of Masons Lane were levelled out and a high wall removed on the sharp bend opposite Newtown to improve visibility for motorists. The long established Knees shop at the junction of Silver Street and Market Street (familiarly known as Knees Corner) was demolished for the same reason. Cottages were pulled down above Tory so that U.D.C. garages could be built for nearby residents. As deliveries from shops decreased, residents had to find other ways of getting their heavy shopping home.

> *Gradually by degrees from the middle '60s we got less and less delivered. In the end it was only the milk. We lost Nichols and Bushell (now a public house, The Dandelion) and that's when it hit us. It was a wonderful grocer who sent a man up every week for your order and then sent the groceries up. A real old fashioned grocer who'd say "I've got a nice cut of ham I know you'd like". Come the 70s these old fashioned services began to disappear. I got a council garage which was near St. Mary Tory. Then I could hump my shopping down the steps and go along a path at the back of Tory and in the back door. But it was still down three flights of stairs to the kitchen. (UB97)*

The 1970s brought further changes to the town. One was the transformation of Barton Farm into a Country Park when, in 1971, Wiltshire County Council bought this ancient farm, its buildings and land from Sir Charles Hobhouse, whose family had been its owners for generations. The Countryside Commission gave a grant of 75% towards the cost of the land. One of the first grants to be made throughout the whole country by this newly formed body, this indicates yet again that Bradford on Avon was gaining even more national attention. The great fourteenth century Tithe Barn had received public notice as long ago as 1914 when the Hobhouse family had handed it over to the Wiltshire Archaeological Society. The society undertook to repair the structure, which at that time was in a very poor condition. But only the most necessary repairs could be made during the Great War, and the building had continued to deteriorate until it was presented to the Ministry of Public Building and Works in 1939. Its most major restoration took place over a ten-year period, being completed in 1960, and thus, 11 years later, was handed over in a good state of repair:

> The entire roof had been taken off, and every single timber inspected, and where necessary renewed. The north west wall had been taken down and photographed for any damage, and under the north centre wall 80 tons of concrete had been sunk for support. At that point there were found to be no foundations at all. The walls had "bowed" out about a yard, and had sunk about nine inches. The roof had been re-lathed and retiled, and the windows were to have perspex inserted to keep birds out. (WT 22.7.60)

It is only when one stands inside this 168 feet long building, that the enormity of these renovations, especially those on the roof, become fully apparent. Alec Clifton-Taylor emphasised its grandeur in his programme 'Six More English Towns' which was broadcast on television in 1981:

> Bradford's Tithe Barn is one of the most spectacular in England. It is larger than many churches with its massive oak roof with three tiers of oak windbraces. Its roof is one of the great sights of Bradford, stone slates in their thousands on an unusually steep pitch.

Retiling such a roof is no mean achievement. Later the Tithe Barn was transferred into the safe keeping of English Heritage and its condition has been carefully monitored and maintained ever since. Now the building has returned to being one of the glories of Bradford and a fitting centre piece for the Country Park itself.

The Wiltshire Historic Building Trust took over Barton farmhouse, its farmyard and all the surrounding farm buildings, none of which was in such good state of repair as the Tithe Barn itself. The Historic Buildings Trust restored the Granary Barn, recouping the cost of the work in the subsequent sale of the entire complex. After some work on the farmhouse, this was sold, together with the farmyard and all other associated buildings to a private purchaser. But the Tithe Barn remained in public hands and Farmer Chard's cows continued to graze the land until he retired. Then for Bradfordians, who had always felt free to wander the Barton Farm fields, the major change was in the loss of the animals, some sixty or seventy head of cattle. Not only were the fields now empty but the pigsties and cowsheds, or skillins, to use the local word, were turned into the little shops and showplaces which are with us today. Sadly the little Victorian dairy which stood alongside the farmhouse was later demolished.

Throughout this period, the Kennet and Avon Canal alongside the Country

Above: Three generations of the Chard farming family in the 1920s: Joseph Chard, his son Ernest "Joe" Chard and his granddaughter, Hilary;
Left: The interior of the Tithe Barn before its restoration. At this stage, extra timbers were needed to secure the roof.

The Tithe Barn and the stack yard when it was a working area.

Park remained unnavigable in spite of the vigorous campaign by the Inland Waterways Association, which had been formed with the avowed intention of restoring the near-derelict system of canals throughout the country. The Kennet and Avon branch was one of the first to be formed. But the canal's condition had continued to deteriorate, especially on the section between Winsley bridge and the Avoncliff aqueduct. Due to the steep incline of the hill and its unstable composition, this part of the canal had given trouble ever since it was first opened in 1810. Now part of the section had subsided and had been partly drained. However the towpath was still in place and inhabitants remember the wealth of wild life and bird song which could be enjoyed along its peaceful banks. It would take some 25 years to bring the canal back into full operation although the band of canal enthusiasts determined to do so was already at work. The restoration of the lock gates on the great flight of locks at Caen Hill, Devizes began in 1969.

This same year saw the contract signed for the development of a considerable number of council flats on Budbury, the site which had aroused so much public controversy back in 1945 when the U.D.C. wanted to reduce the housing waiting list quickly by building prefabs on the area. Now, with the caution of hindsight, a careful and scientific excavation was organised over eight weeks in the summer of 1969. Budbury Circle was found to be a fort, built sometime in the Iron Age (600BC-100AD), yielding good quality Iron Age pottery, clay sling missiles and many domestic remains. A great many spindle whorls and part of a big clay loom weight also came to light, demonstrating the length of time that the making of cloth has been part of local industry.

Mr. Peter Donaldson and his students also managed to excavate the central part of the site which turned out to be a rectangular enclosure with rounded corners.

> *The remainder of the fortress probably stretched across towards Wine Street on the south-western slope of the hill. Natural defences were used to the south and west, and to the north and south they built a ditch and bank complex. The rounded shape of the bank would have given rise to the very natural original theory of a barrow. (WT 1.8.69)*

Perhaps Guy Underwood would have felt his enthusiastic misreading of his earlier excavation was justified.

There were rumblings of a different kind of controversy through the late 1960s and early 1970s while plans were being made across the whole of the country for a vast shake-up in the organisation of local government. In 1969 there was public horror, vehemently expressed, at the Redcliffe-Maude Commission's proposals which recommended that some West Wiltshire towns should be merged into a new unitary authority with Bristol and Bath. U.D.C. Minutes from Council meetings throughout this period make it clear that yoking Chippenham, Trowbridge, Melksham and Bradford into one organisation along with part of Somerset and with Bristol was not an option Bradford or its fellow Wiltshire towns was prepared to accept. The proposals were rejected. Bristol and Bath found themselves unwilling partners in the new county of Avon in 1974 but Bradford became part of West Wiltshire District Council.

This new administrative system was to have a far-reaching effect on every town throughout the country. Bradford, for example, still had its Town Council, but this had much more limited powers than its predecessor. Instead of being one small unit, an Urban District Council whose councillors lived and worked within its vicinity, Bradford was now amalgamated into one District Council together with six other different local authorities These were four neighbouring Urban District Councils – Melksham, Trowbridge, Warminster and Westbury; and two Rural District Councils – Bradford & Melksham (including Winsley and Atworth) and Warminster & Westbury.

It seems that a decision was made to pool the individual assets of the seven previous Councils. Thus Westbury House, for example, became the property of the West Wiltshire District Council (W.W.D.C.) and even St. Margaret's Hall was handed over, though later retrieved. This arrangement was not followed by all other District Councils in Wiltshire where individual towns retained their local, potentially money raising, assets, for future use. For example, Devizes still kept its Corn Exchange and did not hand it over to Kennet District Council. Nor did the new District Council of North Wiltshire receive any town assets from Wootton Basset or from Chippenham which kept its Borough Fields under its own control. Perhaps it was assumed in West Wiltshire that pooling assets would simplify administration. But it has produced its own set of complications. St. Margaret's Hall was originally handed over, then its management was returned to the Town Council: currently it is once more in the administration of Direct Leisure, the contractual arm of the W.W.D.C..

Planning for the change had been in progress over the previous two years. Generally it was felt that the seven Councils settled down together reasonably well, keen to make the new system work. But inevitably every one of those Councils suffered a loss of its traditional autonomy, and local town personalities, familiar to all and fully committed to Bradford's specific needs, were no longer totally in charge of its future. Now the overall requirements of the much larger District were paramount. The repercussions of such a radical change became ever more significant as the twentieth century wore on and are discussed more fully in the final chapter.

The immediate result, visible to all, was the change at Westbury House. This

Above: Officers and councillors at thr final meeting of the Bradford Urban District Council when it was disbanded in 1974. The mayor in the centre of the row nearest the camera is Colonel Dudley Smith.

Left: Abbey House, Church Street, while still in the occupation of the Bradford and Melksham Rural District Council.

building had been the U.D.C. premises ever since those stormy meetings back in 1911. Now Westbury House was sold and the Town Council took up residence in the annex beside it in Westbury House gardens. Bradford and Melksham Rural District Council left Abbey House in Church Street and the new West Wiltshire District Council was settled in custom-built premises, already finished, in Bradley Road, Trowbridge. However Bradford's Town Scheme stayed firmly in place, the principle by now having been extended to other Wiltshire towns:

> In 1974 the County Council carried on funding Town Schemes, the W.W.D.C. took over part funding, and new Town Councils were invited to participate. As time has gone on it is the Town Councils and the District Councils that have put in the lion's share of the money because it was more in their own interests to do so. In 1996 Bradford Town Council put in about £6,000 entirely for use in the town. (CJ97)

The value of a designated Conservation Area in a town also became more fully appreciated. Until a town had a Conservation Area there was no control over demolition unless the buildings were individually listed:

> When Fitzmaurice Grammar School closed in 1980 it was realised that the old building wasn't included on the list of buildings of special and architectural interest. With no such protection it could have been pulled down there and then, there was no control over it whatsoever. It was outside the Conservation Area and unfortunately what this meant was that there were VAT benefits in pulling it down. The Preservation Trust tried very hard to get the building listed, but the investigator who came from London looked at it and said well, it's just an ordinary Victorian building. The arguments about its importance as part of the social development of Bradford didn't persuade him that it was worth listing so he declined to list it. Eventually, in order to preserve the building, the W.W.D.C. decided in 1984 that the best thing was to extend the Conservation Area because once this was done then demolition could be controlled. So extending the Conservation Area persuaded the people who developed the Fitzmaurice Place retirement apartments that the school building was worth keeping. (CJ97)

While some solutions to local difficulties could be found, Bradford faced other problems, some of which were common across the entire country. For example, the year 1982 did not start well. There was severe winter weather throughout January and snow clearance work was continuous in West Wiltshire from 6 January for three exhausting weeks. The maximum daytime temperature on 13

January was minus 8.6 degrees C and the minimum night-time temperature was minus 17.5 degrees C, the lowest figures since records began and well below those of the disastrous winter of 1963. To compound the misery, there were national rail strikes and the entire rail system was shut down for two days in mid-January.

Newspaper reports at the time are full of stories of troubles brought about by these bitter weather conditions. The steep streets of the town were inevitably impassable as had happened many times in its past history. But we also get some indication of how life had changed since that memorable winter nearly twenty years previously. In 1963 many people had struggled to work on foot. But by 1982 getting to the workplace would probably mean going by car. W.W.D.C. tried with snowploughs and diggers to keep local roads open, but with little success:

> *Compared with the winter of 1962-3, the most significant difference was the volume of traffic, 80% higher now than then, with consequential damage to roads less able to carry the burden. Kerbside overnight parking and abandoned vehicles caused many problems. (WT 15.1.82)*

A lorry, fortunately without a heavy load, which crashed into a building in Market Street in August 1982. Only one of the many accidents on the steep hill. Opposite is the shop belonging to Dible and Roy who subsequently moved to larger premises in Bridge Street. (Photo reproduced by kind permission of Bath Chronicle)

With such a huge growth in traffic movement, it is not surprising that this period in Bradford's history becomes dominated by efforts to keep Bradford's streets open to vehicles and yet safe for pedestrians. Juggernauts of up to 40 tonnes were regularly passing over the town bridge, negotiating the Market Street turn with varying levels of success. In February 1982, the Town Council met the M.P. Dennis Walters to enlist his support for solving the town's traffic problems. The conclusion was that:

> ...*a bypass is necessary...but immediate action is needed as irreparable damage will be done in the meantime. At least 4 premises already damaged quite considerably by physical impact have been refused insurance coverage, one in the region of £10,000. A lot of heavy traffic also comes through Bradford, as a short cut to the motorway. (WT 5.2.82)*

Wiltshire County Council announced:

> *Plans for a bypass are in the W.C.C.'s forward programme for the next 10 years. It is one of the schemes that perhaps has more of a priority than others. (WT 6.8.82)*

In the same summer there was a series of dramatic accidents on Masons Lane and in Market Street. Firstly a lorry careered out of control down the 1 in 7 hill and smashed into Rodway & Green, solicitors, near the bottom; in July a car burst into flames at the foot of the hill after brake failure; and in August a runaway mechanical digger crashed into buildings in Masons Lane, causing thousands of pounds of damage. Other years could produce a list of similar events There were even more urgent calls for something to be done. A W.C.C. spokesman reaffirmed that a bypass was in place in County planning but stressed it was not likely to happen until 1991. Fortunately townspeople did not hold their breath for the next nine years. They waited to see what would happen next.

Opposite: An overall view of the town centre taken in late 1966 and showing the medieval jumble of buildings on the north side of the river. The size and complexity of the rubber factory site is very apparent. The old Swimming Baths in Bridge Street are still there, but the houses in St. Margaret's Hill on the south side of the river have been demolished, opening up some empty space soon to be filled with garages and St. Margaret's Court.

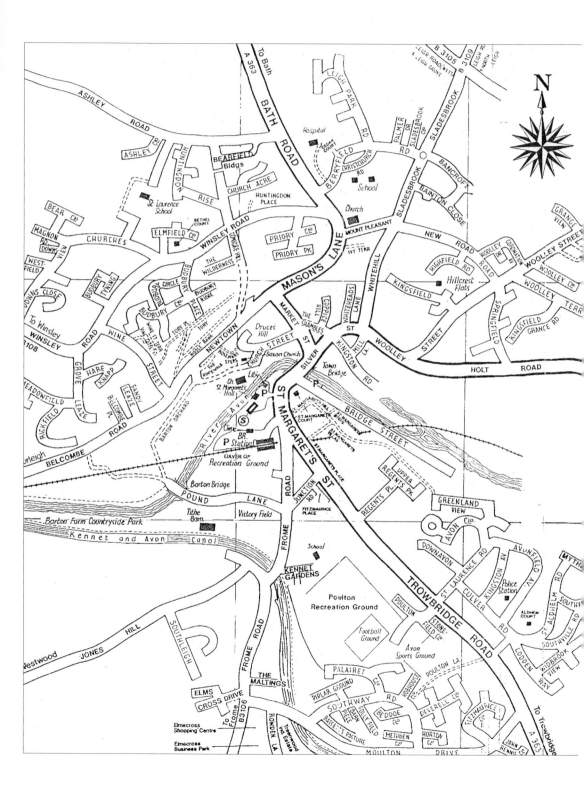

CHAPTER SEVEN

1986 -1997
The Old Order Changeth, Yielding Place to New

The Bypass Scheme ~ Recession and Closures ~ Avon Rubber Ceases Production in Bradford ~ Kingston Mill and Problems with Redevelopment ~ Town Entertainments ~ The Community Play ~ Incomers and Housing ~ Llewellen Palmer Trust ~ The Growth of Tourism ~ Retirement Apartments ~ Employment and Commuting ~ Looking Back at the Past and Forward to the Future.

HOW TO SORT OUT TRAFFIC HAS been a constant preoccupation in Bradford's affairs. The A363 through the centre of town, the ancient narrow town bridge and the steep hills on the north side of the river have never offered any easy answers. The huge growth in numbers of cars and heavy lorries in the late 1980s caused the Town Council to propose one possible solution to the problem – namely a one-way system around the town. The scheme was to route all traffic up Market Street and Masons Lane, along Mount Pleasant, New Road and Springfield and back down the Holt Road and Silver Street. It was argued that this would speed up the flow of traffic which would then be through the town and out of the way much more quickly.

Not everyone accepted this proposal, the residents of New Road finding it particularly unappealing. Another argument against it, one which has continued to gather force in the last years of the twentieth century, was that by encouraging traffic flow, more vehicles would come into the town and aggravate the heavy use of the bridge. At a public meeting in St. Margaret's Hall called by the Town Council in 1988, strong opposition to the one-way system caused the scheme to be dropped.

Creating a bypass to the town had long been the ideal solution and now a Bypass Committee of local residents began to press more urgently for this as a means of relief to the town's escalating traffic problems. Martin Davies was part of that group:

Our policy was to work with the authorities as much as we possibly could – Town Council, District Council, County Council and if necessary central Government. About 1988/9 we actually saw a plan, a route which was to us a perfectly reasonable one, going east round the town. It was single carriageway and 7 metres wide which is the normal, standard width for a small local road. But the cost was enormous, estimated at £4 or 5 million, most of which was for building a new bridge over the railway and the river. The Bradford bypass kept slipping down the County's priority list because other bypasses were considered more important or less costly – or both. But we really thought that the proposed realignment of the Staverton bridge would go ahead. And that would have helped towards the bypass.

When it became public news that the Government was planning a Batheaston bypass our question was what happens when that traffic gets to Bathford. Does it all come down the A363 and through Bradford? The Department of Transport's answer was that it would go round Bradford to the east and that would be your bypass. But I was unhappy with this. To have a small bypass is one thing; to have an enormous dual carriageway very near the town is quite a different matter and probably it would not serve as a bypass for the town at all. (MD2/97)

The public enquiry into the building of the Batheaston bypass was held in 1990 and, after immense argument and protest, the road was operational by 1996. During this period anxieties and negotiations over the proposed A36 East of Bath to Beckington route, the Department of Transport trunk road which would lock into the Batheaston bypass and have a profound effect on Bradford, were constant. The A36 Beckington bypass was already in place. Many saw it as inevitable that the missing section, east of Bradford and north of Trowbridge, would follow. But nothing is certain in this world. There was a general public change of mood and a growing campaign against the endless building of more and more roads, most violently expressed by groups who physically held up construction by taking up residence in trees and tunnels on site. The Government was also very short of money. A change of government policy followed and the A36 East of Bath to Beckington road was cancelled.

But, quite separately, something significant was achieved by the town's persistence. For the first time ever a weight limit on the bridge was introduced. This was only achieved by tremendous pressure being exerted at a County Council meeting by a determined consortium of Bradford traders and residents who came together to insist that something must be done. Evidence of the need for some positive measure came from the survey which detailed the kind of traffic interfering with ordinary life in Bradford:

Above: A typical scene in the 1980s on the town bridge. A two-axle lorry meets a three-axle articulated lorry carrying Avon Rubber materials.

Below: When an articulated lorry meets a Badgerline bus in Silver Street, mounting the pavement is the only solution.

In 1990 we did a very thorough survey of traffic crossing the bridge: we analysed and categorised it. We did the same survey on two separate days, and they more or less coincided. There were around 13,000 vehicles in the 12 hours from 7.30am to 7.30pm on each day. Of those, 80 were certainly over 16 tons, nearly all articulated lorries. If it's got three axles it's almost certainly over 16 tons. (MD2/97)

Vicki Landell Mills, who as a County Councillor represented Bradford at this meeting made it clear that it would be impossible to return to Bradford without something having been achieved which would improve an intolerable situation. At the end of a lengthy and seemingly intractable meeting, the County Council agreed to put a weight limit of 17 tons on Bradford town bridge:

As a result of that meeting anything with three axles – all the articulated lorries – were now banned. People still complain, but they have forgotten what it was like. You may get two or three huge vehicles a day now. But it was eighty articulated lorries a day and they'd meet head on on the bridge. (MD2.97)

There were other matters to worry about in the early 1990s which were not a good time in Bradford's economic history. Once again the town mirrored the problems of the entire country where recession was biting deep. Houses seemed impossible to sell, the inflated prices of the late 1980s had collapsed and "negative equity" was the phrase which politely disguised serious financial hardship. Geoffrey Saxty, the town's estate agent, summarises the situation:

We had this great surge in the property market and we saw prices soar and soar in the late 80s. And I don't doubt that by 1989 the whole market had blown itself out completely. And with interest rates going up to 15% , the Gulf War and the withdrawal of the Ministry of Defence people the whole place went in total recession.

In that decline I think one of the great shames – old-fashioned of me – was to see the Co-op disappear. Simply because it was like a little honeycomb. People buzzed in and out and it was a centre. If you want places to develop you need central places like that. (GS97)

The range of individual shops throughout the town which were part of the Co-op network had been very extensive, especially in the first half of the century. Members of the Co-op gained "a divi" on their purchases and could buy anything the family needed in one or other of the many local Co-op shops. For example there was a Co-op butcher, a grocer and a draper in the Shambles; a Co-op boot

The Co-op grocery in Silver Street not long before its closure. The site is now a range of shops, one with a flourishing little café.

& shoe shop and a separate men's outfitters in St. Margaret's Street and a Co-op bakery in Whitehill which in the 1920s and 1930s had also contained a Penny Bank and a meeting room upstairs for the Co-op Club. At one time they had a furniture shop (now a teashop) at the bottom of Silver Street near the town bridge. They also delivered coal. Their large stables, now a private house, were in Whiteheads Lane. The Co-op even arranged trips by charabanc to Weston super Mare in the 1930s and sometimes put on a Co-op train which ran from Westbury and through other local stations to collect children whose parents were members of the Co-op for a trip to the seaside. By 1990 only the grocery shop at the bottom of Silver Street remained and local residents fought hard to keep alive this last little bit of a previous empire, organising petitions and telephoning the Head Office, seeking reprieve, but with no success.

One shop which finally closed down in 1986 was Christopher's, the chemists which had been founded in 1863 and on the same premises in Silver Street since 1908. With the positive involvement of Miss Angela Christopher, some enlightened people retained and stored the entire fittings and contents of its fascinating interior. There was no town museum already in place to display this special piece of Bradford's past. But with a new library in the planning stage, there was now further impetus to create a town museum. This finally happened

Christophers Chemist shop in Silver Street which R.T. Christopher took over from Norris in 1908. Its contents now form the central display in the Museum which is housed in the Library building in Bridge Street. The Museum is an independent charitable trust and is run by unpaid volunteers with the help of grants, donations and subscriptions of members of the Museum Society.

when the new library was built on the old swimming bath site in 1990.

Not only shops but also businesses which had been significant sources of local employment for as long as most people could remember also closed The mushroom business in Bethel Quarry, Frome Road was one. Some 40 people lost their jobs and the compost making yard in the Frome Road eventually became another site for housing. But Bethel Quarry was reopened some time later as a much smaller operation. It still sells mushrooms within the locality.

The most serious closure came from Avon Rubber in the Autumn of 1991 when they announced that they would be ceasing production in their Bradford factory. Its administrative offices had long been based in the splendid Abbey Mill, originally built as a cloth mill in 1875 and dominating the down-river view from the town bridge. The two sites, once vacant, would be sold. This was devastating news. The manufacture of rubber had been in Bradford since 1848 and had swiftly become the most significant industry in the town. Generations of Bradford men and women had worked there on the astonishing range of goods produced during its long history. Many men had clocked up 51 years of service, joining at 14 and retiring at 65. No women seemed to have achieved the same total, their continuous record in work being traditionally interrupted by marriage, childbirth and caring for relatives.

Three members of the Vennell family began working for Spencer Moulton as long ago as 1850 and they with their descendants are on record as having achieved a combined service of 900 years. Members of the family to the fifth generation are still working at Avon Rubber, Melksham to this day. The longest serving was Bob Vennell (1870-1932) who started work at the age of 10, combining work at the factory with being valet to Stephen Moulton himself.

Mrs. Holbrook, born Lily Banks, worked at Spencer Moulton for some 20 years: her husband, "Woppit" Holbrook, was employed there for all his working life. She describes something of the complex nature of family relationships among the workforce:

> *My mother worked there, and <u>her</u> father had worked there. Their name was Viles and a lot of the Viles worked for Spencer Moulton. Some of my father's family, the Bankses, they worked down there. Then there were the Vennells who were my husband's people. Auntie Lil, she used to work there, and Auntie Agnes – that's my husband's mother's sister – she was a forewoman down there. My husband and, to start with, his two brothers were there. My daughter was the fourth generation to work there and my granddaughter she was in the laboratory and her husband works in the laboratory over at Melksham as well. There were the Vileses and the Bankses and the Vennells and the Holbrooks, and they all intermarried and worked in Spencer Moulton and Avon Rubber.*
>
> *My husband worked his way up and became a production manager but when he was quite young, his uncle Vennell locked him out one morning because he was late for going in at 6 o'clock. Fancy! His uncle! My husband was a foreman when my mother worked down there. When he come over to see me, my mother said to him "Ah, you've made me cry many a time". But my husband was a real Holbrook and he always said, "A spade's a spade and when I know I'm right, I'm right, there's no mucking about." Of course he had to time them on piece work and they didn't like that, but he was fair, no doubt about it. (LH97)*

The closure was not unexpected for it was well understood that developments in modern production methods were difficult to implement on the Bradford site. While ever larger transport vehicles could be accommodated at Melksham, the narrow, intricate streets of Bradford made access to the factory site ever more difficult. By the time the last workers left in 1994 the long and difficult quest for positive means to regenerate the site and take Bradford into the twenty-first century had already begun.

Avon Rubber continued to manufacture in much the same ways as Spencer Moulton, making intricate mouldings for the aircraft and automotive industries as well as for the railway. They specialised in large extrusions for the engineering industry and a variety of reinforced hoses. Here we see workers filling moulds as part of the complicated processes required for the finished product.

Abbey Mill and its related buildings in Church Street became another development for retirement apartments, and began selling in 1997. But the difficult question of the future use of the Kingston Mill site has continued to reverberate around the town. Everyone had different ideas and, indeed, the Town Council went out of its way to canvass public opinion. One obvious way of developing the land along the river was seen, especially by Avon Rubber, as the provision of a supermarket and quality houses although there was strong feeling throughout the town that community and employment needs were more important. In the event, Avon Rubber and their partners were unable to find a supermarket operator who felt that Kingston Mill was a suitable site. Inevitably some of the factors which had caused Avon Rubber to cease production remained just as awkward whatever new schemes were put forward. In particular there was the difficulty of access for modern vehicles of commercial size. The National Rivers Authority also had its own constraints to impose: no construction should take place below the highest flood level of the previous one hundred years. Not even a car park could be allowed on such land. From a developer's point of view, the attractive and substantial 5.5 acres was thus dramatically decreased in usable size and therefore in potential.

There was also the question of what should be done with the buildings already there. For the purpose-built industrial units from the 1960s and 1970s demolition was not a significant problem. But what about the range of nineteenth century buildings on the site, including those which were listed for preservation? Should they all be preserved as part of the town's heritage and regenerated in new ways? The thick walls and floors of some of these buildings were impregnated with carbon black which would be expensive, perhaps impossible, to remove. The ground on which they stood had absorbed nearly 150 years of chemical usage – creating another concern expressed by the National Rivers Authority, anxious that no pollution should enter the river. If no developer was prepared to take over the whole site, how could the site be split up? Most crucially of all, who would produce the vast amount of funding necessary for any regeneration?

Various initiatives have been promoted, but eventually rejected. The most ambitious scheme was created through Bradford 2000. This body had been working for several years on ways to ensure that re-use of the site should generate sources of employment and activity to boost the long-term vitality of the town centre. It was also concerned to save those buildings with character and historic importance from further decay. The Town Council had already funded, in 1995, an objective study by the Urban and Economic Development Group which had reinforced the views of the community that what Bradford desperately needed was the development of opportunities for local employment.

The next move was an application for funding made by Bradford 2000 to the Millennium Commission,[1] based on partnership with Bath University which had become positively engaged in plans to develop two thirds of the site for its post-graduate students. The one third nearest to Silver Street, known as the Lamb's Yard Centre, was left to the town's initiative. This New Mills Partnership, as it came to be called, raised high hopes among the many townsfolk who worked on its presentation. Avon Rubber, the Town Council, the Chamber of Commerce, Moulton Estates and the Preservation Trust as well as the District and County Councils were involved. At last there was a coherent scheme for the entire site which could bring about new forms of work and opportunities in the heart of the town, create new cultural and leisure facilities, establish a centre of higher education and research, provide public open spaces and riverside walks in a town which was becoming more and more of a tourist centre.

The application, which took as its theme Design and Innovation and brought together art and computer technology in innovative and commercially productive ways, was turned down by the Millennium Commission. A vast sum of many millions of pounds had been allocated to the Millennium Centre in Greenwich, London and so the five million pounds (a modest wave in this financial ocean) which was all that was needed to reinvigorate the life of Bradford was just not available. By early 1997, when this decision was made public, the disappointment felt around the town can easily be imagined. By then much of the site had been empty for over five years. However Avon Rubber, loath to relinquish totally its association with the town, had restored one fine building on the site, Manvers House, as its Head Office. A group of other factory buildings was demolished, creating a large open space which it was agreed would make a magnificent Town Square. But, at the time of writing, some buildings remain, carbon black and lifeless, waiting to be given a positive use which will take Bradford into the twenty-first century.

The blackened entrance to the Lamb Yard at Avon Rubber in 1992. A motorised extractor fan inside the main building sucked out air which was laden with carbon dust from the factory floors above. The tubular metal duct from the first floor of the main building then carried carbon black dust down into the large container on the left. This device was demolished after 1994.

But not everything was gloom at the beginning of the 1990s. Bradford was creating its own community play, an ambitious venture which came to involve a large majority of the town in one way or another. Such community efforts were not new in a town which has a long tradition of creating its own entertainment in some style. Coronations and royal occasions were celebrated in the ways described in Chapter 1. In the earlier parts of the century town events were enhanced by floral arches across the main streets. Every summer would bring a fête at the Hall; both the Liberal Club in St. Margaret's Street and the Conservative Club (now the Riverside public house) held flower shows, each being followed by a public dance in the evening

Processions through the town, for events of all kinds were also quite frequent and could include elaborate floats, each decorated by an enthusiastic group from a local firm. Sometimes the final point would be Priory Park, above Newtown or, for the Rogation Sunday procession from Christ Church and Holy Trinity, the destination would be Barton Farm. The special Sunday School Anniversary children's services and their processions have already been mentioned in Chapter 3 and were significant features on the town's calendar for over fifty years. Jo Uncles can remember when the Congregational Church (now United Church) was full with children (upstairs and down) for the Sunday afternoon service. She also remembers going through the town on hot Sunday afternoons from St. Margaret's Street with fifty or more children to walk up Conigre to Zion Baptist Chapel and also up to Bearfield Congregational and then back again. For King George V's Silver Jubilee in 1935, the children all had to meet at their various Sunday Schools and then they marched to the Victory Field with their Sunday School banners where they were presented with Silver Jubilee mugs.

In 1963 there had been an Elizabethan Festival week, funded by the U.D.C. People from all over the town had taken part, putting on different events in various places around the town. Whole families dressed up in Elizabethan costume and processed through the town in the normal Bradford way to the central venue, which was the lavish Fair in Culver Close.

So when the Colway Theatre Trust, a charity and a non profit-making body, came to Bradford to see if the town would be interested in evolving its own play about itself, the initial public meeting attracted a wide audience:

When I moved to Bradford in the Autumn of 1988 I didn't know a single soul in the town, although I loved the place as soon as I moved here because of its buildings and its sense of history. Then that same Autumn there was notice of a meeting at St. Laurence School about the possibility of the Colway Theatre Trust providing the expertise to help the town create its own Community Play. There must have been about two hundred people there from all kinds of walks of life and all different ages, lots of school children and their parents and just a great feeling of curiosity, interest and growing enthusiasm for this ambitious idea of a play which would probably take some two years to bring to fruition.

So we signed up for various areas we were interested in – fund raising of course, publicity and PR, research and general dogsbodying as well. We had to discover what we wanted the play to be about, once we had done the preliminary organisation and felt we would raise enough money for a production. Then the Colway Trust would provide us with a writer to put the play together. For me it was a marvellous introduction to the town because I met lots of people I might not have met otherwise. And what is more we didn't just sit around making polite conversation: we actually had to work together which is a very good way to get to know each other.

Of course not everybody in the town got directly involved. But think, for example, of making the costumes. The Colway Theatre Trust provided us with a brilliant costume designer who stayed in the town for six months and could create most convincing period costumes out of piles of donated clothes, material and stuff we found at jumble sales. Lots of local ladies came into the premises we took over in St. Margaret's Street to do the actual sewing. Then there was all the scenery painting and props to be found – countless people found themselves lending a helping hand. (MD3/97)

The Colway Theatre Trust estimated that £42,000 was the sum needed to put on a community play of this magnitude. Sally Beale, the Town Clerk, raised £10,250 through sponsorship and small grants and the town began on a series of events – such as dances, concerts, fairs, guided walks, raffles, a Victorian evening and a French and a Greek evening to raise funds. Such activities and many, many more, not only raised money but also helped to publicise the enterprise and achieve its real goal – the working together of a community. Almost every firm and business in the vicinity, as well as nearly all local voluntary groups were drawn in.

The Colway Theatre Trust had already provided the framework for some fifteen Community Plays and from its experience brought in the successful playwright, Peter Terson, to write the play itself *Under the Fish and Over the Water*. The title was the old Bradford euphemism for being put into the town lock-up on the bridge and focused on the local riot that took place on the town bridge in 1791. The play is already well documented through a video and a tape recording of its songs, which were of course written by a local man Mark Davies and a book containing the entire text.[2] Acting workshops started early and the eventual polished production ran from 26 November to 8 December 1990 at St. Laurence School where the Sports Hall was transformed into a professional

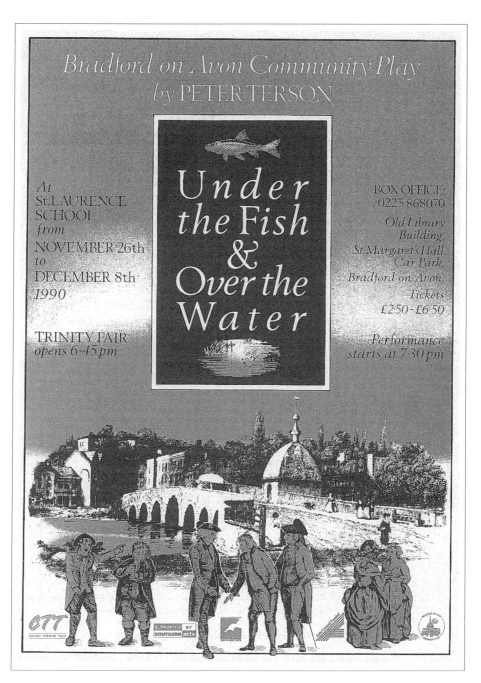

Publicity for the Community Play in 1990. The design, which incorporates features from an eighteenth century drawing of the town bridge, was by Alan Peacock.

theatre with a special sloping stage and proper raked seating for 389 people. Together with the eventual ticket and programme sales of £17,500, the proceeds from book and other sources, final accounts showed a modest profit of £1,000 which was donated to later town initiatives.

As well as important but indefinable benefits of the enterprise, there were more direct spin-offs. There were nearly a hundred adult actors, together with a cast of some 66 children who performed on alternate nights. "The Bradfordians", the talented local theatre group, gained a fresh influx of enthusiasts and for several years a Drama Workshop was run for the young people of the town who also wanted to continue in more informal ways. In 1993 Bradford Community Music produced "Carmina Burana" in the Tithe Barn with a cast of 200 adults and children. This was followed in 1996 by "African Sanctus" with again over 200 adults and children and 1997 by "Sir Gawain and The Green Knight" with about 150 adults and children.

In a town which had by 1990 grown to nearly nine thousand inhabitants,[3] the Community Play provided ways for the many new inhabitants to become part of the town. In general terms, there have been waves of incomers, all attracted by Bradford's charms. Through the 1980s many ladies of mature years, living on their own, found Bradford provided small comfortable homes at sensible prices. Drawn, first of all, to Bath, the charms of a smaller town with its own strong identity made them settle in Bradford. They quickly began to set up their own social networks, the Arts Association providing an ideal vehicle for their shared interests. One such lady is Mavis Earnshaw:

> *I was convalescing at a place near Chippenham after a hip operation. My daughter came down and we decided to go and look at Bath. On the way I saw a sign to Bradford on Avon which I'd never heard of. So I said to Lynn, "Let's go and have a look". So we come into Bradford and I'm fascinated, charmed with everything the minute I see it. The houses, the stone, the whole atmosphere was so welcoming. And as we came over the bridge and saw that wonderful tree, that huge plane tree in Westbury Gardens I said to Lynn "Just look at that, I'd love to live here, this is my home, I think I've really arrived home and I'd like to live near that tree."*

> *I went back to Chiswick and a friend of mine wanted to have a place outside London, so I said the best place to move to is Bradford on Avon. He and his wife loved it and bought a house in Lower Westwood. They didn't come for eight months so I used it as my country house and in the meantime I put my name down with all the estate agents. We were in Bradford when a man came running out from Tilley and Noad and said "I've found you a property near your tree." "Near that tree?" said my friends. "You mean you told an estate*

agent you wanted to live near that tree? Aren't you worried people will think you're strange?" So I said, "Well I'm coming to live here so they might as well know I'm a bit strange." And so it was I got a flat in Westbury House. I felt an affinity to the tree, so that was it. I felt Bradford was really my home and it's proved so really. (ME97)

But for others, including many whose families had been in Bradford for generations, finding somewhere to live in the town was proving difficult. Tim Williams, born in 1944 and still living in the house his parents bought in 1961, speaks about many who have had to go elsewhere.

There's very few of us who grew up together who live in Bradford now. You've got the ones who voluntarily moved out: they went to university and very few who go to university come back because they get jobs elsewhere. Most people would have liked to have stayed but they can't afford it. There are two main reasons – firstly, this is such a beautiful place, everyone wants to live here. It's close to Bath and house prices always get aligned, so if prices go up in Bath they go up in Bradford. And secondly of course there was the selling off of council houses. This has had a big, big effect. Because people have been in these houses for years, you can't say keep your prices down when you sell so that local people can buy them. So when they sell, outside people move in.

Newly weds have to move into Trowbridge, Melksham, Westbury; many of my friends live in those places. You talk to them and they all want to move back. They still look on themselves as Bradfordians because they've still got parents and grandparents living here; they were brought up here and went to school here. Every time I look out of the window I thank my lucky stars I was able to stay here. I'm sure it was a stroke of luck. (TW97)

Geoffrey Saxty estimates that, as a rough rule of thumb, house prices in Bradford have increased more than six-fold since the 1970s: the same house in Tyning Road which sold for £15,250 in 1976 cost £93,950 in 1997; a particular Newtown cottage, priced at £10,000 in 1970 sold for £74,000 in 1997; three-bedroom cottages in Woolley Street which were selling at £7,000 or £8,000 in the 1970s, now fetch £70,000 or £80,000 depending on their condition. But not all that many old cottages changed hands in the 1970s. It was, of course, partly the explosion of new financial institutions in the 1980s, offering highly competitive and attractive mortgages which pushed up the prices. The Old School House on Mount Pleasant was £18,000 in March 1976; in June 1997 it was sold for a sum in the region of £130,000. The Old Cottage in Silver Street, advertised in the summer of 1997 for £160,000 had been sold by Geoffrey Saxty in 1976 for £14,500.

2 Church Street which underwent repairs which were completed in 1994. A small grant towards the cost of this work was available from the Town Scheme. This interesting view of the property demonstrates how so often in Bradford an orderly eighteenth century façade may disguise a more complicated collection of earlier buildings.

The positive council housing programme which Bradford U.D.C. had managed to pursue through the 1950s and 1960s was brought to a standstill by the Conservative government's decision that no new council housing should be built in the country and that council homes should be sold to sitting tenants wherever possible. District Councils consequently amassed large sums of unexpendable money but could not provide new dwellings to replace the ones now sold on. One eventual solution was to allow developers to buy Council land and build houses within housing association schemes. Such associations were committed to the provision of affordable rented accommodation for those who previously might have benefited from the traditional system of council housing. To this end, in 1989, W.W.D.C. in conjunction with a housing association sought and obtained planning permission for residential development on part of the Sladesbrook allotment area. Over the following two years the developers paid some £800,000 for the site.

It was only when negotiations were well on the way to completion that it was discovered that this land had not become the property of W.W.D.C. at the changeover in 1974, even though the District Council had assumed responsibility for it as an open space in 1979. The land had originally belonged to Colonel Llewellen Palmer of Berryfield House who had kept up the traditions of a big house into the 1930s:

> When I was a boy we used to go there carol singing at Christmas, carrying our candles in jars. And they'd have you in the big entrance hall and if you sang the carol correctly, the maid would bring round a mince pie or a lump of stale cake. (JL97)

Colonel Palmer had always taken a close interest in the children of the poor farmworkers on the north side of town:

> We lived on Maplecroft Farm and we weren't qualified to go to the Bearfield sports day; if we went in there we were turfed out because we weren't in their district. Colonel Palmer used to be very friendly with Mr. Knight at Frankleigh and used to walk up from Berryfield House through the fields to see him. He came up on this Saturday and he said, "Why aren't you children down at the Bearfield Recreation sports tea-party?" I explained that we were sort of in between. Mr. Curtis's children could go there because they were on the other side of the road and the children in Nettlecreep Cottages were included for anything in Bradford Leigh. "In other words," he said "you're in no man's land. Oh I'll see about this." So the next year we had notification come that we were included in Bearfield's sports day. (SS97)

It was, therefore, quite in character when, in 1931, Colonel Palmer gave over eight acres in trust to the County Council, the land to be used as a school garden and playing field for the benefit of the young people of Bradford. From the 1930s onwards, Trinity School used the ground nearest to Sladesbrook as a school garden, teaching agricultural skills to generations of boys. Many a lad had toiled up there from Newtown, hoping it might rain so they could all go and play cribbage instead in 4B's classroom – more usually thought of as the Sladesbrook Temperance Hall. The school's garden had eventually become well tended private allotments. Another of Colonel Palmer's fields had been made into a sports field. Trinity School pupils played football and cricket on it until St. Laurence school was built, whereupon it became a general recreational area. It was a third area, which had also been turned into allotments, which had been sold by W.W.D.C. in 1989 as the new housing association building site.

The yearly income from the sale of the land was proving to be over £50,000.

A lot of money was involved. Who should benefit? Bradford or the District Council? Much discussion followed. But although Colonel Palmer could never have envisaged his gift achieving such a financial return, his lawyers had made his wishes quite explicit. His gift must be used for the benefit of the youth of Bradford. It could not be used for any purposes outside of the town.

Having established the beneficiaries of what was now a substantial Bradford charity, a formal Charitable Trust became essential and was duly set up by the County Council and the Charity Commissioners. The administration of the Trust and the composition of its board of Trustees were two important matters to be settled. Naturally Bradford Town Council felt it should be fully represented. But Colonel Palmer's original gift had been left in the hands of the County Council who argued that Trustees could only be appointed from County Councillors. After some negotiations, it was agreed that Bradford's one County Councillor should be included among the Trustees, thus ensuring that local experience is involved in decisions on how the yearly income can best be used for young people in Bradford. All applications by groups for grants over £500 are referred to Bradford Town Council for recommendation. Money goes on such grants to sports clubs and additional sports facilities; Poulton has gained a skateboard rink and Sladesbrook Recreational ground, most appropriately, has been completely redesigned. The Trust cannot pay for anything which has to be provided as a normal part of educational funding, but grants can be made for musical instruments or other extra school equipment. Low income families can also benefit from money towards school uniforms. A very substantial capital sum has been granted to the Wiltshire Music Centre which is based at St. Laurence School. Over seventy years after his original gift, Colonel Palmer's generosity continues.

As the whole country began to recover some financial equilibrium in the second half of the decade, an interesting new wave of incomers were arriving in Bradford:

Now that Bradford is discovered we've seen a lot of people coming in who are professional people, managerial people, writers and artists with a wide range of skills – people who've come into the town and actually help the town breathe, help the town develop. You'll find woodworkers, carvers, painters; you'll find writers, you'll find poets and actors. There's a tremendous amount of talent in Bradford. (GS97)

There is undoubtedly a new wave of settlers in the town and around the area, and there are at least two reasons for this. One must be the way in which we now regard easy mobility as a factor in the choice of a home. Thus one new inhabitant has chosen Bradford because it is a conveniently central location from which to fulfil work and family commitments in Torbay, South Wales and London. What would an inhabitant in 1902 have made of that? Secondly, the astonishing growth in digital technology in recent years has suddenly made it possible for many more people to work from home than was possible before. One current trend is for cottages to be bought with such usage in mind – with a consequent swing to younger, professional people as the latest incomers.

Michael Darlow, a film maker, moved here from Islington in 1994, having visited the town previously when he was location hunting with Peter Ustinov:

It is interesting that many of my friends and acquaintances have also moved down here. My next door neighbour in London, a very well known film producer with his actress wife moved here completely independently of us. A number of actor, writer and other colleagues actually live within ten miles of Bradford.

Basically what I do is make TV programmes but if I made films or gramophone records I could do it here. Technology is altering in ways which were inconceivable even five years ago. Now all I need is a communications base, which is only a computer and e-mail and a fax and a telephone. The equipment gets lighter and lighter, smaller and smaller, I now have a broadcast camera here which I wouldn't have been able to use before. Firstly the unions wouldn't have let me, but we've had a freeing up of all those restrictive practices of the late 1970s and 1980s. Secondly cameras were too big and the technology itself was too complicated so I couldn't have processed the material when it was shot. Now I can: it's digital technology so it will go into a computer. My broadcast camera is no bigger than a small box and it produces absolutely wonderful pictures. Now I can pick it up and go and use it and the result's accepted – it's put out on the air.

I work in a technological industry which can be here as well as anywhere. Peter Gabriel, in Box, has one of the best record studios in the world and I use it. There are good specialised cameramen around, there are actually pretty good post production facilities in Bristol; there aren't any yet in Bath although we are discussing converting a place in Bath into a film studio. I work for the South West Media Development Agency and occasionally in Bristol. But equally we're doing development for Channel 4 TV. The last film I shot in America and it looks as if it's sold in the United Stat es – sold from here. I can do it all from here – why be in London?

At the moment I bring editors – which is a highly skilled job – down from London. The equipment comes with them for the length of time I want. A lot of the work is very specialist, and I have to train people but in other ways the overheads are cheaper and it's a very much better life style. There are a lot of good things about this place: not only is there the talent but where are all the

classic serials being shot? At Lacock, in Bath, Stonehenge and in the Welsh
mountains. (MD1/97)

And how do the old Bradford families who have been here for many
generations feel about these different waves of incomers who have settled in
their town? After all, no one likes to see their space swamped by too many
strangers. The older generations particularly regret today's lack of the
neighbourliness they remember so vividly from the past. Once they knew not
only the names but also much of the personal lives of those who lived around
them. What they now recall is the companionship and support in such familiarity:

> *My dad, he used to go and polish all the names on the war memorial, all*
> *voluntarily. He had known so many of them, he took it upon himself to do it. I*
> *can hear my mum saying now,"there he is, going off with my polish". My mum*
> *used to wash all the pavement down in Whiteheads Lane for all the people, she*
> *used to do all their brass on their doors: I've never known such kindness, you*
> *don't find it today. We used to have an open fire and she used to do these*
> *bloaters down beside the fire and she'd say, "I've been down town and I've been*
> *and bought a bloater and I've been and bought one for Mr. Smith, next door,*
> *I'm sure he'd like one". And she used to do this bloater and take it in to old Mr.*
> *Smith – all out of love. Everything was done for nothing in those days. (LH97)*

Such reminiscences, real as they are, encourage us to imagine the "good old
days", to see old Bradford through a haze of a dreamy hankering for life as it
will never be again. Some detailed examination of the past century provides us
with a much more complex picture. Undoubtedly there used to be far more
picturesque cottages than there are now: but they were cramped little dwellings,
sometimes literally piled on top of one another, frequently rented from landlords
who did little to maintain them. Those who lived in them had to toil over domestic
chores we now leave to a range of machines. A few gave up the struggle and
tolerated the inevitable muck and smells that followed – and their neighbours
endured it with them. Staying on good terms with your close neighbours meant
mutual support in any domestic hazards. But such communities did not welcome
"strangers" from other parts of Bradford into their area, as many accounts of
growing up in Bradford between the wars make only too clear. Bradford was
never one close-knit community. On the contrary it seems to have been a series
of separate territories: folk shared the same town centre and local employment
but firmly kept to their own little patches for everything else.

Such enclaves have vanished, being replaced now by networks of people who
may live anywhere in the town but come together through friendships, shared

interests or occupations. There must now be much more relaxed wandering about in all areas of the town, visiting on both sides of the river than ever there used to be, although older Bradfordians continue to feel they belong firmly either one side of the river or the other:

I lived at the other end of the town just after I was married in 1952. I just couldn't settle there, in Trowbridge Road, it was a different sort of atmosphere somehow. So I did eventually get back to the top end of the town. This feeling of north and south had still carried on, it's still here now. It was all little districts years ago. Ashley and Bearfield, Woolley, Tory. Of course the rest was all fields. (JL97)

Nostalgia is a strong colourant to our picture of the past. We hark back to a Bradford where children walked to school, chanted their tables in class and filled their free time with the seasonal games which were being repeated all over the country. We like to think of a time when children could play in the streets, could spend their holidays in the fields and woods around the town, unsupervised and devising their own ways of passing the time. We imagine their mothers, domestic chores finally completed, finding a few minutes to sit outside their picturesque little homes, admiring the views across green fields and talking with their neighbours: a time when men came home from work and spent their evenings peacefully working on the family allotment close to home. For those in work, perhaps with several wage earners at the factories, mushroom quarries or shops, life could be good, with local food and home grown fruit and vegetables to keep everyone fit and healthy.

All this may be true. But such a panorama needs to be balanced against some of the other factors in daily life. Work was uncertain. Men could be and were laid off when national recessions affected Bradford's industries. The support systems for the poor and the out of work were limited and could be humiliating to those who had to ask for assistance. And what happened to such people when they fell ill? Some kindly doctors, such as Dr. Adye and Dr. Jean Murray, who treated the sick and asked little remuneration are still remembered in the town. Bradford also worked long and hard to fund its own hospital at Berryfield House. Even so, we need to compare our contemporary access to care and medication (however imperfect it may seem) with some description of poverty in the 1930s:

From Christchurch School they used to take you over to the Lambert Rooms to look at your teeth. And they'd say, "You've got a tooth there that needs seeing to – you bring 6d and you can have that done". Now where was my mother going to get sixpence? I didn't get it, did I? Couldn't afford it. Couldn't afford

to live, let alone have a tooth done. I can never remember my mother having a
doctor for herself, she just couldn't afford it. (JL97)

Toothbrushes and toothpaste being an unobtainable luxury, teeth were cleaned
with salt or soot – if at all. The poor of the town concocted their own remedies. A
chilblain would be rubbed with an onion dipped in salt, a heavy cold required a
draught of dark beer, first boiled up on the fire together with a piece of stem
ginger and for indigestion (or worse) there would be a supply of orange peel,
baked hard in the oven, to be chewed by the sufferer. When John Ludlow's mother
bought six Oxo cubes in a tin, the plaster seal around the tin was carefully
unwound and kept on a cotton reel to serve as a sticking plaster for cuts. Living
off the land was part of normal life. John recalls his pleasure in foraging for
extra food. There was a field above Bearfield where they could pick wild
asparagus at certain times of the year and the running stream in the next field
where there was a good supply of watercress to supplement a meagre diet. Rabbits
abounded, so his grandmother could look forward to her favourite dish - rabbit
brains. The head of the rabbit was roasted in the oven, which turned the brains
into a soft and tasty paste to be spread on bread. It sounds strange, but is it so
very different from gourmet delicacies like caviare or goose liver paté?

Today there are pubs, luncheon clubs, church groups and natural informal
gatherings where memories are still shared, sometimes with the prompt of an
old Bradford Directory with the names of families and the streets in which they
lived. When old Bradfordians talk about their town, they talk about the people.
More recent settlers who talk about the town are far more likely to discuss the
buildings. On the whole, Bradfordians seem to have accepted the inevitable,
recognising that changes have taken place throughout the country and not just
in their own home town. The self sufficient, somewhat insular, industrial
Bradford has gone for ever. The long battle to regenerate the industrial area in
and around Greenland Mill in Bridge Street emphasises the change. After lying
derelict for many years, the site has become another housing development. Tim
Williams takes a realistic view of Bradford at the end of the century:

Not in a million years will you get heavy industry back to a place like
Bradford. It's not a case of industry not wanting to come to Bradford – there's
not the industry to come here. You're not going to get it back to a place like
Birmingham, so you're certainly not going to get it back into a place like
Bradford.
The town needs money, tourists have got money, so do you encourage tourists?
I think you've got to, to a certain extent. That's the way ahead for Bradford.
(TW97)

BRADFORD on AVON

Touring Guide

Tourist Information

Tourism brochure of 1997

There is no doubt that tourism has been a steadily growing source of income to the town. Back in 1982 its first Tourist Information Centre was opened in the reception area of the Swan Hotel. Since then, it has been rehoused several times and in 1996 the astonishing figure of 38,678 tourists made use of its services. Since many other visitors explore the town without using these facilities, the overall figure must be much larger and the number grows each year. Interestingly many Australians in particular come to Bradford, some of them descendants of those earlier Bradfordians who emigrated. The attraction of the town needs no emphasis – the Saxon Church, the fourteenth century Tithe Barn, the town itself and the Country Park providing interest for specialist and general visitors alike. Bradford is twinned with Norden in Germany and Sully in France which brings other groups to the town. The Kennet and Avon Canal was finally fully restored in the early 1990s and is naturally another leisure attraction.

Considering the ways in which so many people have discovered and settled in Bradford in the last fifteen years of the twentieth century, it is remarkable that Bradford seems in many ways to remain unchanged, although those born here see it differently. Many old names around the town have now disappeared. Some people know of Piano Row in the Trowbridge Road, but the nickname Co-op Row for the long line of semi-detached houses built along Bath Road in the 1930s is probably now forgotten. This local name came about because so many people who worked in the various Co-op shops in Bradford were among the first purchasers. And who remembers the evocative name of Nettlecreep Cottages, now demolished, out at North Leigh?

Then there were names for local streets: Frying Pan Hill, part of Woolley Street; Morgan's Hill on St. Margaret's Hill; Town Hill, the upper part of Market Street; and Horse Street, already mentioned as the bottom end of Market Street. Further out there was Jericho Hill now just part of the A363 road to Bath near Maplecroft; Dead Man's Lane opposite Leigh Park; Quarters Lane from Leigh Park to Woolley; Quarry Lane, now part of the Holt Road and Coombquar Hill which was the hill in Holt Road just above the much newer Springfield junction. Some field names are preserved as roads in post war estates – Avonfield, Kingsfield, Elmfield, Churches (one of two large fields belonging to the church), Grove Leaze and Sandy Leaze. On the south side of the river the Southway Park estate retains the name of Folly Field. Others seem to have disappeared – Tasleys, the field the children played on between Sladesbrook and Woolley Street, and Pinchmead, the name of a field between Woolley Street and the Holt Road. There must be many more.

Relatively recent newcomers to the town delight in the amount of the past which is still here. Those who have always lived here are more aware of what has been lost. Geoffrey Saxty puts the point:

> *Last night as I walked over Tory I said to someone, this view doesn't change does it, it's lovely all the time. And she began to talk about the library and how ghastly that was and how the town is full of estate agents and building societies. There's an awful lot of antique dealers, about fourteen. I said, well there are five estate agents but only two building societies. But we would like to see more things in the town which service the needs of Bradford; whether you can buy clothes, shoes, food from these shops is very debatable. It's all geared towards tourism. (GS97)*

Now that tourism is a major industry in Britain, will Bradford become no more than a tourist venue in the next century, a sort of free theme park which tour operators will promote in glossy brochures to their own advantage? Possibly. This has happened to places in the Cotswolds. As a National Trust village, Lacock is an example even closer to home. Without any deliberate policy in this direction, the ways in which planning decisions on housing and employment are taken and funding is allocated for leisure facilities also pushes Bradford, almost insidiously, towards this role. Until 1974 everything at Urban District Council level was done for the benefit of the town; since the creation of West Wiltshire District Council, decisions have to be taken for the benefit of West Wilts as a one unit:

> *We want employment in the town: Until twenty-five years ago, the U.D.C.*

could choose a part of the town where it would try to create and maintain employment for those living in Bradford. But since 1974, when these matters are discussed at District level, then Bradford is not seen as the best place for such expansion for the District as a whole. Bradford is difficult, transport is difficult and there is a danger of spoiling the fabric of the town. Also it lacks land suitable for development, due to the tightly drawn Green Belt boundary around the town. Inevitably, roles are allocated to different towns in the District and Bradford becomes seen as the "preserved" town, the "tourist" town, the "commuter" town. These words aren't used necessarily, but these conclusions are the ones arrived at. Thus business parks and industrial estates are built around Trowbridge, Westbury and Melksham rather than close to Bradford. (DV97)

This picture of the south side of the river was taken from the Bullpit in 1992. It was photographed from exactly the same spot in 1890. The two pictures, separated by more than a hundred years, are almost identical.

The north side of the town bridge in 1992. Empty buildings wait for a new use. – or for demolition.

The unemployment rate in Bradford in 1997 is around 6%, which is below the national average. The town with its environs has far more places of work than is generally recognised. In 1994 the list of business employers registered within the Bradford BA15 postcode (which includes surrounding villages such as Winsley and South Wraxall) numbered 182.[4] But not all work is within local walking distance. Recent surveys by the County Council suggest that about four-fifths of the working population of Bradford is employed outside the town and over 85% of these commuters travel by car. Like so many other small towns, Bradford has become dependent for employment and much of its leisure on easy mobility. As financial resources seem to diminish even further, the question of how money is allocated becomes more and more important. Donald Vass has been involved with attempts to redevelop the Kingston Mill site as a Town Councillor and subsequently on Bradford 2000:

> *When you have to ask what is best for the District, you're going to be putting certain things in one area and certain things in another because that creates a*

kind of critical mass and there's a good deal of logic to that. The W.W.D.C. has had to allocate scarce resources for, say, leisure. Bradford has a swimming pool so it's not going to get a sports centre; Melksham has a sports centre and is not going to get a swimming pool. The whole idea had been to try and redraw this District and make it one unit instead of five separate units. That's all right as long as there's complete mobility of people within its five towns. If people are prepared and can afford to live in Westbury, take their leisure in Melksham, shall we say, swim in Bradford and work in Trowbridge, that's going to be alright. But a lot depends on the motor car and I feel sure that such mobility is probably going to decline. The last Conservative government said it was going to increase petrol taxes at a higher rate than inflation, the present Labour government will almost certainly carry that on as part of their transport policy.

It seems to me that we're moving towards a stage where people are not going to be able to afford easily to go and do low paid jobs if it means owning a car to get there. At the moment someone on a very low wage may just be able to do so. If those costs are going to rise faster than their pay there's going to come a time when that ceases to be the case. That's another strong reason for saying that what we must do in Bradford is create employment opportunities wherever we possibly can. But just when we should be trying to do that we've got this local government system which is inimical to that way of looking at things. (DV97)

Road and transport policies also come into any discussion of the future needs of the town and the District. This usually takes us swiftly beyond measures which can be introduced locally. Following the concern over the proposed A36 East of Bath to Beckington trunk road, an Open Forum on Traffic and Transport, involving local volunteers and supported by County, District and Town Councils and local businesses, was formed. Traffic in Wiltshire is increasing even faster than the national forecast of 3% per annum Two-thirds of the traffic in Bradford which crosses the bridge is estimated to be locally generated. These are daunting statistics, but the Open Forum is not only looking at the local traffic problems; it is also attempting to find viable solutions which can be presented to the authorities. Any bold initiative is certain to arouse opposition from some section of the community. Therefore it remains to be seen whether any practicable scheme will achieve consensus or even majority acceptance, let alone attract the necessary finance. However, the Open Forum does ensure that Bradford's constant concern about traffic continues to be brought firmly to the attention of those in charge of transport issues in the county.

Another fear frequently expressed is that Bradford will turn into a retirement

Left and below right: Pupils at Christchurch School, which has remained a Church of England controlled school throughout its long life. After several reorganizations, a new building was opened in 1957, and the Berryfields Infant school building then was added in 1968.

Left and below: Education of the whole child at Fitzmaurice Primary School.

St. Laurence Comprehensive School came into existence in 1980 when Trinity School in Ashley Road and Fitzmaurice Grammar School in Junction Road both closed. The new school then opened on the Trinity School site.

town, "a sort of inland Bournemouth" as one Bradfordian put it. It is true that buildings which previously served a range of the town's needs – for example, Fitzmaurice Grammar School, Trinity School, now The Ropewalk in Newtown, and Abbey Mill – are now replaced with retirement apartments. Retirement and commuter housing comes to Bradford: industrial estates and business parks are built elsewhere. It can only be hoped that this trend will not continue. Since the particular attractions of the old town and the growth in computer technology are bringing in new energetic people, once again the future development of the Kingston Mill site, so central to the town's affairs, becomes more and more significant. It could become a working area where people could also meet informally, where ideas could be transferred across from those with one set of skills to another:

> If we want to consolidate the current trend for technologically based small firms to live and work in Bradford, we need to find a central place where such small businesses can expand when successful and where like minded people can meet and make contacts with those in similar fields. The Kingston Mill site would be an ideal space. (DV97)

At the end of this century, Bradford has several options. It may become mostly a residential town, it may put its future wellbeing into the tourist industry, it may be able to attract and develop small businesses in its town centre and environs. Ideally it will manage an amalgam of all these possibilities, continuing as a diverse community. The town is full of busy, energetic people. Local voluntary organisations invited to the Town Gathering in 1996 numbered 70.[5] Remembering that this figure could be easily augmented if many other informal groups were included, it is clear that Bradford, still only a small town, has a healthy range of flourishing groups to carry it forward.

The 1997 Town Survey[6] provides a remarkable catalogue of the diversity of present day Bradford. The churches in Bradford have been central to many people's lives for generations. That continues to be so and in 1997 the town still has twelve church organisations, many of which work in unison in their Churches Together programme. Religious worship in Bradford embraces Church of England, Roman Catholic, Non-Conformists, the Quakers and the Christian Fellowship as well as a thriving community of Buddhists. There are two primary schools and one comprehensive school which lives up to sound educational aims and serves the entire community. Indeed, there is evidence that families nowadays choose to move to Bradford to take advantage of St. Laurence School. The great social divide in old Bradford between the Grammar School and Trinity School in Newtown so frequently mentioned in the past is long gone. There are

64 sports groups from Archery to Yoga active in the town and the civic parish of Bradford contains the astonishing number of 89 retail outlets. As this second figure may take some readers by surprise, Appendix IV gives further details which are worth contemplating. The character of the town has undoubtedly changed since 1900 but its spread of activities and its self sufficiency may be more actively present than we sometimes assume.

Poised at the entry to the new millennium, we continue to mull over what has happened in Bradford's past, to enjoy what it offers at the present and to look forward, with some determination, to its positive future.

Notes & References

Abbreviations and Sources
CRO: County Record Office, Bythesea Road, Trowbridge, BA14 8BS
CLSL:County Local Studies Library, Bythesea Road, Trowbridge, BA14 8BS

A range of local newspapers has been used: these appear, where necessary, as references in the text. A most promising source, *The Bradford on Avon Observer and District Intelligence*, which began weekly publication in July 1905, price 1d, unfortunately only lasted until December 1905 and has only provided background information. Those used are as follows:

Wiltshire Times (WT): A collection of fully bound copies is available at the WT Office in Trowbridge. Volumes 1881-1902; 1921-19929 (ex. 1921/2); 1931-1963 (ex.1936) are also in the County Record Office in Trowbridge. Allowing for small changes in the title, microfilms of issues for 1881-1940 and 1944 to the current date are in the County Local Studies Library, Trowbridge.
Devizes & Wiltshire Gazette (DWG): Its name became altered to The Wiltshire Gazette, but for consistency the same abbreviation has been retained. Microfilms of all issues are in the Local Studies Centre, Trowbridge. There is very little about Bradford after November 1918
Salisbury & Winchester Journal (SWJ): Issues for 1915 are in the County Record Office
Wiltshire News (WN): CLSL

CHAPTER ONE
1   That a total population of only 4,500 could include as many as 1,200 school children might seem unlikely, but the census return for 1901 seems to give some support to this figure. The school leaving age in 1901 was 12 years, but in those days the term "school children" could also include older children already at work but still attending a Sunday school, as many young people did. Children also frequently started school at two and a half. The number of children under the age of 13 in Bradford in 1901 was 1,228. See Appendix I for more information on age ranges in the population in 1901 and 1991
2   Area redivided in 1934. Powell, W.R., *Bradford on Avon: A History to 1950*, Wilts County Library & Museum Service, Trowbridge 1990 (reprinted from Victoria County History Vol V11) p.5.
3   *Kelly's Directory*, 1903
4   Byelaws made by the Urban District Council for the Management, Use & Regulation of the Bradford on Avon Public Baths (CRO. Cat:G13/123/9)

5   Bradford U.D.C. Records (CRO. Cat:G13/154/26)
6   *Dotesio's Directory and Year Book*, 1900
7   Fassnidge, Harold: *Bradford on Avon Past and Present*, Ex Libris Press, 2nd ed., 1993, p.28
8   Powell, L, W.R., *Ibid*, p.45.
9   Ponting, K., *Wool & Water*, Moonraker, 1975, p.20
10 Two letters, handwritten by Isambard Kingdom Brunel, to Stephen Moulton, in March 1857, in the private possession of the Moulton family
11 *George Spencer, Moulton & Co, Ltd.: 1848-1948, A Hundred Years of Rubber Manufacture*, p.30 (private publication)
12 Woodruff, William: *The Rise of the Rubber Industry*, Liverpool University Press, 1958, ch. V1
13 Bradford on Avon Poor Law Union, 1902: (CRO. Cat: H/3/140/1)
14 As members of this family still live in Bradford, the surname has been omitted
15 "oakum": loose fibre, obtained by untwisting and picking old rope and then frequently used for stopping up the seams of a ship.
16 Fassnidge, H., *Ibid*, pp.113 & 153.
17 *Kelly's Directory*, 1935
18 Platt, Brigadier: *Royal Wilts Yeomanry 1907-67*, p.28 cont. (CRO)

CHAPTER TWO
1   Through the kindness of a number of ladies and gentlemen of the town, the five national flags of the Allies have been purchased and placed on the Drill Hall (DWG 1.4.15). The Imperial War Museum has provided the following helpful comment on this report in the local newspaper: "It seems likely that the five flags of the Allies consisted of those for Britain, France, Belgium, Russia and Serbia. Italy did not declare war on Austria until May 1915, and Portugal did not officially enter the conflict until 1916. Japan did declare war on Germany in 1914 but her operations did little to affect the European theatre. This, perhaps, helped to ensure that she was not widely perceived as a major ally as far as public opnion was concerned."
2   Kenrick, Col. N.G.C., *The Story of the Wiltshire Regiment*, Gale & Polden, Ltd., 1963, pp.143-146.
3   Platt, Brigadier, *Royal Wilts Yeomanry 1907-67* (CRO)
4   The account is taken from papers now in the possession of Miss Foxcroft's niece, Mrs Isla Tuck
5   I am indebted to Major John Peters, M.B.E at The Royal Gloucestershire, Berkshire and Wiltshire Museum at Salisbury for confirmation of these and other details about the Wiltshire Regiment.

CHAPTER THREE

1 Bradford U.D.C. Records (CRO Cat: G13/100/110)

2 The Bell Inn was at 62 Newtown. It is now a private house. A list of the 16 public houses in around the town in 1935 appears as Appendix III.

3 "staves" a temporary structure of long, thin removable boards placed around the sides of a cart so that bulky loads can be more easily supported while in transit.

4 Joyce (Jo) Uncles, whose family has lived in the Trowbridge Road for since the end of the nineteenth century has kindly provided this, and much other, information about this area.

5 "Co-op": This was a shop on the corner of Bath Road and the original Winsley Road. There is now a new junction between Winsley Road and Bath Road The shop was demolished and replaced with a small paved area in what is now a cul de sac.

6 Census of England & Wales; 1921: County of Wilts. H.M.S.O. 1923 (CLSC).

7 As yet there were no other domestic electrical appliances for the ordinary home. When the wireless became the next innovation a few years later, it was aptly named, its source of power being a portable battery accumulator, regularly recharged with acid at a local hardware shop.

8 The King's Arms, now renamed, was on the corner of Coppice Hill and Silver Street. See Appendix 111.

9 *Guardian Angel*: The Priory, Bradford on Avon, article by Margaret Dobson: Journal of the Bradford on Avon Preservation Trust Issue no.21.Autumn 1996.

CHAPTER FOUR

1. Mock, J.H., *Bradford on Avon and District, The War Years (1939-1945)*, Makjok Publishing 1997.

2. Some of the Rubber articles manufactured by Messrs George Spencer, Moulton & Co. Ltd during World War Two: Petrol Hose, Water Hose, Hot Oil Joints, Various Sleeving, Fin Damper Pads, for Aircraft Engines, Flexible Black Out Curtaining, for Railways, Cylinder Air Seals, High Tension Ignition Harness Sleeves, Electrical Lead Bushes, Moulded Cable Connectors, for Rocket Firing Apparatus & Field Wireless Sets, Sealing for Radios for use in Tropical Conditions, Containers for Oil Immersed Transformers, Parts for Airborne Wireless Equipment, Parts for Radiolocation Apparatus : Neoprene Bottles, Washers for Aircraft, Tubing for Gun Mantles, Sealing Rings for Tanks, Suction Hose for Filling Bombs, Buoyant Hose, Rings for Depth Charges & Mines, Buffers for Paravanes, used for cutting the moorings of submerged mines, Air Seals for Aero Engine Cylinders, Buffer & Draw Springs for Railways, Vacuum Hose for Railways, Engine Mountings, Transformer Assemblies, Sea Fuelling Hose (60 ft.),

3. City Archives, Guildhall, Bath.

4. British Restaurant Government sponsored restaurants created to supply cheap meals to evacuees, workers, townspeople and troops. Particularly useful because people could buy meals without having to use their ration books.

CHAPTER FIVE

1 It seems that nowadays "skillins" is solely a Wiltshire dialect word for a cowshed with one open side, although at one time the term had a wider distribution into neighbouring counties.

2 Census 1951 England & Wales County Report; Wiltshire, part 1, HMSO 1955,Table 13.

3 "glebe": a portion of land assigned to a clergyman, originally often used for producing food.

4. This sequence of production is taken from the *Proceedings of the Institution of Mechanical Engineers* 1979, vol.193, no. 9, 'From Hydrolastic to Hydrogas Suspension', p.18. This publication reviews the development of fluid interconnected Hydrolastic and Hydagas suspension systems and describes their principles.

CHAPTER SEVEN

1 Application to the Millenium Commission, November 1996. The intention was to establish a Town Trust as a development trust in the form of a company limited by guarantee, membership of the Trust to be open to all residents of the town. The total cost over three years at then current prices was estimated at £12.90 million. The Millenium Commission was asked to provide Bradford with a grant of £4.95 million: the balance of £7.95 million was costed out among Avon Rubber plc, University of Bath, West Wilts District Council and County Council and charitable fundings & donations.

2 Terson, P., *Under the Fish & Over the Water*: Ex Libris Press, 1990.

3 County Electoral Division;1991 Census Profile, no7. Wilts.County Council.

4 Information supplied by the County Council's Careers and Guidance Service.

5 Bradford Town Council Town Gathering Invitation List, 1996.

6 Bradford Town Council returns to 1997 Survey of Rural Services for the Rural Development Commission..

Appendix I

Information from Census Returns, 1901-1991: Full census returns are not made available for 100 years. But some material is available and is used for the following tables.

Much census information becomes an approximation and is likely to have inbuilt errors. Returns are dependent upon what the head of household chooses to reveal and the attitude of the enumerator to the task. Exact comparisons between different census years can also be difficult. For example, the geographical area under examination may vary and official definitions of terms used in making returns can also change. In 1921 the census was taken at a different time of year, thus bringing into play a subtle set of altered circumstances. Therefore the tables which follow should be seen as of general interest for comparison between different periods in the town's social history.

The 1901 census listed the population ages numerically. The 1991 census produced returns in broader age bands and as percentages (to one decimal point) of the total population. While keeping the original raw data for 1901 in Table 1, corresponding percentages have been calculated and added. For 1991 a numerical figure has been calculated and added to correspond with the percentage figures available; calculations are in italics. But as these percentages are only to one decimal point, calculations of the number of individuals can not produce an exact result. However it is hoped that this presentation in Table 1 will allow for some interesting comparisons between the two periods. For example in 1901 just on 24% were aged between 5 and 15 plus. By 1991 the percentage figure had dropped to 13.4%.

References

1   Census of England & Wales 1901; County of Wiltshire (63 VICT C.4) (CLSL).
2   1991 Census Reports: A series of booklets published by Wilts County Council 1992 (BoA Library)
3   1981 Census; Key Statistics Urban Areas South West and Wales, HMSO (BoA Library)
4   Higgs, E., *Making Sense of the Census Manuscript Returns: England & Wales, 1801-1901:* HMSO, 1989 (CLSL).
5   *Victoria County History*, Vol. 4

AGE	1901 CENSUS GROUP DATA		1991 CENSUS GROUP DATA	
	NUMBER	% POPln. calculated	NUMBER calculated	% POPln.
Under 5 GROUP	456	*10.1%*	*423*	4.8%
5-15 GROUP	1083	*24.0%*	*1181*	13.4%
16-17 GROUP	191	*4.2%*	*247*	2.8%
18-29 GROUP	818	*18.1%*	*1208*	13.7%
30-44 GROUP	883	*19.6%*	*1834*	20.8%
45-59 GROUP	612	*13.5%*	*1737*	19.7%
60-74 GROUP	356	*7.9%*	*1472*	16.7%
75+ GROUP	116	*2.6%*	*714*	8.1%
ALL AGES	4514	*100%*	*8815*	100%

An Overview of Population from Census Returns: 1901-91 (Crown Copyrught reserved):

Date	Total	Male	Female	POPULATION Under 16	POPULATION Over 60	Type	AREA Acres	AREA Hectares
1901	4514	2058	2456	34%	10%	PCN*	1990	
1911	4501	2085	2416	28%	12%	PCN	1990	
1921	4624	2114	2510	28%	13%	PCN	1990	
1931	4735	2201	2534	23%	15%		1990	
1941	No census taken due to war							
1951	5628	2687	2941	25%	19%	PCN	2148	
1961	5760	2722	3038	24%	20%	PCN	2148	
1971	8002	3844	4158	26%	19%		2148	869
1981	8921	4282	4639	23%	20%	NR**	2145	868
1991	8815	4169	4646	18%	25...%	NR	2142	867

*   PCN = Present on Census Night   ** NR = Normally Resident

Appendix II

Roll of Honour: Bradford on Avon men who joined the services in the first weeks of the 1914-18 war. This is as printed in the *Devizes & Wiltshire Gazette* on 27 August 1914 as part of a much longer list for other adjacent towns in Wiltshire. The inconsistent way in which names are listed shows the speed with which it was compiled. The names of the many Bradford men who joined the services after 27 August 1914 are, of course, not included.

BRADFORD: Population 4,501

C.K. Merewether, Lieutent, 4th Wiltshire Battalion

J. Ewence, Col. Sergeant, 4th Wilts

A.E. Hillard, Sergeant 4th Wilts

F. Huntley, Sergeant, 4th Wilts

W.J. Banks, Sergeant, 4th Wilts

W. Drew, Corporal 4th Wilts

F. Brown, Private, 4th Wilts

G. Gibson, Corporal, 4th Wilts

Holbrook, Lance Corporal, 4th Wilts

W.C. Holbrook, Private, 4th Wilts

E. Huntley, Private 4th Wilts

G.H. Stafford, Sergeant, 4th Wilts

F.A. Stevens, Private 4th Wilts

W. Whatley, Private 4th Wilts

S. Totten Private 4th Wilts

P.J. Bilby, Private 4th Wilts

R. Jones, Private 4th Wilts

K.R. James aznce Coroporal 4th Wilts

W.E. Sadd, Private 4th Wilts

L.J. Fricker, Lance Corporal, 4th Wilts

W.C. Vennell, Private 4th Wilts

N.G. Banks, private 4th Wilts

C.L. Bray, Private 4th Wilts

H.J.Clark, Private 4th Wilts

M.C. Bray, Private 4th Wilts

H.S. Hart, Private 4th Wilts

P.H. Tucker, Private 4th Wilts

R. Doddington, Private 4th Wilts

J.C. Raine, Private 4th Wilts

E. Keevil, Private 4th Wilts

J.E. Willis, Private 4th Wilts

G.A. Crouch, Private 4th Wilts

R.J. Hannay, Private 4th Wilts

W.J. Howell, Private 4th Wilts

W. Spender, Private 4th Wilts

W.A. Blick, Private 4th Wilts

C.H. Carrier, Private 4th Wilts

L.A.Smith, Private 4th Wilts

S.V. Sartain, Private 4th Wilts

R.J. Willis, Private 4th Wilts

W. Bees, Private 4th Wilts

H. Howell, Private 4th Wilts

P. Lowe, Private 4th Wilts

H.J. Jones, Private 4th Wilts

H.J. Brown, Private 4th Wilts

F.S. Redman, Private 4th Wilts

E. Wilkins, Private 4th Wilts

F. Taverner, Private 4th Wilts

H.H. Foster, Private 4th Wilts

S. Gerrish, Private 4th Wilts

E. Kettlety, Private 4th Wilts

A. Burt, Private 4th Wilts

A. Leslie, Private 4th Wilts

E.H. Blake, Private 4th Wilts

F.C. Potter, Private 4th Wilts

T.E. Hodges,Private 4th Wilts

E.V. Gane, Private 4th Wilts

R. Mizen, Private 4th Wilts

J. Booker, Private 4th Wilts

E. Say, Private 4th Wilts

A.C. Phelps, Private 4th Wilts

S. Lintern, Private 4th Wilts

W.G. Leslie, Private 4th Wilts

P.W. Douglas, Commander, *HMS Audacious*

- Tothill, Commander, Royal Navy

- Eyre, Commander, Royal Navy

T.F.S. Fleming, Lieutenant, *HMS Vigilant*

C.C. Flemming, Midshipman, *HMS Audacious*

R.N.R.Ward, Lieutenant, Naval Reserve

E. Hugh Richardson, Lieutenant 1st Wilts. Battalion

J.H. Jennings, 9th Hants Batt. Motor Cyclist Section

George F.Harris, Chief eoman of Signals, *HMS Venus* (?)

Ernest Collier, Coldstream Guards

Frank Pratten, *HMS Birmingham*

Fred Fielding, Coldstream Guards

George Cox 10th Hussars

Walter Garten, 3rd Hussars

Fred Moore, *HMS Queen Mary*

- Wiltshire, Col. Sergeant, Wiltshire Regiment

- Busby, Band Sergeant, Wiltshire Regiment

G. King, Sergeant, Wiltshire Regiment

L. Budd, 7th Fuseliers

E. Escott, Hussars
Fred Underhill, 2nd West Kent Battalion
J. Doddington, Corporal Wilts Regiment
George Allen, 1st Wilts Battalion
W. Daggar, Army Service Corps
F.K. Bricker, Wilts Regiment
- Ratcliffe, Royal Army Medical Corps
Lot Ewence. Wilts Battalion
Herbert Reason, Northumberland Fuseliers
Jack Dixon, Wilts Regiment
Herbert Turtle, 1st Wilts
Henry Bigwood, 1st Wilts
Jack Brown, Scottish Rifles
H.H. Brown, Argyle & Sutherland
  Highlanders
Herbert Cable, Royal Field Artillery
Bert Powney, 3rd Wilts
H.G.Moore, 2nd Wilts
Seymour Moore, Royal Field Artillery
George Sherman, Royal Field Artillery
Fred Coles, Royal Artillery
Robert Spackman, Royal Engineers
L. Underwood, Somerset Light Infantry
S.F. Wenham, Royal Engineers
George Niblett, 1st Wilts
George Bryant, Royal Field Artillery
A.J. Appleby, Royal Field Artillery
W.J. Bright, 1st Wiltshire Battalion
Joseph Caines, CPO *HMS Monarch*
Herbert Smith, Wiltshire Regiment
- Hinton, Royal Naval Reserve
Edward Harford, Regular Army
M. Pullen, *HMS Minotaur*
William Lansdown, Naval Reserve
- Penny, Lance Corporal, 2nd Wilts
Reginald S.Moore, 3rd Wilts
- Walker, Somerset Light Infantry
Edward Bainton, Wilts
Percy Bainton, Wilts
Arthur Knapp, Wilts Regiment

C. Young, Royal Horse Artillery
G. Burton, 1st Wilts
W. Sprules, 1st Wilts
W. Locke, 1st Wilts
C.Clift, Royal Navy
F. Mayell, Grenadier Guards
G.King 1st Wilts
F. Franks, Grenedier Guards
R. White, *HMS Niger*
V. Burgess, Wiltshire Yeomanry
G.F. Hobbs, Royal Marines
W. Walton, Sergeant 1st Wilts
Nelson Hart, South Wales Borderers
W. Bigwood, 1st Wilts
S. Totton, 3rd Wilts
H. Morris, 3rd Wilts
Sydney H. Watts, 1st Wessex Royal Engineers
Nelson Hibberd, Hussars
Albert W. Hibberd, Royal Navy
J. Bristow, Royal Horse Artillery
Arthur Hodges, Army Service Corps
E. Bancroft, Royal Navy
W. Bricker, 1st Dorset Battalion
J. Norris, Gloucester Regiment
J. Bigwood, 3rtd Wilts
W.E. Morris, 3rd Wilts
A.J. French, *HMS Temeraire*
A. French, 1st Wilts
W.J.French, 1st Wilts
J.Lock, 1st Dorset Battalion
W. Lock, Wiltshire Regiment
L. Lock, Wiltshire Regiment
- Shell, Lance Corporal 1st Dorest Battalion
F.K. Moore, *HMS Hercules*
- Comely, 3rd Wilts
E. Stafford, 3rd Wilts
W. Chivers, Wiltshire Regiment
J. Allen, 1st Wilts
About 50 young men have also joined
Kitchener's Army

Appendix III

Pubs in Bradford in 1935
Barge Inn: Leslie Masters,17 Frome Road
The Beehive: George Hunt, 51 Trowbridge Road
The Bell: Bill Sturrock, 62 Newtown
Canal Tavern: James Watts, 49 Frome Road
Castle Hotel: James Godden, 10 Mount Pleasant
The George: Harry Mayell, 27 Woolley Street
Kings Arms: George Beasley, Coppice Hill
King's Head: John Bigwood, 16 Whitehill
Masons Arms: John Beese, 52 Newtown
New Bear: Frederick Greenland, 13 Silver Street
Old Bear: John Lowries, 26 Silver Street
The Plough: Francis Sprules, 25 Regent Place
Rising Sun: Frank Mayell, 48 Winsley Road
Seven Stars: John Young, Newtown
Swan Hotel: Trust Houses Ltd., Church Street
Three Horseshoes: William Morris, 55 Frome Rd.

NB   The Dog & Fox does not appear in Kelly's Directory for 1935, but Albert Gerrish is listed as a beer retailer in Ashley Road.

Appendix IV

Bradford on Avon Town Council Returns to 1997 Survey of Rural Services for the Rural Development Commission.
All these figures are for the Civil Parish of Bradford on Avon.

89 retail outlets
    shops in the town centre:
        10 The Shambles
        17 Market Street
        2 Church Street
        22 Silver Street
        2 Bridge Street
        8 St. Margaret Street

    shops outside the town centre, but within the civil parish
        10 around the Tithe Barn
        4 Treenwood Estate, including 1 supermarket
        3 Frome Road
        3 Trowbridge Road
        2 New Road/Winsley Road
        2 Ashley Rd/Leigh Park
        1 Holt Road
        3 garages with shops

3 schools catering for an estimated 1,900 pupils
10 specialist housing schemes for the elderly
2 alternative health clinics
1 spiritual healing centre
12 churches and religious groups, including
  Buddhists & Christian Fellowship
15 children's play areas with equipment
64 sports groups, ranging through archery –
football – rowing – tennis – yoga
35 recreational organizations
19 youth organizations
17 public houses, only 3 of which do not serve meals
12 café/restaurant/take aways
5 full-time banks and building societies

Doreen Hemming of Bradford Town Council, who surveyed the town for these returns to the orginal questionnaire, has most kindly helped to compile the above figures which are specific to 1997.

*Right: **Appendix V***
Bradford on Avon's Roll of Honour, saved for the town in September 1997. It carries the names of 488 Bradfordians who served their country in the First World War.
Photograph by Don Miles.

BRADFORD-ON-AVON ROLL OF HONOUR.

ROYAL NAVY.

ARMY.

Bibliography

Bradford on Avon Poor Law Union, 1902:(CRO. Cat:H/3/140/1).

Byelaws made by the Urban District Council for the Management, Use & Regulation of the Bradford on Avon Public Baths (CRO. Cat:G13/123/9).

Census of England and Wales 1901; County of Wiltshire (63 Vict. Ch.4) (CLSL).

Census Reports: A series of booklets published by Wilts County Council 1992 (BoA Library).

Clew, K.R., *The Kennet and Avon Canal*, David & Charles, 1968.

Dotesio's Directory and Year Book 1900.

Fassnidge, Harold, *Bradford on Avon Past and Present*, Ex Libris Press, 2nd ed., 1993.

George, Spencer Moulton & Co. Ltd., 1848-1948: A Hundred Years of Rubber Manufacture (private publication).

Higgs, E.,*Making Sense of the Census Manuscript Returns: England Wales, 1801-1901*: HMSO   (CLSL).

Jones, J. & Dillon, P.: *Dialect in Wiltshire*, Wiltshire County Council, 1987.

Kelly's Directory, 1900.

Kenrick, Col. N.G.C., *The Story of the Wiltshire Regiment*, Gale & Polden, Ltd., 1963.

Key Statistics Urban Areas South West and Wales (HMSO).

Platt, Brigadier, J.R.I.,R*oyal Wilts Yeomanry 1907-67*, Garnstone Press 1972 (CRO).

Ponting, K., *Wool & Water*, Moonraker, 1975.

Powell, W.R., *Bradford on Avon: A History to 1950*, Wilts County Library & Museum Service, Trowbridge 1990 (reprinted from *Victoria County History* Vol V11).

Victoria County History, Vol. 4.

Woodruff, William: *The Rise of the Rubber Industry,* Liverpool University Press, 1958.

References used for Population Figures, etc.:
Only in County Local Studies Library (CLSL), Trowbridge:
Census of England & Wales 1901 County of Wilts: HMSO, 1902
Census of England & Wales 1911 County of Wilts: HMSO, 1914
Census of England & Wales 1921 County of Wilts: HMSO, 1923
Census of England & Wales 1931 County of Wilts part 1: HMSO, 1933
Census of England & Wales County Report Wiltshire part 1: HMSO, 1955
Census of England & Wales County Report Wiltshire part 1: HMSO, 1964
Census of England & Wales County Report Wiltshire parts 1&3: HMSO, 1973
Making Sense of the Census Manuscript Returns England & Wales 1801-1901: HMSO, 1989

In Bradford Library and CLSL
Census 1981 England & Wales County Report; Wiltshire, part 1: HMSO, 1982.
OPCS Monitor; Wards & Civil Parishes, 1984.
Key Statistics to Urban Areas; South West & Wales 1981: HMSO.
Census County Report; Wiltshire, parts 1&2: HMSO, 1992/3.
Census; Local Monitor, WWDC Parishes & Wards: WCC 1992.

INDEX – illustrations are indicated in bold type.

251

EX LIBRIS PRESS

Ex Libris Press has been publishing from Bradford on Avon since 1982. It is based at No.1 The Shambles, where Ex Libris Bookshop has been trading since 1979.

Our first publication was *Where Wiltshire Meets Somerset: 20 Walks in the Country around Bath, Bradford on Avon, Trowbridge, Westbury, Warminster and Frome.* This book first appeared in 1982 and has gone into four editions. It is hoped to publish a new, revised version in 1998.

In 1987 we published *Bradford on Avon: Past and Present* by Bradford historian Harold Fassnidge. A revised edition appeared in 1992; the author died in 1996.

Ex Libris Press now has a list of around sixty titles, in three broad subject areas: West Country, Country Bookshelf and the Seaflower list of books on the Channel Islands. Please ask for a copy of our free, illustrated, complete list of Books in Print.

Copies of our publications may be obtained through your local bookshop or direct from the publisher, post-free, on receipt of net price. See back of title page in this book for our address.